Well and Eager for the Fray

Letters from Northumberland County Soldiers to the
Local Press during the Civil War, 1861–1865

Volume 1

John P. Deeben

LOCAL HISTORY PRESS

an imprint of Sunbury Press, Inc.
Mechanicsburg, PA USA

an imprint of Sunbury Press, Inc.
Mechanicsburg, PA USA

Copyright © 2025 by John P. Deeben.
Cover Copyright © 2025 by Sunbury Press, Inc.

Sunbury Press supports copyright. Copyright fuels creativity, encourages diverse voices, promotes free speech, and creates a vibrant culture. Thank you for buying an authorized edition of this book and for complying with copyright laws. Except for the quotation of short passages for the purpose of criticism and review, no part of this publication may be reproduced, scanned, or distributed in any form without permission. You are supporting writers and allowing Sunbury Press to continue to publish books for every reader. For information contact Sunbury Press, Inc., Subsidiary Rights Dept., PO Box 548, Boiling Springs, PA 17007 USA or legal@sunburypress.com.

For information about special discounts for bulk purchases, please contact Sunbury Press Orders Dept. at (855) 338-8359 or orders@sunburypress.com.

To request one of our authors for speaking engagements or book signings, please contact Sunbury Press Publicity Dept. at publicity@sunburypress.com.

FIRST LOCAL HISTORY PRESS EDITION: December 2025

Set in Adobe Garamond Pro | Interior design by Crystal Devine | Cover by Lawrence Knorr | Edited by Sarah Peachey.

Publisher's Cataloging-in-Publication Data
Names: Deeben, John P., author.
Title: Well and eager for the fray : letters from Northumberland County soldiers to the local press during the Civil War, 1861–1865 / John P. Deeben.
Description: First trade paperback edition. | Mechanicsburg, PA : Local History Press, 2025.
Summary: The young men from Northumberland County who went to war in 1861 faithfully shared their military adventures with the home front. While most soldiers corresponded with family and friends, many wrote for a public audience, reporting their actions to the local press. Their accounts ultimately detailed the community's collective role in the Civil War.
Identifiers: ISBN : 979-8-88819-386-6 (paperback).
Subjects: HISTORY / United States / 19th Century | HISTORY / United States / Civil War Period (1850–1877) | HISTORY / United States / State & Local / Middle Atlantic (DC, DE, MD, NJ, NY, PA).

Designed in the USA
0 1 1 2 3 5 8 13 21 34 55

For the Love of Books!

This work is dedicated to all the
Fighting Men of Northumberland County, Pennsylvania
Past, Present, and Future

Including my own:

Adam Diehl
(1762–1825)
Revolutionary War

Daniel S. Heilman
(1795–1875)
War of 1812

David Hodge
(1830–1901)
Civil War

Frederick Paul Deeben
(1892–1934)
World War I

Paul Earnest Deeben
(1925–2005)
World War II,
Korean War

"The real heroes of this war are the great, brave, patient, nameless people."

—Whitelaw Reid, war correspondent

"If I had my choice I would kill every reporter in the world, but I am sure we would be getting reports from Hell before breakfast."

—Maj. Gen. William Tecumseh Sherman

CONTENTS

Acknowledgments	vii
Introduction	1
1. Lincoln's Three-Month Volunteers, April–July 1861	29
2. The Army Reorganizes, August 1861–January 1862	149
3. To Key West and the Peninsula, February–July 1862	219
Bibliography	280
About the Author	283

ACKNOWLEDGMENTS

As most authors usually recognize, a research project like this requires a fair amount of support from multiple quarters. First and foremost, I wish to thank my place of employment, the National Archives and Records Administration, and in particular my immediate supervisors, T. Juliette Arai, Chief of the Archives 1 Reference Branch (RR1R), and Trevor Plante, Director of the Archives 1 Textual Records Division (RR1), for their support and encouragement in allowing me to explore and pursue professional activities beyond my routine responsibilities. Federal employees are generally held to a higher standard when it comes to work or activities outside their official duties, and I am grateful that my supervisors readily recognized and approved the need for such professional development. A similar nod goes to NARA's Ethics Office for acknowledging that this project did not in any way conflict with my official work as a government reference archivist.

A research project of this nature also benefits from having friends in scholarly places. In that respect, I heartily thank Dr. Jonathan Berkey, Professor of History at Concord University in Athens, West Virginia, for his careful reading and critique of the manuscript during the editing phase. Jon is not only a friend and fellow alum of both Gettysburg College and Penn State, but also a native of the Susquehanna Valley in Central Pennsylvania. He thus holds a unique perspective and familiar understanding of the local history surrounding Northumberland County. Another Gettysburg classmate and history major, the Rt. Rev. Matthew Lynn Riegel, S.T.M., Bishop of the West Virginia-Western Maryland Synod (ELCA), also graciously read and commented on the introductory material. Whether it be history or theology, Matt is a consummate scholar and offered reassurances on the soundness of my historical analysis. I had also reached out to fellow Penn State graduate school classmate Peter S. Carmichael, Director of the Civil War Institute at Gettysburg College, for advice and manuscript review, but sadly his unexpected and untimely passing in July 2024 precluded any hoped-for collaboration and robbed the entire Civil War community of the benefit of his insight and wisdom. Rest well, Pete, you are sorely missed.

While editing and annotating these letters, I also benefited tremendously from the research of others, particularly regarding information about the regiments and soldiers featured in this history. The 47th Pennsylvania Volunteers, of course, played a central role in the story of Northumberland County during the Civil War, and therefore I am indebted to the exhaustive work already compiled on this exemplary unit by Laurie Snyder, who maintains one of the best regimental websites I have yet discovered on the internet, the "47th Pennsylvania Volunteers: One Civil War Regiment's Story" (https://47thpennsylvaniavolunteers.com/). Laurie's thorough and ongoing research offered invaluable details about the service of the 47th as well as its two top-notch correspondents, John Peter Shindel Gobin and Henry D. Wharton. Following a very informative and gratifying phone conversation, Laurie graciously gave me permission to use her website as a central reference source. I emphatically encourage everyone to visit the URL above, peruse the many fine articles and biographies she has created, and support her continuing research efforts. One particular photograph on the website, a wartime image of Captain John Peter Shindel Gobin, came from the David L. Sloan Archive Collection, and so I thank David Sloan of Key West, Florida, for granting permission to reuse the image for this publication.

Finally, I would like to pay tribute to two of the most important early mentors from my undergraduate years at Gettysburg College, Dr. Gabor Boritt and the late Dr. Charles H. Glatfelter. As my academic advisor, Gabor Boritt—one of the Civil War community's preeminent Lincoln scholars—fueled my already well-developed passion for Civil War history, giving it a scholarly focus I have carried with me ever since. My time as his work-study student opened doors and allowed me to witness the beginnings of the strong Civil War Era Studies program that thrives at Gettysburg College today. My only regret is that the many wonderful opportunities for Civil War scholarship—from the Civil War minor to the Brian C. Pohanka summer internships, among others—that exist today were not already in place when I began my college career way back in the fall of 1983! And as for Dr. Glatfelter, what can I say about a man who towered as a historian over the Gettysburg campus, master of the required Historical Methods class that every sophomore history major dreaded! Aside from an equally meticulous approach to research, it was Glatfelter who instilled in me my abiding preference for footnotes over endnotes. As he once famously said in class: "A footnote [dramatic pause for emphasis] should be exactly what it says it is: a note at the foot of the page!"

INTRODUCTION

I. "At your request," the letter began, "and to fulfill my promise made by me to keep you posted in the movements of our regiment . . . I can think of nothing with which to pass the time more profitably than by describing to a friend some of our regiment's movements."[1] So wrote Isaiah S. Gossler to Emanuel Wilvert, editor of the *Sunbury American*, upon his arrival at Camp Pierpont in Fairfax County, Virginia, on November 3, 1861. One of the early recruits of the war, traveling to Camp Curtin in Harrisburg, Pennsylvania, to enlist on May 27, Gossler had made a pledge to send reports of his adventures in the Army back to the local newspaper of his hometown in Northumberland County. He dutifully proceeded to describe the actions of his unit, the 32nd Pennsylvania Volunteer Infantry (3rd Reserves), as it participated in several excursions into the Virginia hinterland, hoping for its first clash with the enemy, while also taking care of the more routine duties of camp life. "The intervening time" between marching "is taken up by the men performing fatigue duty, cutting down woods, building forts," Gossler noted at one point. "[O]n the 11th of Sept., the greater portion of the regiment were clearing and cleaning ground so as to extend the limits of our camp."[2]

Gossler's offer to correspond with the local press was not uncommon. As the United States embarked upon the uncharted experience of a civil war, many fresh-faced volunteers on both sides of the conflict pledged with enthusiasm to keep friends and family apprised of their well-being while regaling them with accounts of military exploits. The war, after all, represented a new adventure—as another Northumberland

---

1. Isaiah S. Gossler to Emanuel Wilvert, *Sunbury American*, November 16, 1861.
2. Gossler to Wilvert, *Sunbury American*, November 16, 1861.

County soldier eventually admitted, "I have seen more since I have been in the service than I would otherwise have seen in a whole lifetime."[3] And newspapers, naturally, offered an ideal vehicle to keep in touch. In an age in which information traveled largely by horsepower (stagecoach), wind (sailing ship), or steam (railroad), each with its own limitations in terms of speed, the printed word still provided the best way to connect local populations with important regional, national, or foreign events. (Even though the telegraph had been invented in 1844, by the outbreak of the Civil War it had yet to be utilized for disseminating news on a regular basis.[4]) To be sure, newspapers at this time remained highly partisan in nature, with each organ promoting a particular political bent—and the local press in Sunbury was certainly no exception—but they still offered the most practical venue for individuals to be informed.[5]

Most newspapers in the antebellum period were small-scale enterprises, consisting of four-page broadsides that were largely printed by hand, with each sheet set individually between rolling cylinders and then re-fed after the print had dried to set the reverse side. Separate machines then folded the broadsides into the requisite four-page format. Most were printed daily or weekly. They were simple affairs, containing few illustrations aside from occasional woodcuts. At least one or two full pages, sometimes including the front page (sensational, attention-grabbing headlines had not yet become a staple of the trade), were usually given over to advertisements, mostly local in nature but sometimes enticing readers with goods available for order from nearby metropolitan centers. Since news reports were only occasionally shared by wire, most papers relied on volunteer correspondents to share local news and literary submissions, while some copied stories verbatim from neighboring journals. The dailies, quite often, simply repeated the same news items from one issue to the next until new headlines came along.[6]

The Civil War, of course, changed the nature of journalism. Once the fighting began, the public's insatiable desire for information from the front led to an explosion of newsgathering by wire, as well as a dramatic

---

3. See letter of William A. Fetter, *Sunbury Gazette*, May 31, 1862.

4. J. Cutler Andrews, *The North Reports the Civil War* (Pittsburgh: University of Pittsburgh Press, 1955, 1983), 6.

5. As historian Daniel Walker Howe has observed, "As early as 1822, the United States had more newspaper readers than any other country, regardless of population." See Howe, *What Hath God Wrought: The Transformation of America, 1815–1848* (New York: Oxford University Press, 2007), 227.

6. Andrews, *North Reports the Civil War*, 6–9; Howe, *What Hath God Wrought*, 227–229.

increase in the space allotted for telegraphic news in the printed press. War correspondents suddenly became a major component of the journalist profession as papers hired individuals—the *New York Herald* alone reportedly had over forty people in the field—to go out and report the movements of the armies (before the war, most papers had only engaged a small handful of paid reporters and writers). Although most were never formally trained, these correspondents often assumed the mantle of professionals, honing values and skills—such as attention to detail, dedication to facts, preference for eyewitness accounts, speed and accuracy—that would come to define modern journalism. Inexperience, however, proved no hindrance; as historian Carol Reardon has noted in reviewing contemporary news coverage about Pickett's Charge at Gettysburg, "The correspondents' inability to portray the horrors of battle did not seem to bother them much. They compensated for gaps in information and inadequacies of perspective with literary artistry, the real soul of this journalistic era's craft."[7] As competition increased, reporters also mastered the art of logistics (working the telegraph network) while resisting War Department attempts to impose censorship, all to get their stories in print as soon as possible.[8] As Reardon likewise noted, "As long as their colorful and impressionistic stories reached their editors on time, reporters believed they had discharged their obligations."[9]

The war did produce some first-rate journalists, such as Whitelaw Reid of the *Cincinnati Gazette*. Even though he often downplayed his own skills, admitting once that he was "a poor hand to describe battles I do not see,"[10] Reid's war reporting achieved attention for its accuracy, dedication to detail, and descriptive language. Historian Frederic F. Endres has described Reid's dispatches, particularly about Shiloh and Gettysburg, as "superlative efforts, widely reprinted."[11] These war correspondents were often accompanied by talented artists who produced visual depictions of the war for the popular illustrated papers of the day, including *Harper's*

---

7. Carol Reardon, *Pickett's Charge in History and Memory* (Chapel Hill: The University of North Carolina Press, 1997), 40.
8. Andrews, *North Reports the Civil War*, 6–9.; "Civil War Reporting and Reporters," American Antiquarian Society website, https://collections.americanantiquarian.org/earlyamericannewsmedia/exhibits/show/news-and-the-civil-war/civil-war-reporting-and-report (accessed May 9, 2024).
9. Reardon, *Pickett's Charge*, 40.
10. Whitlaw Reid to the *Cincinnati Gazette*, as quoted in Reardon, *Pickett's Charge*, 40.
11. Endres, Fredric F., Review of *A Radical View: The "Agate" Dispatches of Whitelaw Reid, 1861-1865*. *Civil War History* 22, no. 4 (1976): 361-362. https://doi.org/10.1353/cwh.1976.0029 (accessed May 9, 2024).

Weekly and *Frank Leslie's Illustrated Newspaper*. Photography was coming into its own as a visual medium but had not yet been applied to field reporting, much less the normal venues of journalism (in fact, no workable methods existed yet to transfer photographs to a printing plate). Sketch artists or illustrators therefore stepped in to create drawings of the armies in the field or reproduce photographs as wood engravings for the printed page. Alfred R. Waud became perhaps the best known of these war artists, working for the *New York Illustrated News* in April 1861, and then later for *Harper's Weekly*. Waud produced memorable images that displayed both an artist's talent for composition as well as a reporter's attention to detail. Perhaps most importantly, Waud understood the historical weight of the events he drew, leading him sometimes dangerously close to the fighting to capture the drama and horror of the moment.[12]

In the company of such budding professionals, soldiers in the field acting as correspondents for their home journals became an added feature of war reporting. It almost seemed like a logical outcome, since most small-town newspapers did not have the ability to embed their own reporters.[13] Aside from writing directly to family and friends, the opportunity to correspond with the local press filled a necessary void as these young men left home to fight, offering them an additional way to stay connected. As historian Zachary A. Fry has observed, many soldiers contributed "regular columns to hometown newspapers about events at the front" in an effort to "replicate prewar civilian culture within the confines of military discipline."[14] Assisting in that effort, many regimental companies fostered at least one budding writer—usually a friend or acquaintance of a local printer or editor back home—who was willing to report the military news on a regular basis (or as frequently as Army life allowed). Often with colorful enthusiasm, they described the comings and goings of their regiments, related humorous anecdotes about camp life, explained the larger military movements of the Army, sometimes waxed philosophically about the nature of the war, and in no uncertain terms vilified the enemy at every opportunity. Without exception, they

---

12. Meg Groeling, "Drawing the War, Part 1: Alfred Waud," Emerging Civil War: Providing Fresh Perspectives on America's Defining Event, https://emergingcivilwar.com/2012/03/12/drawing-the-war-part-1-alfred-waud/ (accessed May 9, 2024).

13. Brian Matthew Jordan, *A Thousand May Fall: Life, Death, and Survival in the Union Army* (New York: Liveright Publishing Corp., 2021), 142.

14. Zachary A. Fry, *A Republic in the Ranks: Loyalty and Dissent in the Army of the Potomac* (Chapel Hill: University of North Carolina Press, 2020), 44.

reassured the home audience about the welfare of themselves, their company, and their eagerness to serve. As another Northumberland soldier in the 5th Pennsylvania Reserves declared, "The Boys are all well, excepting a few that have bad colds, which we are all liable to take anywhere; but in every other respect they are well and eager for the fray."[15]

Most volunteer soldiers only had a rudimentary, if any, understanding of military operations (and likely no grasp of larger strategies and tactics), so their descriptions of Army activities were often limited, confined to movements that were known to them or uncensored by the War Department.[16] Speaking to the latter point, one soldier from Columbia County observed in his own letters to the local newspapers in Bloomsburg, Pennsylvania, that "I have not given you as much information in regard to our forces, their disposition or their destination as I should like or as I could were it not for an order . . . forbidding reporters of papers giving any details that is calculated in any way to give the enemy any information whatever, under pain of arrest and trial by court martial." "So, you see," he added, "our mouths are almost sealed on this."[17] A notice in the *Sunbury American*, entitled "CAUTION TO SOLDIER LETTER-WRITERS," further advised soldiers against writing or publishing "any article praising or blaming, or discussing the conduct of any officer or man."[18] Personal observations of military personnel aside, most common soldiers held limited knowledge of the larger course of the war. As another soldier put it more bluntly about his unit's future movements: "Vague rumors, are astir amongst the privates, in regard to our departure and destination. Privates know nothing of the future, and will not."[19]

Operating under such uncertainty, some soldiers' recollections, of course, could be subject to unconscious, or sometimes even deliberate, bias. In many of the letters to follow, the reader may detect a collective effort to put a positive spin on the Union war effort, regardless of the actual circumstances. Whether intentional or not—perhaps an attempt to allay fears at home or bolster continued support from the home front—remains hard to determine, but the tones are definitely noticeable. The uncertainty

---

15. *Sunbury Gazette*, February 8, 1862.
16. Jordan, *A Thousand May Fall*, 143.
17. Thomas E. Swinton, 84th Pennsylvania Volunteer Infantry, to Williamson H. Jacoby, February 11, 1862, in *The* (Bloomsburg) *Star of the North*, February 19, 1862.
18. *Sunbury American*, June 1, 1861.
19. *Columbia Democrat & Bloomsburg General Advertiser*, January 11, 1862.

stems directly from the inherently personal nature of individual recollection, which is often influenced by one's own particular life experience and consciousness. Confederate Lt. James Simons, Jr. (1839–1919) cautioned about this very point in discussing the movements of his own unit, the German (South Carolina) Artillery, in the Maryland Campaign with post-war Antietam historian Ezra C. Carman (who was himself a former Confederate officer). "As a rule," Simons observed in a letter to Carman in 1897, "I abstain from War narrations, because they frequently involve the too free use of the personal pronoun, which is undesirable." Such recollections "are sometimes evolved from the depths of one's moral consciousness,—and perhaps sometimes from the depths of one's want of moral consciousness."[20] Emphasizing the soldier's limited knowledge as well, Simons added, "The field of vision of any man in a big battle, is limited, especially that of a subaltern—and whilst I had my opinion, I doubt if the opinion of a subaltern would be of much value."[21]

Despite such potential limitations, soldiers wrote from the heart and attempted to convey information as accurately as their abilities allowed. Speaking mainly of things they experienced personally, soldiers often did not shy away from the more somber aspects of the war as well, such as the death of friends and neighbors in the ranks. In the pages that follow, the reader will discover some of the most forlorn episodes of grief conveyed in mournful messages to families on the loss of loved ones. At times, the letters also described tragic incidents that occurred outside the maelstrom of battle. Indeed, Isaiah Gossler's lone contribution to this anthology carried the unfortunate story of an accidental death in camp, an almost bizarre incident that deserves to be quoted at length:

> October 14th, a sad and fatal accident occurred. A Battery of Artillery was stationed on the hill in front of our lines, and as usual, many were looking on. A young man was lying down, his head resting on his right arm. Orders were given for the first time for "ground arms," our muskets were all loaded with ball and three buck-shot. One was accidentally discharged, the ball passing through the young man's arm near the elbow joint, making a

---

20. James Simons, Jr. to Erza C. Carman, August 25, 1897; Antietam Studies (entry UD 324); Records of the Adjutant General's Office, Record Group 94; National Archives Building, Washington, DC.
21. Simons to Carman, August 25, 1897.

compound fracture, passed through the tent and into the heart of an elderly man, who was writing a letter home, he staggered out of the tent and fell dead. The body was sent home the next day, escorted part of the way by two of our companies and band.[22]

On occasion, such news was also reported in private letters to family that were, in turn, passed along to the press for public consumption.[23]

II.

This work seeks to present soldier correspondence shared with the local news market of the small northern town of Sunbury in Northumberland County, Pennsylvania. Founded at the same time as the county on March 3, 1772, Sunbury was laid out to serve as the county seat, making it the political and social center of the frontier community. Located at the confluence of the north and west branches of the Susquehanna River, where the former Indian town of Shamokin—once the capital of the Iroquois Confederacy in Pennsylvania—had been located, it was also the former site of Fort Augusta, a French and Indian War-era military post that had been dismantled by 1796. Northumberland itself had once been known as the "Mother of Counties," occupying a huge swath of territory in Pennsylvania's interior from the Lehigh River in the east to the Allegheny in the west and stretching northward all the way to the New York border. By the time of the Civil War, the county had been whittled down by partition to a mere fraction of its former self, with no less than nineteen counties being carved out of its former boundaries between 1786 and 1855.[24]

When the Civil War erupted in 1861, Northumberland County still represented a typically rural, agrarian northern community. Sparsely populated, the county shared only a very small fraction of the total state

---

22. *Sunbury American*, November 16, 1861.
23. In an era characterized by Victorian sentimentality, emotionally charged letters from citizens affected by the war played right into the sensational nature of news reporting. See "The Reported War: Printed Media and the American Civil War," Special Collections & Archives Research Center (SCARC), Oregon State University Libraries website, https://scarc.library.oregonstate.edu/omeka/exhibits/show/mcdonald/civil-war/war/ (accessed May 2, 2024).
24. Herbert C. Bell, *History of Northumberland County, Pennsylvania* (Chicago: Brown, Runk & Co., 1891), iii. The counties eventually created from former Northumberland territory included Luzerne (1786), Mifflin (1789), Lycoming (1795), Centre (1800), Venango (1805), Bradford (1810), Schuylkill (1811), Susquehanna (1812), Tioga (1812), Columbia (1813), Union (1813), Warren (1819), Clearfield (1822), McKean (1826), Potter (1826), Clinton (1839), Wyoming (1842), Montour (1850), and Snyder (1855). One final county, Lackawanna, was carved from Luzerne County after the Civil War in 1878.

population, according to the 1860 census, containing 28,922 residents out of a total of 2,906,215 people. (By contrast, the county population in 2020 stood at 91,647.)[25] The vast majority was also white; there were only 115 free blacks or mulattos. While the county populace was about evenly split between male and female (14,600 white males compared to 14,207 females, along with 37 black males to 30 females, and 24 mulatto males to 24 females), prime adults comprised the great majority. The largest combined age group (whites and colored, per the census form) included adults between 20 and 29 years old (2,524 males and 2,511 white females). Considered in tandem with adults aged 30 to 39 (1,730 males and 1,524 females) and ages 40 to 49 (1,297 males and 1,194 females), working-age adults in the prime of life made up the largest subset of the population (10,780 people, or 37 percent).[26]

The amount of developed farmland within the county easily reflected its agrarian nature. In 1860, Northumberland boasted 158,865 acres of improved land supporting farms, versus 41,250 of unimproved acreage (79 percent of the total county landmass of 200,115 acres). Even though the county was small, the cash value of its working farms totaled a respectable sum of $8,085,626. The overall value of the county's farming implements and machinery equaled $265,085. Swine comprised the largest category of livestock (16,961 hogs), followed distantly by milk (dairy) cows (6,509), sheep (6,169), horses (5,230), and cattle (4,603). Other beasts of burden brought up the rear with asses and mules (77) and working oxen (22). The total value of the county's livestock was $708,109. Indian corn made up the great majority of the county's field produce, with 598,308 bushels harvested in 1860. Grain or cereal crops followed close behind, including oats (349,389 bushels), wheat (242,231 bushels), rye (90,674), and buckwheat (60,240 bushels). The county also hauled in 52,959 pounds of tobacco and 23,390 tons of hay.[27]

Despite the primary focus on agriculture, manufactures—defined as principal industries and trades—still played a large role in the county's economy. In 1860 Northumberland supported 212 business

---

25. U.S. Census Bureau QuickFacts: Northumberland County, Pennsylvania, https://www.census.gov/quickfacts/fact/table/northumberlandcountypennsylvania/PST045221 (accessed May 4, 2024).
26. Joseph C. G. Kennedy, *Population of the United States in 1860* (Washington: Government Printing Office, 1864), 406–411.
27. Joseph C. G. Kennedy, *Agriculture of the United States in 1860* (Washington: Government Printing Office, 1864), 122–124.

establishments with a capital investment of $901,605 and expenditures of $560,028 in raw materials. These businesses employed 1,673 hands (1,657 men and 16 women) at a labor cost of $449,802. The annual value of their products totaled $1,171,829 (representing .0004 percent of Pennsylvania's total manufacturing income of $290,121,188). Since the county straddled the edge of the eastern anthracite coal fields, mining comprised the most lucrative industry even though there were only 13 mines in operation. Collectively, they employed 1,119 men at an annual cost of $284,808 and produced $359,474 worth of anthracite coal. Grist mills constituted the largest industry in terms of the number of establishments—31 mills employing 46 men—and generated the second-largest amount of income, $261,547 worth of flour and meal. A single pig iron foundry employing 100 men recorded the third largest income at $100,000. Otherwise, lumber mills represented the second-largest business in the county (23 mills employing 59 men), closely followed by lime manufacturing (22 kilns employing 33 men).[28]

By the time the Civil War began, Northumberland County thus stood ready to supply its share of men, foodstuffs, and material. Once the fighting commenced, Northumberland contributed manpower to twenty-one different Pennsylvania regiments. A few units contained companies recruited from across the general county population, including the 53rd Pennsylvania Volunteers (Company H), 56th Pennsylvania (Companies C, D, G, and K), 7th Pennsylvania Cavalry (Company D), 3rd Pennsylvania Heavy Artillery (Battery D), 74th Pennsylvania (Company C), and the 37th Pennsylvania Emergency Militia (Company I), while the 51st Pennsylvania and the 2nd Pennsylvania Heavy Artillery had Northumberland volunteers peppered throughout their regiments. Most county volunteers, however, enlisted from specific communities, often forming companies around existing militia organizations. The Sunbury Guards, a local unit originally founded in 1818, went off to war in April 1861 as Company F of the 11th Pennsylvania Infantry, a three-month regiment, then later reorganized as Company C of the three-year 47th Pennsylvania Volunteers. Similarly, the pre-war Shamokin Guards became Company A, 8th Pennsylvania Infantry, and then Company K, 46th Pennsylvania Volunteers, while the Taggart Guards of Northumberland and the

---

28. Joseph C. G. Kennedy, *Manufactures of the United States in 1860* (Washington: Government Printing Office, 1865), 521–522, 544.

Pollock Guards of Milton became Companies B and H, respectively, of the 5th Pennsylvania Reserves (34th Volunteers).[29]

Collectively, these units served through most of the major campaigns of the Civil War, from the fledgling maneuvers of the ninety-day volunteers called up by Lincoln in the aftermath of Fort Sumter, to the slogging, brutal fighting that characterized the late-war campaigns of the veteran three-year regiments. While most fought in the Eastern Theater, particularly from the Peninsula in 1862 through the Petersburg and Shenandoah campaigns in late 1864, a few also served in coastal and western operations from the Florida Keys to the Louisiana swamps. The nine-month regiments raised in 1862, including the 131st Pennsylvania Volunteers and its four Northumberland companies (C, D, E, and F) recruited from Sunbury, Snydertown, and neighboring townships, just missed Antietam but received their brutal baptism of fire at Fredericksburg before finishing their service in the aftermath of Chancellorsville. Several Northumberland companies also comprised the temporary state emergency militias that were called up to counter the northward incursions by the Confederates during both the Antietam and Gettysburg campaigns.

This record of local service certainly belied the initial great uncertainty that gripped the country after the 1860 presidential contest. As the nation descended into the crisis of the Secession Winter, witnessing the defection of the states of the Lower South from the Union, that uncertainty affected the people of Northumberland County no less than the rest of the Northern population. The bombardment of Fort Sumter the following spring, however, galvanized the county with equal fervor. As local historian Herbert C. Bell described it, "Every latent instinct of patriotism was stirred to action, and public sentiment crystalized into a united determination to maintain the honor of the flag and the integrity of the government."[30] What follows is a collective first-hand accounting of that experience as men from at least a dozen companies chronicled their wartime service for the local press.

---

29. Bell, *History of Northumberland County*, 402–441. Other companies recruited locally included Company I (Sunbury), 58th Pennsylvania; Company A (Milton), 3rd Pennsylvania Militia of 1862; Company B (Trevorton) and Company E (Sunbury), 18th Pennsylvania Militia of 1862; and the following 1863 Emergency Militias: Company E (Milton), 28th Pennsylvania; and Company F (Sunbury) and Company K (Shamokin), 36th Pennsylvania Militia. Sunbury's local cornet band also served one year as the regimental band for the 45th Pennsylvania Volunteers, while men across the entire county selected from the 1862 state draft formed Company D, 172nd Pennsylvania Drafted Militia (see page 253).

30. Bell, *History of Northumberland County*, 400.

III.

Civil War soldiers from across Northumberland County penned letters for publication in two of the principal local newspapers of the day, the *Sunbury Gazette* and the *Sunbury American*. John G. Youngman and his son, George B. Youngman, originally founded the *Gazette* in 1838 as "The Sunbury Gazette & Miner's Register." The elder publisher had been a longtime participant in the Sunbury print trade, having established one of the earliest papers, the Sunbury *Amerikaner*, in 1812. He was also active in local politics, serving as county treasurer in 1814, county commissioner in 1818–21, and register and recorder in 1839. In 1855, George B. Youngman became senior publisher and his brother, Andrew A., assumed the role of junior partner. John B. Youngman (to whom many of the soldier letters are personally addressed) remained active with the paper even after his retirement in 1868; he was reported to "take great delight in type-setting, and worked at this in the composing room of the *Gazette*" until shortly before his death on September 13, 1871.[31] During the Civil War, the *Gazette* published a weekly edition every Saturday evening.

The *Sunbury American*, founded by Henry B. Masser and Joseph Eisely as a Saturday morning weekly, began operation soon after the *Gazette* on September 12, 1840. Masser became the sole proprietor after Eisely retired in 1848 and published the paper on his own until his editor, Emanuel Wilvert, acquired an interest in 1864. A native of Sunbury, born August 17, 1809, Masser initially pursued a career as an attorney, studying law under Alexander Jordan. He was admitted to the Northumberland County Bar on November 5, 1833, along with James Pollock (who would eventually become governor of the commonwealth), and was appointed deputy attorney general for the county in 1839, a post Masser held until 1845. "Although thus established in the practice of the law," later histories recounted, Masser's "natural talent as a writer early found expression in contributions to the local papers and eventually led him to devote the best activities of his life to the work of journalism. . . . Masser was recognized as a trenchant and forcible writer, and a sagacious observer of the political and social movements of the day."[32]

---

31. Bell, *History of Northumberland County*, 280–281.
32. Bell, *History of Northumberland County*, 806–807.

Initially, both the *Gazette* and the *American* were staunch Democratic mouthpieces. Masser steered the *American* in a more nuanced approach, however, showing a willingness to support opposition party positions and candidates when circumstances warranted. The most noticeable example occurred when the *American* endorsed James Pollock (the Whig candidate) for Congress in 1843. Campaigning in favor of a protective tariff, Pollock's position aligned with Masser's own advocacy for internal improvements in the state, and so the paper's endorsement helped carry the county and the election for the Milton native. As well, Masser supported the "Free Soil" movement in the Democratic Party during the Buchanan administration. With the election of Republican Abraham Lincoln in 1860, however, both newspapers came out as solid pro-administration organs virulently opposed to the rising national threat of secession. Their sudden reverse course led to the founding of a new Democratic paper, the *Northumberland County Democrat*, under proprietor Truman H. Purdy in March 1861. Equally fierce in his political views, Purdy found himself regularly at loggerheads with both Masser and the Youngmans, so much so that their editorials frequently traded vicious (and often deprecating, sometimes humorous) barbs. It seems very telling, and hardly surprising, then, that the *Democrat* never carried a single soldier letter during the entire course of the war.[33]

Both the *Gazette* and the *American* usually printed letters from at least one soldier correspondent every issue. The letters published were authored overall by average young men. Although they came of age during the single most traumatic event of their generation, most did not achieve much notoriety beyond the shared experience of joining the Army and going off to war. Those who returned home after surviving the physical and psychological trauma of war carried on with their civilian lives in relative anonymity, leaving their published letters as the only record of their life-defining experience. The identities of some, who only signed their missives with initials or a pen name, such as "Union," remain lost to history. Of course, there were a few exceptions that should be noted. A few authors came from backgrounds that fostered a more polished, mature understanding of the conflict and enabled them to convey information with greater clarity and, sometimes, literary flair. Perhaps the most notable and gifted of such local war correspondents was John Peter Shindel Gobin (1837–1910).

---

33. Bell, *History of Northumberland County*, 280–283, 807.

A native of Sunbury and the son of Samuel Shoemaker Gobin, a prominent contractor and wagonmaker in the county, and Susanna M. Shindel, John P. S. Gobin—or Shindel, as he sometimes referred to himself—seemed almost predestined to achieve martial as well as intellectual success. By his father's family, Gobin descended from a long line of soldiers, including his great-grandfather, Charles Gobin, a captain in the 6th Battalion of Berks County Militia in the Revolutionary War, who later defended frontier settlements against Native and British incursions from New York, and his grandfather, Edward Gobin, who fought in the second war against Great Britain between 1812 and 1814. Gobin's maternal relatives followed a religious calling. His grandfather, Rev. John Peter Shindel Jr., was a prominent clergyman who served as the principal Lutheran minister in the Sunbury area from 1812 to 1851. Gobin's great-grandfather, John Peter Shindel Sr., likewise a Lutheran pastor, was also a veteran of the Lancaster County Militia in the Revolution (he later served in several political positions such as justice of the peace and chief burgess of Lebanon, Pennsylvania, and as a member of the Pennsylvania Senate). As one later biographer summarized, Gobin thus "inherited the martial spirit of his paternal ancestors, and the scholarly characteristics of those on the maternal side."[34]

Early training as an apprentice in the printing trade in Sunbury contributed to Gobin's penchant for coherent, descriptive writing as well as his predisposition to chronicle his future exploits in the war. He honed his skills as a newspaperman with the *Sunbury American* and briefly as publisher of the *Philadelphia Star of Youth*. He also became a protégé and close associate of publisher John Youngman (in fact, most of the war letters he wrote for publication would be addressed to "Dear John" at the *Gazette*). Later, Gobin studied law in Sunbury under attorneys Martin Luther Shindel—a maternal uncle who subsequently joined the Lutheran clergy—and John Kay Clement, joining the Northumberland County Bar in 1858. Including a stint as a teacher in the local schools as well, Gobin's pre-war career positioned him to be an educated, articulate observer of facts.[35]

---

34. *Biographical Annals of Lebanon County, Pennsylvania* (Chicago: J. H. Beers & Co., 1904), 3–4; Laurie Snyder, "The Honorable John Peter Shindel Gobin," 47th Pennsylvania Volunteers: One Civil War Regiment's Story, https://47thpennsylvaniavolunteers.com/officers/roster-field-and-staff-officers-47th-pennsylvania-volunteers/the-honorable-john-peter-shindel gobin/ (accessed May 12, 2024).

35. *Annals of Lebanon County*, 5; Snyder, "Honorable John Peter Shindel Gobin."

14   Well and Eager for the Fray

Wartime image of John Peter Shindel Gobin. (Credit: David L. Sloan Archive Collection)

When the Civil War broke out in April 1861, Gobin immediately left his law practice to help organize the local militia company, the Sunbury Guards, for service, first as Company F of the 11th Pennsylvania Infantry, and then as Company C, 47th Pennsylvania Volunteers. As the details of his military career play out in the following pages, it is useful to note here that Gobin became an exemplary soldier while rising through the ranks from first lieutenant to colonel of the 47th. Gobin performed his duties with considerable integrity, so much so that he was cited for gallantry in action at the Battle of Pocotaligo in October 1862, distinguished himself again at Cedar Creek in October 1864, and finally earned a brevet promotion to brigadier general of U.S. Volunteers for meritorious services on March 13, 1865. After the fighting ended, Gobin served for a time as Judge Advocate General for the Department of the South while commanding the First Sub-District in Charleston, where he also acted as the city's Provost Judge until mustering out of service on January 9, 1866.[36]

The other prolific Northumberland County correspondent was Gobin's comrade-in-arms and fellow newspaperman, Henry D. Wharton (1826–1898). Born in Sunbury to Charles Doughty Wharton Sr. and Maria Donnell, Henry entered the printing trade at an early age. He initially worked as an editor for the *Intelligencer*, a newspaper serving the community of Danville in neighboring Montour County. He honed his journalistic skills there for a time before returning to Sunbury to take a position as a compositor (the person who arranges type for printing) with the *Sunbury American*. In that capacity Wharton became a ready acquaintance with John P. S. Gobin at the *Gazette*. When the war erupted in April 1861, Wharton immediately enlisted with the Sunbury Guards on April 23, and then mustered in as a musician under Capt. Charles J. Bruner with Company F, 11th Pennsylvania Volunteer Infantry, at Camp Curtin in Harrisburg.[37]

Wharton's value as a journalist in the ranks became readily apparent. Indeed, as soon as the war began, the *Sunbury American* published a statement to that effect when recognizing several local newspapermen in the Army. Observing that "Printers are generally among our most patriotic men," the *American* called out J. P. Shindel Gobin and William C. Goodrich "of the Danville company" as "graduates from this office" while "Henry D. Wharton, of the GUARDS, was also one of our compositors."[38] Wharton became widely known to the readership of the *Sunbury American* as the correspondent "H.D.W.," the author of regular submissions that chronicled the activities of the Sunbury Guards. As one

---

36. *Annals of Lebanon County*, 5.
37. Laurie Snyder, "Henry D. Wharton—Journalist, Soldier and Public Servant," 47th Pennsylvania Volunteers: One Civil War Regiment's Story, https://47thpennsylvaniavolunteers.com/letters-home/the-scribes-of-the-47th-pennsylvania-volunteers/henry-d-wharton-journalist-soldier-and-public-servant/ (accessed May 18, 2024).
38. *Sunbury American*, April 27, 1861.

biographer has noted, "His riveting prose conveyed the gallant exploits of comrades engaged in small skirmishes and major battles across the South while telegraphing his sorrow as peach fuzz-faced boys were cut down by yellow jack or cannon fire."[39] His writing skills led to special assignments as well, when Wharton was tapped to serve as a clerk for Brig. Gen. John M. Brannan. His letter writing declined in consequence and was duly noticed at home in early 1862: "We have not, of late, heard of our correspondent, H. D. Wharton, who, we understand, acts in the capacity of clerk to Gen. Brannan."[40]

Wharton's correspondence and war reporting eventually resumed its regular frequency, and his words "became a trusted resource for the loved ones of 47th soldiers who were worrying and waiting back home in Pennsylvania."[41] His efforts eventually earned Wharton recognition as an indispensable Army correspondent when he finally mustered out of service on October 12, 1865, and returned home. In welcoming the veteran back to Sunbury, his former employer, the *Sunbury American*, duly observed: "H. D. Wharton, of the 47th Reg't. P. V., our Army Correspondent during the war, returned home to this place on Monday last.—The letters of Mr. Wharton, who is a Printer by profession, were well received. We congratulate him on his safe return."[42]

In the company of veteran journalists Gobin and Wharton stands one other accomplished chronicler that deserves mention, the Rev. Peter Rizer (1812–1886). Educated at Cumberland Academy and Gettysburg Lutheran Seminary, from which he graduated in 1832, Rizer was well polished and compassionate—indeed, as part of his examination for licensure in the Maryland Synod in 1833, Rizer delivered a public address on "The Moral and Intellectual Qualifications of a Gospel Minister"—qualities that positioned him well as an observer of the coming war. After receiving his preaching license, Rizer was formally ordained as a Lutheran pastor in 1834. He initially served a parish in Boonsboro, Maryland, in 1832–1833, and then became a Lutheran missionary to the Cherokee Nation in South Carolina, Alabama, and Georgia for eight years, cultivating fledgling congregations in Monroeville, Flat Creek, and Bogue-Chitto Creek in Alabama. Rizer then served Lutheran parishes

---

39. Snyder, "Henry D. Wharton—Journalist, Soldier and Public Servant."
40. *Sunbury American*, January 18, 1862.
41. Snyder, "Henry D. Wharton—Journalist, Soldier and Public Servant."
42. *Sunbury American*, October 28, 1865.

in Cumberland, Indiana; Dayton, Ohio; and Somerset, Pennsylvania; before relocating to Northumberland County in 1859.[43]

As the primary Lutheran clergyman in the Sunbury area, Rizer served not only as pastor of Zion Evangelical Lutheran Church, the main Lutheran congregation in Sunbury, but he also covered the pulpits of St. John's Lutheran Church in Northumberland and Eden Evangelical Lutheran Church at Plum Creek in neighboring Upper Augusta Township. His position as a public figure brought Rizer into contact with many prominent members of the community, most notably James Cameron of Milton, the younger brother of Pennsylvania politician Simon Cameron (who would go on to become Abraham Lincoln's first secretary of war). When the Civil War began and Cameron was tapped to become colonel of the 79th New York (Highlanders) State Militia due to the strength of his family's Scottish heritage, he immediately offered Rizer the position of regimental chaplain. Rizer resigned his collective pastorates and went to Washington, D.C., to begin his military service.

Rizer's stint with the Union Army proved quite brief compared to others, derailed by ill health before the first year of the war ended. But in the interim, he became a solid and reliable observer of military events, including the first major combat of the war near Manassas, Virginia. Witnessing the First Battle of Bull Run from a nearby abandoned farmhouse, Rizer's correspondence became significant because it provided a moving first-hand account of the death of Northumberland County's favorite son, Colonel Cameron, the first regimental officer of that rank to fall in battle. Rizer returned to his pastorate in Sunbury and became headmaster of Sunbury Classical Academy for one term before resigning both positions to take charge of a Lutheran congregation in Manchester, Maryland. Upon his departure, the editors of the *Sunbury Gazette* pronounced a fitting summary of Rizer's lasting regard within the community: "Both as a man and a Christian he will be esteemed wherever he may be located."[44]

---

43. Rev. Peter Rizer Biography, Spared & Shared website, https://sparedshared4.wordpress.com/letters/1834-rev-stephen-albion-mealy-to-rev-peter-rizer/ (accessed March 27, 2024).

44. *Sunbury Gazette*, April 26, 1862.

IV.

The letters written by Gobin, Wharton, Rizer, and other Northumberland soldiers conveyed a few different yet consistent themes. Collectively, they broadly chronicled the county's participation in the war. Letters from one or several members of the local companies that were raised in Northumberland during the war in response to the various calls from the War Department in Washington, D.C., recounted how the local population responded to, and thus supported, the national war effort. The letters detailed, sometimes graphically, the specific histories of these local companies, offering important primary narratives of the war. In doing so, they generally did not provide an overarching history of the conflict, but rather described specific events from the perspective of the soldiers on the ground as they experienced them. In this respect, they presented an important voice, and oftentimes a symphony of voices, through which present generations can perhaps better understand the war.

Above all else, most of the soldier correspondents offered fierce expressions of patriotism that never seemed to waver over time. Even though historians have firmly established the ebbs and flows of Northern morale in response to battlefield successes or disasters, and the even more complicated attitudes of the soldiers themselves during the war—the recent scholarship of Brian Matthew Jordan and Peter S. Carmichael readily come to mind[45]—one would hardly notice such nuances from the near constant declarations of unflagging loyalty voiced by these soldier-writers in the field. This may have been intentional, as these soldiers, it should be remembered, were clearly writing for a public rather than a private audience. As Carmichael noted in his masterful study on how soldiers thought, they needed "to be seen as men of bravery who proved their character through noble acts of suffering."[46] They perhaps viewed it as part of their duty to sustain the morale of the home front by regularly articulating words of loyalty and bravery.

Their letters home, therefore, conveyed frequent pledges of complete devotion to the Union, the Constitution, the Stars and Stripes, and the freedom embodied in the American form of government. As one early

---

45. See Jordan, *A Thousand May Fall* (as cited in footnote 13), and Peter S. Carmichael, *The War for the Common Soldier: How Men Thought, Fought, and Survived in Civil War Armies* (Chapel Hill: The University of North Carolina Press, 2018).

46. Carmichael, *War for the Common Soldier*, 101.

recruit declared, "I don't believe that there are any here but what consider it an honor to die in defense of their country.... Our soldiers are enthusiastic with patriotism. They fight for the honor of their country, their flag, the ensign of their former glory."[47] Another recruit likewise commented, "To all those who have taken the old constitution and the old flag close to their hearts, give a soldier's blessing, and for those who think the constitution is torn, and our flag is no better than any other piece of muslin, pass them by."[48] Chaplain Rizer, as well, vowed to "maintain our NATIONALITY, our UNITY, and the INTEGRITY OF THE BEST GOVERNMENT ON EARTH [Rizer's emphasis]."[49]

Support for the Union continued even during the most trying times of the war. In the aftermath of Maj. Gen. Ambrose Burnsides's December 1862 military debacle at Fredericksburg, including the abortive advance in January 1863 that ended in the infamous "Mud March," one correspondent remained confident about the war effort: "It is true our brave and well provided army has been defeated twice at this point, but still we hope. A dark cloud seems to hang over the Republic, but we cannot but trust that all will yet be right. It cannot be that our beloved land will be blighted with ruin forever! Surely right will prevail! If our Government has been founded upon truth, and the God of nations is moving the storm that shakes the world, there can be no doubt of the final triumph of our cause." In a subsequent letter the soldier added, "There can be no doubt to a reasonable mind that the FREEDOM OF MAN and the RIGHT OF SELF GOVERNMENT, are the two great principles that move the contest. The stability of the Republican Government will be fixed on a rock of enduring ages."[50] That the men writing these letters were the ones who were placing themselves in harm's way to defend the Union perhaps explains the root of their enduring patriotism.

The belief that God favored the Union cause as righteous offered another sustaining factor. The soldiers' letters are peppered with various references to divine support. Not surprisingly, as befitted his vocation, Chaplain Rizer frequently led the way with these sentiments. Often invoking divine assistance, for both the nation as a whole and for his own

---

47. Letter of Isaac R. Dunkelberger, April 20, 1861, in *Sunbury Gazette*, April 27, 1861.
48. *Sunbury Gazette*, November 16, 1861.
49. *Sunbury American*, July 13, 1861.
50. Letters of Andrew N. Brice, January 29 and February 20, 1863, in the *Sunbury Gazette*, February 7 and February 28, 1863.

personal safety, Rizer observed on one occasion, "God grant that this wicked rebellion may soon be put down," and on another that "I felt that I had embarked in the sacred cause of duty, and that I could trust God for his protection."[51] He also made it a point to emphasize how the Confederate cause was anathema to God's will: "We are going to try to put down treason and rebellion, which is contrary to God's law, and subversive of the best government on earth. Let us then be true to our God, true to our country, and march fearlessly on in the discharge of our duty, land wherever we may."[52] Another Sunbury soldier echoed similar sentiments when reporting home for the first time: "We have the prayers of the young and the old—the males and the females—the sympathies of the civilized world, and have reason to believe that we have the sympathies of God. Under these circumstances who can fight against us?"[53] So in this regard, God's favor and genuine patriotism formed a powerful combination no enemy could overcome.

Such views also instilled in these soldiers a sense of continued optimism despite the various military setbacks that occurred during the war. In the aftermath of Maj. Gen. George B. McClellan's failed campaign on the Virginia Peninsula, one soldier—who also appeared to parrot McClellan's mistaken notions about the enemy's superior forces—voiced his persistent faith in the fight: "My star of hope for the restoration of the Union shines brightly this moment, neither have I lost sight of it since the rebellion broke out. It did not even become dim in the late series of fights before Richmond. Although we were outnumbered, we sustained no disastrous defeats."[54] Said another soldier in the aftermath of the costly Union trouncing at Fredericksburg: "Notwithstanding our retreat and sad loss of men our army is not demoralized. We are all in good order."[55] Even after Chancellorsville, widely regarded as Robert E. Lee's most brilliant and daring victory, an opposite view of the contest persisted. Attributing the defeat to secondary factors, one correspondent proclaimed, "We were, therefore, not defeated at Chancellorsville, but retreated only because Sedgwick failed at Fredericksburg. The enemy certainly suffered the more severely at the first named place, and although

---

51. *Sunbury American*, September 14, 1861; *Sunbury Gazette*, November 30, 1861.
52. *Sunbury American*, November 30, 1861.
53. *Sunbury Gazette*, April 27, 1861.
54. *Sunbury American*, August 23, 1862.
55. *Sunbury Gazette*, January 10, 1863.

we did not advance, we gave them a terrible thrashing."⁵⁶ Despite frequent battlefield reverses, often attributed to unforeseen circumstances, it seems clear that some Northumberland County soldiers did not necessarily believe the war was going badly.

A persistent belief in the superiority of Northern arms, fighting prowess, and bravery likely sustained such optimism as well. Right from the start at Camp Curtin, Gobin offered his own pronouncement on the fighting trim of the Sunbury Guards: "Our men are in fine condition and excellent spirits and are anxious to show their metal [mettle]. For raw recruits the proficiency they have acquired in marching and the manual is astonishing."⁵⁷ "The Sunbury Guards are composed of small men," Henry Wharton likewise noted, "but they are made of the right grit."⁵⁸ In somewhat more flowery language, Chaplain Rizer also declared the superiority of the Union's martial power: "The prancing of noble steeds, the bristling cannon, the sound of the bugle, and the long files of infantry, together with the thousands of baggage wagons, ambulances, &c., show the undreamed of power of this wonderful Republic of the United States."⁵⁹ As the midpoint of the war approached, another soldier considered the Union's fighting ability to be undiminished: "It is well known that the enemy have never whipped us in the open field! In an open fight, the dashing bravery of our troops has always disgraced them."⁶⁰

General terms such as "our brave boys" or "brave soldiers" are repeated liberally throughout these letters. But tales of bravery extended to personal deeds as well. In relating the experience of a friend who fought with the 1st Minnesota at Bull Run, one soldier observed, "His clothes were riddled with bullet holes, yet he received not a scratch. His captain told me that he fought with that cool bravery which knows no fear."⁶¹ While recounting the story of the 11th Pennsylvania's first formal brush with the

---

56. *Sunbury Gazette*, May 16, 1863. The comment "Sedgwick failed at Fredericksburg" likely refers to the action known as the Second Battle of Fredericksburg or Marye's Heights, which occurred on May 3, 1863. While Hooker moved against Lee, Sedgwick was left in front of Fredericksburg with the 1st and 6th Corps, and the 2nd Corps division of Brig. Gen. John Gibbon. Maj. Gen. Jubal Early's Confederate division held Marye's Heights to watch the Union flank. Ordered to demonstrate against the city to mask Hooker's movements, Sedgwick launched several attacks against Marye's Heights on May 3, finally succeeding in driving the Confederates off the ridge. The action was a tactical Union victory, thus indicating that the correspondent was wrong about his understanding of the operation.
57. *Sunbury Gazette*, April 27, 1861.
58. *Sunbury American*, June 15, 1861.
59. *Sunbury American*, July 13, 1861.
60. *Sunbury Gazette*, January 10, 1863.
61. *Sunbury Gazette*, August 3, 1861.

enemy at Falling Waters, Virginia, a few weeks earlier, Wharton likewise noted, "I saw our brave fellows rush into the fight and pour a volley into the enemy that made them scatter."[62] The most revered examples of individual bravery, though, were reserved for those who made the ultimate sacrifice in battle. One local soldier from the 5th Pennsylvania Reserves related at length the noble death of their color-bearer at Fredericksburg:

> Color-Corporal James C. Voris, a man beloved by all who knew him, fell while gallantly bearing our Star-Spangled Banner on to victory. The flag staff was shattered by a ball a few minutes before he received the wound which terminated his existence; but he instantly seized the colors by the remaining stump and by his daring courage and heroic bravery inspired the Regiment with a zeal which caused them to add new glory to the standard under which we are fighting, and win for themselves immortal fame.[63]

One final act of personal bravery thus offered sufficient inspiration for the rest of the regiment to carry on the fight.

These comments point to a comparison that was routinely (and perhaps not surprisingly) disparaging in nature toward the enemy. Many soldiers unabashedly believed that the Union's military strength and bravery were contrasted by Confederate cowardice, including a propensity for skulking and ambush rather than facing the Northerners in a stand-up fight. In hindsight, we know that both sides fought with equal skill, bravery, and conviction, but at the time some soldiers were quite reluctant to admit as much. Seeing nothing honorable about their Confederate adversaries—and the Southern cause in general—these correspondents denigrated the fighting skill and much-vaunted chivalry of these "Secessionists" at every turn. After conducting a few excursions into the Virginia countryside in 1861, Gobin observed, "This is the style of the warfare practiced by the Southern chivalry. They go sneaking among the grass like cowardly skunks, and shoot sentinels, but as soon as a Regiment appears none are to be found. They retreat before one fourth their number."[64] One soldier even attributed this fighting style as a reason for

---

62. *Sunbury American*, July 3, 1861.
63. *Sunbury Gazette*, February 7, 1863.
64. *Sunbury Gazette*, June 29, 1861.

the embarrassing defeat at Fredericksburg: "They always seek the shelter of a woods, or the protection of batteries, fences, and rifle pits. Hence, had they come out from their works, we would certainly have whipped them at the bloody field of Fredericksburg; for our men struck at the very stones behind which the enemy were secreted."[65] And such views, it should be noted, were not just confined to the fighting ranks; soldiers sometimes had nothing good to say about Southern civilians. As one soldier observed after his regiment occupied Suffolk, Virginia:

> The majority of the men in this neighborhood are the meanest traitors I have met with. They have not the manliness to avow their sentiments openly; but maintain a dogged silence, with the exception of an occasional snarl. They are too cowardly to put on the rebel uniform by day, but they frequently disturb the quiet of the town by firing upon the pickets at night. It is believed these latter named cowards wear the garb of farmers by day and reside not far from the suburbs of Suffolk.[66]

One anti-Southern bias that recurs throughout these letters is a reference to the "sacred soil" of Virginia. The term appears to have been originally coined by the *New York Times*, and was made in response to Governor John Letcher's message to the Virginia General Assembly on January 7, 1861, in which he proclaimed the sanctity of Virginia, inferring that the North would not be allowed to use the Commonwealth as an avenue or throughway to attack or otherwise subdue the seceded states farther south.[67] Once Virginia itself seceded and the fighting actually began, federal troops occupied parts of northern Virginia, leading the *New York Times* to observe, "Last night that event so threateningly denounced by Gov. LETCHER took place. The 'sacred soil' of Virginia received the imprint of thirteen thousand feet on march to the vindication of the Union."[68] Several soldiers writing home to the *Gazette* and the *American* picked up on the phrase and repeated it liberally throughout

---

65. *Sunbury Gazette*, January 10, 1863.
66. *Sunbury American*, October 25, 1862.
67. "Invading Virginia's 'Sacred Soil'," Blue Gray Review website, https://www.bluegrayreview.com/2011/05/25/invading-virginias-sacred-soil/ (accessed May 25, 2024). Governor John Letcher to the Gentlemen of the Senate and House of Delegates, January 7, 1861, is printed as Document No. 1 in the *Journal of the House of Delegates of the State of Virginia, for the Extra Session, 1861* (Richmond, 1861), xx–xxii.
68. *The New York Times*, May 26, 1861.

their correspondence. The phrase appears to have been used in a mocking fashion, although at least one soldier, writing in August 1862, seemed to believe that Virginia soil had been re-sanctified by the baptism of Union blood up to that point: "I felt strangely, as, reaching the Virginia shore of the Potomac, I placed my feet for the first time on the 'sacred soil,'—made sacred at least by the blood and memories of many thousand patriotic soldiers!"[69]

One final observation about these letters seems necessary because it certainly places them, and their authors, firmly within the context of the times in which they were written. The correspondence reveals occasional evidence of racial prejudice—including the casual use of racial slurs now recognized as unacceptable—as soldiers encountered slaves and freedmen, often for the first time, while moving farther into southern territory. Such animus should come as no surprise. It has been well established that most of Northern society in the nineteenth century, while abhorring the institution of slavery, still harbored personal distaste toward African Americans in general.[70] Contrabands—former slaves who escaped to the safety of Union lines—were viewed particularly as inferior, fit only as subjects of derision. Soldiers from Northumberland County, even the more cultured ones such as Captain Gobin, proved no different in this regard, describing contrabands in derogatory terms that seemed inhuman.[71] As Henry Wharton marched south with the 11th Pennsylvania in 1861, what he noticed about the black population of southern Maryland suggested, to him, a level of unruliness that needed physical (i.e., violent) correction: "Indeed the colored people here think that the entire army of the North have come to liberate them, so much so that they have become impudent. If that is their style, and keep on in the manner they are doing, we will have to 'pop' them instead of the people of the 'Confederate States.'"[72]

A curious offshoot of the racial (or perhaps in this case, ethnic) attitudes of the soldiers appeared among those who ended up stationed

---

69. *Sunbury Gazette*, August 30, 1862.

70. Christy Clark-Pujara and Anna-Lisa Cox, "How the Myth of a Liberal North Erases a Long History of White Violence," *Smithsonian Magazine*, August 27, 2020, https://www.smithsonianmag.com/smithsonian-institution/how-myth-liberal-north-erases-long-history-white-violence-180975661/ (accessed May 25, 2024).

71. In one of his letters from Key West, after the 47th Pennsylvania moved south, Gobin wrote, "Of the 7000 contrabands on this Island, nearly all are field hands, and a blacker, uglier lot of mortals were never seen together since the days of Adam." *Sunbury Gazette*, September 13, 1862.

72. *Sunbury American*, June 16, 1861.

in Key West at the beginning of 1862. There, the soldiers of the 47th Pennsylvania, including both Gobin and Wharton, encountered local inhabitants who were descendants of British Tories who had fled Charleston, South Carolina, for the Bahamas during the Revolutionary War. The Bahamians then began emigrating to Key West in large numbers after 1830. These locals, the soldiers learned, were known as "conks," which appeared to be a misspelling (or phonetic spelling) of the word "conch," a common saltwater snail native to the local waters. The term may have originally been derogatory, as many eighteenth-century loyalists in the Bahamas reportedly looked down upon the original white inhabitants of the island, calling them "conchs" because the snail formed such a large part of their diet. At the time of the Civil War, however, the moniker appeared to have become a label of pride.[73] Wharton used the word liberally in his chronicles of military service on the island. Another description he (unfortunately) employed, which was much more demeaning in nature (then as well as now) was the term "dago" in reference to the Spanish inhabitants of the Keys.

Racial prejudice certainly extended, at least during the first half of the war, to the suitability of contrabands for military service. While we now know that African Americans—over two hundred thousand of them—made very capable soldiers, contributing in no small way to the preservation of the Union while taking an active role in their own emancipation, the opposite view persisted among some soldiers in the field. In particular, when Maj. Gen. David Hunter attempted in 1862 to organize contrabands in the Department of the South into a formal brigade, outfitted with their own uniforms, as part of his larger plan to liberate all slaves in the department—a plan quickly quashed by Lincoln as he wrestled with his own emancipation policy—the effort was met with general opposition among the soldiery. Considering contrabands more suited for menial tasks, Wharton noted at length:

> I am happy to inform you that General Hunter's Brigade of people of color, different in hue from Uncle Sam's legitimate soldiers, has been disbanded, and their occupation now is that of "hewers of wood and carriers of water," . . . The idea of clothing

---

73. Thelma Peters, "The Loyalist Migration from East Florida to the Bahama Islands," *The Florida Historical Quarterly* 40:2 (October 1961): 140.

the contraband in the same style with regular and volunteer, did not take with the boys—they thinking it was an insult. The colored man "may be good in his way," but he neither "keep a hotel" or fight along-side of the Yankee boys for the preservation of the Union. Horace Greeley and Wendell Phillips to the contrary, notwithstanding.[74]

Echoing the sentiment, Gobin doubted the fighting ability of the contrabands as well: "Of their fighting qualities I have no idea, but I am satisfied there is not a single Regiment in this Department that would go into a fight with them, or have any confidence in them."[75]

After the Emancipation Proclamation went into effect, however, some soldiers eventually came around to the idea of former slaves being able to support themselves, as well as fight for the Union. Watching the freedmen of Key West celebrate the first anniversary of Emancipation in January 1864, Wharton commented, "If those at home who are continually crying that a negro, when freed, cannot take care of himself and would come to want, had seen these freedmen and women in their gay clothes and the comfortable condition in which they appeared, they would have altered their opinion and come to the conclusion that slavery is a curse and should not be tolerated in a free government."[76] In the last month of the war, one soldier stationed in front of Richmond wondered whether Confederate authorities would finally recognize the benefit black soldiers provided the Union war effort, to the detriment of their own: "And more bitter still [for Rebel leaders] to admit that menial slaves will make good soldiers! The Rebels, from their lines in front of Fort Harrison, can see, every day, regiments and brigades of colored troops going through military evolutions inside of our lines." The military ability of freedmen had become universally evident, the soldier added, as both sides "have been struck with their quick movements, the pride they take in their military bearing, and their aptness in acquiring the duties of a soldier. You would be surprised to see them on the skirmish line, or in

---

74. *Sunbury American*, September 6, 1862. Horace Greeley (1811–1872), founding editor of the *New-York Tribune*, and Wendell Phillips (1811–1884) were both prominent abolitionists who favored raising black regiments for the Union war effort. Phillips, in particular, was one of the main sponsors of the famed all-black 54th Massachusetts Regiment.

75. *Sunbury Gazette*, September 13, 1862.

76. *Sunbury American*, January 30, 1864.

the M'Clellan bayonet exercise, or in the ordinary company drill."[77] By the end of the war, there was some evidence that racial attitudes, at least in terms of final victory and the preservation of the Union, had begun to soften (even if only momentarily, as the ensuing struggle over post-war Reconstruction would quickly demonstrate that racial tensions were far from extinct).

V.

Much thought has gone into the best way to organize these soldiers' letters for publication. The primary consideration has always been to allow the soldiers to tell the story of Northumberland County in the Civil War in their own words. To that end, the correspondence has been grouped into chapters that roughly correspond to general periods of the war. Some of the parts may be more evident than others—such as the initial section that just covers the letters from the three-month regiments, or Chapter 3, which deals with events of the first half of 1862 that culminate with McClellan's Peninsula Campaign in Virginia. Sometimes the sporadic nature of letter-writing dictated how and when letters would be grouped together to convey a cohesive and understandable narrative. In each section, however, the letters are presented in chronological order as they originally appeared in the printed newspapers (even when multiple authors are at work within the same regiment). For the most part, the letters speak from the perspective of the boots on the ground; they do not attempt to place the events they describe into any greater context. The soldiers reported the war as they saw and lived it.

In much the same vein, the commentary that accompanies each section of letters does not seek to explain the overall history of the Civil War—it is assumed that much of the broad details of the conflict are already understood by the reader—but instead provide the necessary context to place the narrative of the letters within the specific actions of the authors' regiments as events unfolded. Contextual annotations are used in reference to names and events mentioned in passing, offering details that the writers would have assumed were common knowledge to their audiences but may not be familiar to modern readers. The text, finally, has been lightly edited for clarity. On a few occasions, some words

---

77. *Sunbury American*, March 25, 1865.

or passages were missing due to damaged newspapers (water stains being a particular hindrance in some editions) or poor microfilming. These gaps are also noted where they occur. That such blemishes exist is truly regrettable. But otherwise, most colloquial spellings, syntax, and terminology—including the derogatory racial vocabulary that was normal for the time but would be considered offensive today—have been retained. The editor begs the reader's indulgence in this last regard, so that these letters may be understood properly, and perhaps appreciated, as speaking truth to the people and the times—an era especially fraught with much division, controversy, and prejudice, as well as great pride and patriotism—in which they were created. Any mistakes that may have occurred in the transcription or interpretation of the correspondence I gladly accept as my own.

1

Lincoln's Three-Month Volunteers, April–July 1861

In the early morning hours of April 12, 1861, Confederate batteries in Charleston harbor opened fire on the federal garrison at Fort Sumter, ultimately forcing the instillation to surrender unconditionally two days later. This unprecedented attack on federal property, by the military forces of a state deemed to be in open rebellion against the United States, provoked an outpouring of patriotic fervor. Local communities across the North responded immediately to President Abraham Lincoln's call on April 15 for seventy-five thousand three-month volunteers to put down the insurrection. In Northumberland County, situated in Central Pennsylvania some fifty miles north of the state capital, residents from the towns and farmlands along the North and West branches of the Susquehanna River to the edge of the anthracite coal fields answered the call with equal enthusiasm. Following a series of local Union meetings, men from Sunbury, Northumberland, Milton, Shamokin, Mount Carmel, and outlying townships, organized themselves into companies and headed off to Camp Curtin in Harrisburg to offer their services to the Union.

The three-month men were placed under the authority of Gen. Robert Patterson. A veteran of the War of 1812, where he served as a colonel in the Pennsylvania militia and a captain in the Regular Army, Patterson also fought in the Mexican War in command of the 2nd Division of the Army of Occupation, and as second-in-command to Winfield Scott. Commissioned as a major general of volunteers in April 1861, Patterson assumed command of all Pennsylvania troops on April 16. A few days later Winfield Scott placed Patterson in charge of the Department of Washington, which comprised the

Gen. Robert Patterson (1792–1881), the oldest general in the Union Army at age sixty-nine at the start of the Civil War, commanded Pennsylvania's three-month regiments in 1861. (Credit: Virginia Tech University Libraries)

Pennsylvania Governor Andrew Gregg Curtin (1815–1894), for whom Camp Curtin in Harrisburg was named. (Credit: Library of Congress)

states of Pennsylvania, Delaware, Maryland, and the District of Columbia. As regiments assembled in Camp Curtin, Patterson funneled them to Chambersburg, where he himself went on June 2 to assume command in the field. Tasked with protecting Pennsylvania and Maryland from invasion and keeping the lines of communication to Washington open and secure, Patterson intended to achieve his objectives by taking the fight to the enemy gathering in the Shenandoah Valley.[1]

Letters From Isaac R. Dunkelberger

*A*s recruits assembled in camp, the first Northumberland resident to reach Harrisburg and enlist was Isaac Rothermel Dunkelberger. The son of Solomon Dunkelberger, a county justice of the peace, and Catherine Rothermel, Isaac was studying law in Sunbury under John B. Packer when Sumter

---

1. Samuel P. Bates, *History of the Pennsylvania Volunteers, 1861–1865*, 5 vols. (Harrisburg: B. Singerly, State Printer, 1870), 1:23.

fell. The day after Lincoln's call for volunteers, Dunkelberger set out on his own for Harrisburg. After reaching Camp Curtin on April 18, he fell in with a local militia outfit, the Cameron Guards, which became Company E of the 1st Pennsylvania Regiment.[2] Although Dunkelberger enlisted with a noncommissioned rank as first sergeant, he did not stay long with the regiment. On April 26, Dunkelberger received an appointment as second lieutenant in the 1st U.S. Dragoons (later designated as the 1st U.S. Cavalry). He accepted the commission on May 13, 1861.[3] Since the 1st Dragoons were then stationed in California, Dunkelberger reported for duty at Carlisle Barracks—a major assembly point for Regular Army units in Pennsylvania—until his regiment returned to the East Coast. During this early phase of the war, Dunkelberger became the first soldier to correspond with the Sunbury newspapers about his martial exploits.

Camp Curtin,
Harrisburg, Pa.,
April 20, [1861], 12 o'clock.[4]

Dear Gazette:—We have an exciting time here. I am a member of the Cameron Guards of this place. Yesterday-noon we were called out in double quick time to the R.R. Depot, with a view of a forced march on Baltimore, an attack having been made by a Baltimore mob on the 7th Regiment of New York, but the riot was quelled and the order remanded. We expect to go on this afternoon with between 6000 and 7000 men. If they attack us, they will meet with a warm reception. We all expect to have warm and bloody times. But I don't believe that there are any here but what consider it an honor to die in defense of their country. We have the prayers of the young and the old—the males and the females—the sympathies of the civilized world, and

---

2. Jaqueline B. Nein, *Dunkelbergers in America, 1728–1997: The Dunkelberger Genealogy* (Reading, PA: Dunkelbergers in America Association, 1997): 14, 25; Cooper H. Wingert, *Harrisburg and the Civil War: Defending the Keystone of the Union* (Charleston: The History Press, 2013), 26–27.

3. Francis B. Heitman, *Historical Register and Dictionary of the U.S. Army*, (Washington: Government Printing Office, 1903): 2:388. Consolidated Officer's File (R506-CB-1870); Fold3, *US, Letters Received by the Commission Branch of the Adjutant General's Office, 1863-1870* (https://www.fold3.com/publication/833/us-letters-received-by-commission-branch-1863-1870 : (accessed June 11, 2024), database and images, https://www.fold3.com/publication/833/us-letters-received-by-commission-branch-1863-1870.

4. *Sunbury Gazette*, April 27, 1861.

have reason to believe that we have the sympathies of God. Under these circumstances who can fight against us? Our soldiers are enthusiastic with patriotism. They fight for the honor of their country, their flag, the ensign of their former glory. I care not for myself if only all traitors meet a traitor's doom. If an American citizen should in after years harbor a traitor's sentiment, may he tremble when he thinks of the doom the traitors met in '61. May we achieve a victory that will form the palladium of our future strength, unity and perpetuity. They are making preparations in the South to throw a strong force into Washington by Sunday or Monday. We expect to be on by that time to give them a hearty welcome.

I have been writing this letter on my knees in the camp. We are now called on to fall in ranks, I suppose to march off.

Past 4 o'clock, P. M.—Troops not off yet; getting ready to go. Raised a flag over the head-quarters a few minutes ago, when an eagle majestically wended its way eastward. It was hailed with enthusiastic cheering that made the welkin ring.[5] It is deemed an auspicious omen. I write this while standing in the ranks.

ISAAC R. DUNKELBERGER

* * * * *

Camp Scott,
York, Pa.,
April 25, 1861.[6]

DEAR EDITOR—Agreeably to promise, I shall endeavor to give you some news that came under my particular observation in regard to the army. I joined, as you are, I presume, already aware, the Cameron Guards, in Harrisburg. In the evening of Saturday, the 21st inst., we formed three Regiments at Camp Curtin, to wit: 1st, 2d and 3d Regiments of Pennsylvania volunteers. The 1st Regiment was composed of companies A, Washington Greys, of Bethlehem; B, City Artillery, Easton; C, Easton Fencibles; D, Scott Greys, Easton; E, Cameron

---

5. "Made the welkin ring" was an idiomatic phrase common at the time that simply meant to make a loud noise or celebration.
6. *Sunbury Gazette*, May 4, 1861.

Guards, Harrisburg; F, Lancaster Fencibles; G, Reading Artillery; H, National Guards; I, Union Rifles, Allentown; J, Jackson Rifles, Lancaster. Each company containing 78 men, rank and file. We were boxed up in a number of freight cars at Harrisburg, on Saturday evening, and after a sleepless and very tedious night's ride, arrived at Cockeysville on Sunday morning, 15 miles north of Baltimore, the point where the rebels had burned down the railroad bridges, to impede our further progress. We took up our position on an eminence, about half a mile north of Cockeysville, a beautiful place to please the eye, but a miserable one in a military view, as our camp was surrounded on three sides by high and almost perpendicular hills, by each of which our camp could have been commanded with artillery, without the slightest possibility of resistance on our part. This gross oversight on the part of our superior officer, may be in part excusable, on the ground that he did not expect to see enemies to the Stars and Stripes, so near the border of the Keystone State. During Sunday afternoon couriers were sent through the country far and wide, apprising the people that the enemy had invaded the soil of Maryland. Horsemen (all secessionists) passed our camp in great haste to apprise the Baltimoreans of the impending danger, telling them that a northern army of 8 or 10 thousand men had camped at Cockeysville, threatening to kill and burn everything before them. This was a wise scheme in the secessionists, to force the loyal men under their banner. Churches were closed in Baltimore, and mustering of troops became the order of the day. While these miserable rebels were boiling over with rage, entirely unprovoked, we were coolly partaking of some crackers, and a little cold beef, which every man carried with him in his haversack. After the inner man was strengthened and invigorated, the men gathered stones and various other conveniences on which to lay their heads, as we neglected to bring houses, tents and beds with us. In the afternoon we were visited by a number of fine and intelligent ladies. We soon learned that they sympathized with the country's (Stars and Stripe's) cause. Whilst the band played the "Star-Spangled Banner," I noticed tears—warm and affectionate tears—trickle down the cheeks of many of the ladies that were present. I felt happy to learn that the tender chord that binds

Brigadier General George C. Wynkoop, commander of Pennsylvania Volunteers in 1861. (Credit: Pennsylvania Volunteers in the Civil War, www.pacivilwar.com)

millions of hearts to the flag—the ensign of our country's glory—was not entirely rent asunder even in Baltimore. On one occasion, the following Monday, I took the liberty to speak to two of the ladies I had noticed the day previous. I asked them what impression the northern troops had made upon them. They answered me frankly the impression was favorable; that the northern people had been misrepresented to them; that they sympathized with the flag of our common country. They said most emphatically that they felt perfectly safe so long as we were among them, but no longer, as that part of the country is in the hands of traitors and rebels. A tear of patriotic sympathy from *such* ladies, is worth more than the co-operation of a million of outlaw thieves, traitors and rebels. Our troops, 2340 in number, were commanded by Gen. Wynkoop[7] (not of Mexico notoriety). As twilight had fairly disappeared, and the exhausted soldiers had fairly nestled themselves for a night's repose, we were unceremoniously aroused by the clamors of war. The emergency found everyone at his post, 1st Regiment in front, whilst the click of hammers was heard in our ranks. The sound of the bugle, the drums, and hurrahs for Jeff. Davis, very forcibly struck our ears from the ranks of the rebels. Our Officers went around encouraging their men to wit: "keep cool," "aim low at the word fire, &c.," to which I heard the following response from a soldier in company E, 1st Regiment: "let them come, we'll give them the best we've got in the shop, &c." But their noise soon abated; although they had several thousand men, fully equipped, with sufficient artillery &c., yet the cowardly rascals dared not attack us. We slept all night on our arms, being aroused at regular intervals of about an hour each, till daylight. The soldiers, of course, got tired of this kind of nonsense, and would rather have had a fight than be kept in such suspense, so one in the 1st Regiment offered a cheer for the "Stars and Stripes," which was responded to with deafening applause, for nearly five minutes, notwithstanding the remonstrances and calls of order by the superior officers. One man fell dead in company A, caused by excitement; another had both his heels shot off by accident, by a man in his rear; another had his finger shot off; another had his side grazed by a bullet, and slightly wounded—all accidental. Our company has had one deserter. I am glad we have got rid of the cowardly poltroon. On Monday evening we marched for the cars to return, and arrived in York, Pa., on Tuesday at 9 o'clock. Here we are well taken care of, and our camp has been christened Camp Pleasant, contrasting considerably in comfort with Camp Misery, Cockeysville. I don't know how soon we shall be called off; we are ready in an hour's notice. I think we shall go to Washington via Philadelphia. I have no more to communicate at present. This has been written on

---

7. George C. Wynkoop (1806–1882). Commissioned as a brigadier general of Pennsylvania Volunteers by Governor Andrew Curtin on April 19, 1861, Wynkoop was in command of the 2nd Brigade of General William Keim's division in Major General Robert Patterson's Department of Pennsylvania. The "not of Mexico notoriety" comment following Wynkoop's name may have been a reference to Pennsylvania (Pottsville) native Francis M. Wynkoop (1820–1857), who served as colonel of the 1st Pennsylvania Infantry in the Mexican War and was later promoted to brigadier general and made Governor of Castle de Perote, the military district where Mexico subsequently surrendered to Winfield Scott.

the head of a drum. I am well and in good spirits, hoping that I may help to haul down the Palmetto flag.

I. R. DUNKELBERGER

* * * * *

Camp Scott,
York, Pa.,
May 4, 1861.[8]

FRIEND JOHN.—We have now 7 full regiments encamped here, all from this State, numbering 780 men, rank and file, in each regiment. The men are all armed, but a number of them have not yet got their uniforms. We have 5 field pieces in camp, and more are expected daily. If we march again[,] we shall undoubtedly be prepared to defend ourselves effectually against any attack that may be made at any point intervening between here and Washington. Our situation here is a very pleasant one—citizens very sociable, generous and patriotic. We have plenty of good, substantial and wholesome provisions. We have no tents, and our lodgings were rather deficient until this morning. We had nothing but temporary huts, not enclosed and poorly roofed—they leaked like sieves—layed on the ground, thinly covered with feathers (straw.) The nights have been very cold for the past week, and on Thursday night I was really compelled to run around the camp for three hours to keep warm. I met hundreds of others who passed the greater part of the night in the same way, or in other words, who like myself became industrious through necessity. Yesterday noon it commenced to snow and rain, and continued incessantly till this morning, ten o'clock. Such inclement weather, this time of the year, was very unexpected, and the soldiers suffered very severely here last night. The majority of them slept on the wet ground, covered with wet blankets. I myself passed the night in that condition, although I had a pass from General Wynkoop to lodge in town, but I made up my mind that so long as I belonged to the Cameron Guards, I would share their fate, and share in reaping their laurels. Whilst we were suffering in Camp last night, the good citizens of York were

---

8. *Sunbury Gazette*, May 11, 1861.

vigorously preparing better quarters for us. Churches, school houses, court houses and other buildings were thrown open for our reception, this morning. We took possession of the Presbyterian church. The streets were lined with men and women who sympathized heartily with the soldiers. They soon furnished us with hot coffee, pies, cakes and other delicacies, which they brought in great abundance to our new places of rendezvous. Our apartment was furnished with a stove, plenty of fuel and the room well warmed. Tears of gratitude filled the eyes of some of the soldiers. Who would not feel grateful for such favors at such a time? We are now very comfortably situated, and the soldiers are in good spirits.

I just now noticed an article in the "Philadelphia Inquirer," speaking very laudably of the Sunbury ladies, stating that they were very active in furnishing the soldiers with edibles and other comforts. For such generous actions, they will gain the respect of every patriotic American citizen, and may the blessing of God rest upon them for every noble deed. Ladies, we ask but your sympathies and your prayers, and the Stars and Stripes shall wave over generations yet unborn. Long may it remain the emblem of our glory—the pride of every American!

I noticed in the "New York Herald" yesterday the appointment of Isaac Dunkelberger as 2nd Lieutenant in the U. S. army, published. I wonder whether it is Isaac Dunkelberger of Cameron township (!)[9] If so he will be very apt to have the Cameron Guards of that place called into active service, knowing them to be brave and well drilled, as well as having been strenuous supporters of Old Abe, and have made themselves conspicuous, by uttering strong Union sentiments. For the present, I remain, sir, your obedient servant.

ISAAC R. DUNKELBERGER

* * * * *

---

9. Dunkelberger here is likely making a facetious reference to himself, after being appointed second lieutenant in the 1st U.S. Cavalry. He formally accepted the appointment on May 13, 1861.

Carlisle, Pa.,
June 4, 1861.[10]

Dear Gazette.—I have been sick for some time, but have now again become able for duty. My indisposition is the only apology I shall make for not writing to you sooner. I am now stationed at Carlisle Barracks. This is a beautiful place, quarters clean, roomy and comfortable. Upwards of ten thousand soldiers have passed through this place enroute for Chambersburg. The Pennsylvania 1st Regiment (Col. Yohe) was recalled from Baltimore and passed through here last night—destination Chambersburg. (I suppose finally Harper's Ferry.) This is the regiment to which I was attached while in the volunteer service. Four companies, eighty men each, of the Second Cavalry, U. S. Army, left this barracks on Friday last, also for Chambersburg. They were fine men, mounted and well drilled. Three hundred and fifty regulars left here yesterday for New Mexico. My company, company E, 1st Dragoons, U. S. A., is stationed in California. I expect I shall be ordered there in a few months.

This day we executed the orders of a Court Martial held here a few days ago. Three deserters had the letter D branded on their left hip, were then marched up to a cannon, there stripped of their coat, shirt, &c., and tied hands and feet to the gun carriage, after which thirty lashes, well laid on with a raw-hide, were applied to their bare backs. The flesh was much lacerated and the blood oozed out quite freely. They were then marched out of the barracks bare-headed to the tune of the Rogue's March played by the band. They have learned that the "way of the transgressor is hard." Although I could shed a tear for a cruelly killed sparrow, I felt no sympathy for the *Deserters*. They deserved all they got. Yea, a deserter these times deserves *death*, and that shall be my vote when I am on a court martial. He who would *now* shirk from the duties he owes to his country is not fit to live under the protection of the stars and stripes, the emblem of our fathers' patriotism.

We have here about fifteen new appointees out of the ranks of the volunteers. They differ materially from the Cadets of West Point. The latter are haughty, proud, overbearing, and some of them, if you

---
10. *Sunbury Gazette*, June 8, 1861.

may judge from their language, not any too loyal. The appointees are sociable, genteel, and firmly devoted to their country.

More anon.
I. R. D.

* * * * *

Carlisle, Pa.,
June 9, 1861.[11]

Dear Gazette:—On Saturday, five companies of the 3rd United States Infantry to wit: company B, Capt. Shepherd; company D, Lieut. Bell commanding; company G, Lieut. Williams commanding; company H, Capt. Sheridan; and company -----, Capt. Sykes, accompanied by a fine band, arrived at this place en route for Chambersburg. They had a good night's rest in the Barracks, when on Sunday morning they again took the cars. They are a part of the troops that were commanded by the traitor Twiggs in Texas.[12] They are a fine set of men, have apparently seen much hard service, but look as if they could stand much more. They denounce Twiggs in strong terms, and express their anxiety to meet the foe. Company F of the 4th United States Artillery, is now stationed here, and had an accession of 45 men to their company from the ranks of the recruits of this place. They will soon join the army under command of General Patterson, which is now under marching orders for Northern Virginia. The column is headed by Col. Thomas, 2nd Regiment of U. S. Cavalry.

All the new appointees are held under strict military discipline. We recite daily to some experienced officer, after which we drill, so that we can obtain both theoretical and practical knowledge of our future duties.

I have been attending divine worship in the various Churches since my sojourn here, and must say that I was particularly struck with the sermon I heard on Sabbath morning last. The speaker's bearing was independent, yet noble—unassuming in his appearance,

---

11. *Sunbury Gazette*, June 17, 1861.
12. Brevet Maj. Gen. David E. Twiggs (1790–1862), head of the Department of Texas, surrendered his entire command to Confederate authorities after his native Georgia seceded from the Union. The U.S. Army promptly cashiered him for treason on March 1, 1861.

yet interesting in his manner and eloquent in his arguments; his train of passages were replete with patriotic sentiments, more firmly and fearlessly expressed than I ever heard before. I was as much pleased with his remarks, that I felt a desire of forming his acquaintance, and give him an invitation to accompany me to Sunbury. I did so, and learned that he was Rev. Ross, who told me he preached on the Sunbury circuit some years ago. He accepted my invitation very cordially. So, if no Providential interposition occurs, you may expect us up on Tuesday, the 18th day of June.

I. R. D.

P. S. Mr. Ross had the Star-Spangled Banner sung in Church here last Sabbath. He told them if there were any so religious that they did not like it, they might lump it. He said it was as good a tune as he wanted to hear these times; and if it was offensive to the ears of some, they might go down to South Carolina or Florida, where they would not need to listen to it.

* * * * *

Carlisle, Pa.,
July 28, 1861.[13]

Dear Gazette:—We sent by orders of War Department upwards of two hundred recruits from this place to Washington within the last week, for the purpose of filling up the various companies of regulars to their maximum number. On the 22d inst., I was called to Washington with a squad of men to reinforce company D, 2d Artillery, U. S. A., which gave me a fine opportunity to learn a few particulars in reference to the great battle fought on the previous day. Our soldiers evidently fought with desperation, and achieved prodigies that have no precedent. The right wing of our army, Col. Heintzelman commanding, was called in rank on Sunday morning at one o'clock; they then marched upwards of 12 miles, the last two of which were marched in "double quick time," when they were brought to face the enemy in a fatigued condition. The 1st Minnesota, and New

---

13. *Sunbury Gazette,* August 3, 1861.

Wartime image of Second Lieutenant Isaac Rothermel Dunkelberger. (Credit: U.S. Army History & Education Center)

York Fire Zouaves[14] fought side by side, and now speak of each other in the highest terms. About noon they marched up a hill; when on the eminence they saw four regiments approaching them with the stars and stripes floating over them; thus[,] they marched in disguise till they came within about 80 yards of our brave boys, when they opened a deadly volley which was promptly answered with great effect. One of the four regiments proved to be the Louisiana Zouaves, the balance Georgians and Alabamians. They were repulsed after a severe hand to hand contest. Soon after the celebrated Black Horse Cavalry, about 1000 in number, made a desperate charge against the Ellsworth Zouaves, and left wing of the Minnesota regiment. The N. Y. Zouaves did not fire until they could almost touch them with the muzzles of their guns. They were repulsed with tremendous

---

14. The 11th New York Infantry, also known as the 1st New York Fire Zouaves, commanded by Col. Elmer Ephraim Ellsworth.

slaughter; only seven were seen to return. Our boys were afterwards forced to retreat in consequence of a masked battery which opened on them with terrific effect. On one occasion the N. Y. Zouaves were ordered to charge on one of the enemy's batteries, which they did in the most exemplary manner. They were actually seen to mount the guns, and deal death blows to the enemy with bowie knives, whilst they were applying the matches to their pieces to send their deadly missiles among our brave soldiers. The New York 69, 71, 79 and Wisconsin 2d, and Michigan 1st, fought with equal bravery. They have won for themselves laurels that are imperishable—they have endeared themselves to a grateful people.

    The acquaintance that I had formed with a large number of the men that now compose the 1st Minnesota regiment, enabled me to become on intimate terms with them, through which intimacy they related a few incidents which might be interesting to your readers. On one occasion whilst our column was advancing, they passed a wounded rebel who begged for water, stating that he was dying. Mr. Williams, of the N. York Zouaves, give him some out of his own canteen. After the rebel was sufficiently recuperated, he drew a revolver and shot his benefactor through the heart. On another occasion, when two wounded rebels begged for water, Charles Mansfield, of Mankato, 1st Minnesota, threw them his canteen: after he had advanced some distance, he looked around, and saw one of the same wounded rebels stab one of our wounded men with a bayonet. Wm. McCoy of the 1st Minnesota told me that whilst dragging one of his wounded comrades to the hospital, the enemy fired volley after volley at him, and then after they fired hot shot, and burned it, with the wounded. His clothes were riddled with bullet holes, yet he received not a scratch. His captain told me that he fought with that cool bravery which knows no fear. He was one of my intimate friends during my sojourn in Mankato in 1857. When I left Washington on Wednesday evening, there were missing from the Minnesota Regiment about 350, and from the New York Zouaves upwards of 400. On Tuesday evening a friend and I were setting in a saloon on Pennsylvania Avenue, when a weary soldier entered with a musket slung across his shoulder. He was hungry and fatigued. We soon procured something that strengthened his inner man, after which the quizzing commenced. He said he was from the 1st Michigan. That they were fools for running as there was no enemy after them. He slept soundly alongside the road on Sunday night near Centreville. On Monday he came as far as Fairfax, and on Tuesday evening he entered Washington without meeting with the enemy. He felt very indignant at their precipitate retreat, stating that the road was strewn with arms, knapsacks, &c. Sherman's battery has all returned with the exception of one piece, which is supposed to be in the hands of the enemy. Col. Miles, of the regular army, is under arrest for gross misconduct during the battle. He was beastly intoxicated. Other officers are severely censured in high circles for incapacity, and even cowardice. It is authoritatively stated that those that run first and fastest had rectangles on their shoulders. Time may develop many things that are yet dark. The commander's orders did not reach some of the regiments during the whole of the battle. The quarter master of Washington, instead of sending fifty tons of ammunition, sent five. The consequence was that some of our batteries were short of shot ere the battle was over. The 4th and 5th Pennsylvania regiments did not show that alacrity in moving forward to Bull's Run that we had reason to expect. Neither did Gen. Patterson come up to the lofty expectation of the good "old Keystone." Harrisburg, too, presents a spectacle at present not of the most enviable nature. Hundreds of volunteers are laying around the streets beastly intoxicated, a disgrace to themselves, their State, and the holy cause in which they are engaged. A good soldier must necessarily be a good *man* and a *gentleman*. Yet in all this our leaders may be more justly censured than the private soldiers. Many of the officers were *entirely* deficient in military skill, and showed bad examples to those they had under command. While some of our State political tricksters, and contractors have filled their pockets with ill-gotten money, which was intended to procure clothing, provision and other comforts for our needy soldiers. These are sad truths which there is no use in keeping secret or equivocating. I hope that in future our brave boys will be better cared for, and I feel satisfied that they will give a good account of themselves. I cannot find language sufficient to express my sorrow at the death of our loyal and esteemed friend, Col.

James Cameron.[15] We must bow our heads, and, though sorrowfully, yet with silent assent, submit to the will of God.

Yours, truly,
I. R. D.

* * * * *

Letters From William Wolverton

*A*nother Sunbury resident, William Wolverton, son of Dennis Wolverton of Lower Augusta Township, also made his own way to Camp Curtin, where he fell in with the 10th Pennsylvania Regiment on April 28, 1861. Organized just two days prior under the command of Col. Sullivan A. Meredith, the 10th Pennsylvania remained in camp until May 1, when it was ordered to move by rail to Chambersburg. Upon arrival, the regiment bivouacked at Camp Slifer, named in honor of Pennsylvania's Secretary of the Commonwealth Eli Slifer. Daily drills commenced, and the regiment became part of the 3rd Brigade, 1st Division of Pennsylvania forces under Patterson. Along with the 10th Regiment, the 3rd Brigade included the 7th, 8th, and 20th Pennsylvania Regiments. The 10th remained at Camp Slifer until June 8, when it was ordered to march to Greencastle.[16] Wolverton's association with the 10th Pennsylvania, however, ended before that movement took place, as he had been examined by the regimental surgeons and pronounced unfit for duty. "[T]he Surgeon is examining all in the regiment and if any are found physically unsound, they are immediately discharged," he wrote on May 22, in only the second of two letters Wolverton had time to send home. "And being defective myself," he added, "I am sorry to say I will be home at the last of this week, considered unfit for military duty."[17] After Wolverton returned home, the Sunbury American reported on his unsuccessful effort to enlist, noting he was rejected "on account of a defect caused by a cut severing the muscles of his left arm, which, he had hoped would be overlooked." Although Wolverton

---

15. James Cameron (1800–1861), the younger brother of Secretary of War Simon Cameron, served as colonel of the 79th New York Volunteer Infantry and was killed in action at the First Battle of Bull Run on July 21, 1861. See the Chaplain Peter Rizer letters in the following pages for additional context.
16. Bates, *Pennsylvania Volunteers*, 1:96–98.
17. *Sunbury American*, May 25, 1861.

tried to join the Sunbury Guards as well as two other companies, "fate and the surgeons were against him."[18]

Camp Curtin
April 28, 1861.[19]

MR. EDITOR—*Dear Sir:*—By your permission I send you a few lines of intelligence relative to life in Camp Curtin, and things in general, which seem to me might properly be denominated hardships by anyone else than a soldier.

We live in tents of an area of about 7 feet square, and five or six piled in them to sleep, as they say, but at the most it is only snoozing. Our rations are abundant and rich, and are as follows: One day we get good soft bread, with some raw pork, or cooked, if we happen to have anything to cook it with ourselves. The next day the same thing, with coffee strong enough to bear two eggs, the one on the top of the other. The above is not a very flattering description, but a soldier's bed is not a bed of roses. But the living of the officers and some others is very good, being all that is usually found on our farmers' tables.

By permission of the captain, we sometimes get into Harrisburg, but are required to be back at 9 o'clock or quarter the night outside, and in addition to this we have to guard eight hours the next day, so extreme is our pleasure, if you approve of this kind of pleasure.

Any one just coming into Camp Curtin, would suppose that there was a sufficient number of soldiers in it now to wipe out all Southern traitors with ease, as they present a most animated feeling to the looker on.—But after having been here a few days, the scene becomes common, and would rather depress than enliven the heart, were it not for the daily exceedingly numerous visits of the Harrisburg ladies, the sweet and smiling faces of whom, although unknown, imbues the heart with new life, enjoyed in tranquility and peace, free from the noisy bustle of the world's "busy mart." Yet it is well for us to know that such a life, at so critical a time, is not possible to be enjoyed, and the only way to secure its enjoyment is, (dark as matters

---

18. *Sunbury American*, June 1, 1861.
19. *Sunbury American*, May 4, 1861.

now appear,) to keep the wheels of the government unobstructed, that their advancement may not be impeded. But if the question as to what manner this can be done should arise, let the answer be by calm and decided counsels. But if that fails, let us enforce the right even at the sacrifice of our lives, and if we live through the struggle we will enjoy our own reward. If not, we can terminate our lives with the assurance of a reward by our posterity.

I am happy to say that I have a position at the headquarters, and consequently live very well. But thinking this sufficient for those who peruse your columns, to read without wearied patience, I shall close by informing you that I expect to leave with the Tenth Regiment. Our destination is yet unknown, but I hope to send you another letter before long, more interesting to your readers.

Yours, respectfully,
WM. WOLVERTON.

* * * * *

Letter from Camp Slifer,
Chambersburg, Pa.,
May 22, 1861.[20]

MR. EDITOR:
I undertake to place in your columns a description of things here, both as they have been and still are, with a brief remark of our journey to this place. On the 2nd of May, we left Camp Curtin in the evening for some unknown destiny, to say nothing of the noisy and lively time leaving Harrisburg. We passed on to Mechanicsburg, where we stopped and gave our iron-horse something to drink in order to keep up his spirits in the capacity of steam. By this time we all knew where we were bound for, which had no bad impression upon us. The next place we passed through was Carlisle, where we were cheered and greeted by people of all classes and colors, and after a rapid ride landed at Chambersburg. We immediately marched through the dusty streets to some place called a Camp, where we were placed under some kind of a covering and into a pile of straw. The question whether we would

---

20. *Sunbury American*, May 25, 1861.

ever see daylight or not again, was answered by hoping we might. After sleeping through the remaining part of the night, we awoke in the morning finding ourselves in some place not much unlike a sheep pen. But the next thing was to swallow our breakfasts, which we did without much trouble, on crackers brought from Harrisburg, with us. After a few days of rainy weather[,] we looked for clear skies, but it seemed we got in the wrong quarter for that kind weather, which was very unpleasant, and in addition to this inconvenience, our rations proved not sufficiently plenty, including sour bread at that. But within a short time we have provided a Quartermaster for ourselves, as has each of the two other Regiments here, since which time our rations have been both plenty and sweet. Of course, leaving Sunbury friends at Harrisburg, and coming here among persons, none of whose faces were familiar to me, matters appeared rather unlively at first, but after a few day's companionship, friends were found with as cheerful hearts as ever formed any part of man. We have got used to rainy days now and don't mind them anymore, consequently things move on with all life imaginable. All the boys are in excellent condition, and ready and willing to march to the field of battle at any time. Their greatest sorrow is, that they have not much encouragement of getting into a contest very soon. The exceedingly kind ladies of Chambersburg present the best of all kinds of cakes and pies to the soldiers every week. And last week we had a grand time at the reception of a flag, presented by the ladies of Lancaster. Several speeches were made, rendering thanks to the ladies, and several most beautiful airs were performed, alternately, by the Chambersburg band and a choir of gentlemen and ladies from that place.

The soldiers are nearly equipped, and when entirely so will march southward, for their destined work. Last week two men from Harper's Ferry enlisted here, and were sworn into service, in Company B. They stated that last Sunday there were but two thousand troops there then and poorly equipped.

In conclusion let me say that there is a great time here relative to the enlisting of soldiers for three years or the war, and for that reason the Surgeon is examining all in the regiment and if any are found physically unsound, they are immediately discharged. And being defective myself, I am sorry to say I will be home at the last of this week, considered unfit for military duty by the Surgeon of 10th Regiment.

Yours with Respect,
WM. WOLVERTON.

* * * * *

Letters from the Shamokin Guards
Company A, 8th Pennsylvania Volunteer Regiment

*E*ven though Wolverton missed his opportunity to serve in the field, the exploits of the 3rd Brigade were chronicled by the Shamokin Guards, another Northumberland militia from the anthracite coal region of the county that had first organized in 1854. Upon their arrival at Camp Curtin, the Shamokin Guards under Capt. Cyrus Strouse became Company A of the 8th Pennsylvania Regiment on April 22, 1861. After the 8th moved with the brigade to Camp Slifer near Chambersburg, they proceeded to Greencastle, Pennsylvania, on June 7, where they went into camp for a few days of battalion drill. Then, the 8th Regiment marched to the Potomac River near Williamsport, Maryland, to guard the local fords. The regiment remained on guard duty while the rest of Patterson's army moved into Virginia on July 2.[21] Private Alexander Caldwell penned several letters to the* Gazette *during the company's first month in camp.*

Camp Slifer,
Chambersburg, Pa.,
May 7, 1861.[22]

Friend Youngman—I am attached to Company A, (Shamokin Guards,) 8th Regiment, Pennsylvania Volunteers, now stationed here. We left Sunbury, April 22d, en route for Harrisburg, where we arrived at 3 o'clock in the afternoon. We were enthusiastically greeted all along the route—the citizens of the different towns through which

---

21. Bates, *Pennsylvania Volunteers*, 1:77–78.
22. *Sunbury Gazette*, May 11, 1861.

we passed turning out en masse and bringing us refreshments which were thankfully received as we did not leave the cars until arrived at our destination. Upon our leaving the cars at Harrisburg we were met by Col. A. H. Emley, of the 8th, to which regiment we belong, and marched to Camp Curtin, where we were quartered for the night. Next morning after being drilled for a short time, we returned to our quarters where we received orders to march at an hour's notice. After receiving our arms and having our haversacks filled with crackers and corned beef, we took the cars for Chambersburg, at which place we arrived about 1 o'clock in the morning, and were quartered in the Court House—a very fine building.

No pen can describe the enthusiasm with which we were greeted all along the route. At Mechanicsburg, Newville, Carlisle and Shippensburg the citizens surrounded the cars, and cheered us lustily. At the latter place fair ladies greeted and shook hands with us, wishing us God speed in the good cause. The citizens of Chambersburg did all in their power to make us comfortable while quartered among them. After being quartered for two days in the Court House we marched to Camp Slifer which is on the East of the town. Since our arrival here the ladies have done everything to make us comfortable. All honor to them—and with their presence and smiles to cheer us we are invincible. All our men are healthy and in good spirits. Under the supervision of our excellent Colonel, who is a man of great worth, we are becoming adepts in the military art. Our camp is in a beautiful country, and with such soldiers as we have here stationed, the honor of the old Keystone will be maintained, and her soil kept clear of the foot of the invader. There are here at the present time three regiments or 2340 men. All are in good condition, and if they meet the foe will do good work. Capt. Campbell's company of Flying Artillery left last week for Camp Scott. We will probably march to-morrow. Baltimore is our probable destination. I will write you as to our movements wherever we may be stationed.

Yours respectfully,
ALEX. CALDWELL.

* * * * *

Camp Slifer,
Chambersburg, Pa.,
May 14, 1861.[23]

FRIEND YOUNGMAN.—I wrote you in my last that we were going to leave here and that our destination would probably be Baltimore. The report appears to have been false. As I write there is a report in camp that we are to leave to-night, but it needs confirmation. Last night the 7th Regiment had everything packed up ready to leave, but they are here yet this morning. It is supposed that they leave today.

Last Wednesday the ladies of Chambersburg presented our Regiment with a flag. The men of Col. Emley's command were drawn up in a hollow square to receive it. Ex-Senator Brewer[24] on behalf of the ladies, presented it in a telling speech. Hon. Judge Conyngham[25], of Wilkes-Barre, responded in a brief but eloquent address. It was an impressive sight to see the old man—his gray hairs streaming in the wind—lifting up his voice in behalf of his country and her flag so basely assailed by traitors—traitors of a darker dye than ever was Arnold. On Saturday the ladies again presented us with a flag larger than the first one. J. K. Shyrock on behalf of the ladies presented it. It was received by Capt. Wise, of the Brookville Rifles, who made an eloquent speech. While its folds were still fluttering in his hands, hovering over the flag-staff high in the heavens, was seen the American eagle. When the flag was raised to the top of the staff, he darted far away toward the North as if to bear the tidings of the day's transactions to other camps.

Yesterday the 7th Regiment had a street parade. The avenues through which they passed were densely crowded. They are a well drilled corps, and made a fine display. Good health prevails in camp, and all are in fine spirits. For some days past our provisions have been

---

23. *Sunbury Gazette*, May 18, 1861.
24. This is likely a reference to George W. Brewer (1819–1886), Democrat, who served in the Pennsylvania State Senate from the 11th District (Adams and Franklin Counties), 1857–58, and the 18th District (Adams, Franklin, and Fulton Counties), in 1859.
25. Judge John Nesbitt Conyngham (1798–1871), president judge of the 13th Judicial District (1839–49) and the 11th Judicial District (1851–70) of Pennsylvania.

very indifferent, but arrangements are being made which will bring all things right in a few days. We have had a great deal of rain during the past week, and camp life in consequence is pretty disagreeable. This morning the Sun is shining brightly, and our spirits are rising accordingly.

Every precaution is taken to prevent a surprise, as we are not far from the enemy's border. Picket guards are nightly stationed on the Baltimore Pike and the Hagerstown Road. Last week I formed one of the number. We marched in mud nearly knee deep, about two miles down the Hagerstown Road, and were stationed for the night. No enemy but an old cow appearing, we came back in the morning as bravely as we went out.

From present reports we are likely to go into active service soon. I have no doubt that the soldiers of the 8th, wherever they may be placed, will do their whole duty. The best interests of humanity are at stake in the present struggle, and he is a craven heart who would not hurl back the traitor who attempts to tear down our flag. If the worst comes to the worst—if it is "war to the knife and the knife to the hilt," we will not falter, but keep the folds of our glorious flag free from the polluting touch of traitors.

If we move from here this week I will keep you informed as to our movements.

Yours respectfully,
CALDWELL.

* * * * *

Camp Slifer,
Chambersburg, Pa.,
May 21, 1861.[26]

Friend Youngman:—Reports are so conflicting that we don't know when we shall move, but I see by last night's "Press" that we are to occupy Hagerstown in a few days. Last week the three regiments stationed here had street parades. We were marched about 3 miles into the country for the purpose, I suppose, of testing our marching

---
26. *Sunbury Gazette*, May 25, 1861.

capabilities. On Saturday, His Excellency, Governor Curtin, accompanied by several high dignitaries, reviewed us. On the same day, Hon. Judge Mason[27], late collector of the port of Baltimore and an avowed secessionist, was taken prisoner by Gen. Williams. Next day upon being examined, he was released. A deserter from Harper's Ferry states that the troops there are in a bad condition, being badly provisioned and not so well armed and equipped as is generally supposed. Upon being cross-examined by an experienced lawyer, he did not vary the slightest from his statement.

The monotonous role of camp life presents very poor material for the pen of the correspondent. When the weather is fine, after the duties of the day, however onerous they may be, groups of soldiers may be seen collected on the parade ground tripping the "light fantastic toe" beneath the mild light of the May moon. The German element of the soldiery gather before their tents—or rather shanties—and sing songs of the *Fatherland*. They are uniformly a jovial, merry set of fellows, and have an appreciation of the cause in which they are enlisted; the large majority having fought for Republican principles in their own country.

From reports yesterday mounted patrols were sent forward toward the Maryland line. What the result of their reconnaissance was I know not. The picket and camp guards were last night furnished with several rounds of ball-cartridges each, and great strictness was observed, not even an officer being allowed to leave the camp. All remained quiet, however, during the night, and no visions of a lurking foe stealing upon us disturbed our slumbers, or made our dreams unpleasant.

It rained all day yesterday, and the parade ground is not yet dry enough to allow of any drilling. Several of our members having been discharged on account of sickness, our company was not full. Yesterday three recruits arrived from Shamokin, and we again have the requisite number. As we are daily receiving some part of our

---

27. John Thomson Mason Jr. (1815–1873), a lawyer from Hagerstown, Maryland, served one term in the Maryland House of Representatives (1838) and one term in the U.S. Congress (1841) before becoming a judge on the Court of Appeals of Maryland in 1851. He resigned to become Collector for the Port of Baltimore in 1857. Being warmly sympathetic with the South, Mason retired to private life during the Civil War and was twice imprisoned as a Southern sympathizer. At the close of the war Mason resumed his law practice in Baltimore, and in 1872 became Secretary of State of Maryland under Governor William Pinkney Whyte.

accoutrements, I suppose we will soon leave and go southward. I will write to you wherever we may be stationed.

Yours, respectfully,
CALDWELL.

* * * * *

Camp Slifer, Pa.,
June 1, 1861.[28]

Friend Youngman: —I received a paper from you last night in which you stated that you had not received a letter from me, and asked the reason. I will answer you in a few words. The letters which are mailed by the volunteers are *franked*, and I suppose *that* has occasioned the delay, for previous to this I paid the postage myself, and my letters always arrived in time for the issue of your paper.[29]

Since I wrote you last[,] seven additional regiments have arrived, and there are here at present time of writing, the Second, Third, Sixth, Seventh, Eighth, Tenth, and some others, including a Delaware regiment. They are all well-equipped and ready for action.

This week the Seventh and Eighth received more accoutrements, the Eighth receiving knapsacks and overcoats, and the Seventh the same, with the addition of cartridge boxes.

From what I can learn to-day we will probably march on the enemy very soon. Our destination is Virginia. All the men are healthy, and in good spirits, desiring nothing so much as to meet the enemy. As my time is limited, I must close my hastily written letter. More in my next.

Yours, Respectfully,
CALDWELL

* * * * *

---

28. *Sunbury Gazette*, June 8, 1861.
29. The "franking" privilege allowed users to send letters through the mail without postage. It usually had to be granted to individuals by a government official or legislative body. In this instance it appears the military was utilizing the privilege to send soldier letters through the mail in bulk.

Camp Slifer,
Chambersburg, Pa.,
June 3, 1861.[30]

Friend Youngman:—Last week several regiments arrived and there are here at present writing, the second, third, sixth, sixteenth, twenty-third, seventh, eighth, tenth, and some other regiments, the Irish Brigade and the Scott Legion. On Saturday four companies of United States cavalry, and the Philadelphia City troops, arrived here, bringing fifty baggage wagons each drawn by four horses. On Saturday night the town was thrown into great excitement on account of a disturbance between a negro and some soldiers. Two soldiers were wounded, one slightly, and the other severely. The negro was killed instantly, being riddled with about fourteen balls. I am ignorant of the cause of the riot. Several companies were detailed as a patrol guard, to prevent further disturbance. All, however, remained quiet during the night.

Yesterday, General Patterson arrived and was brought into the town by the eighth and tenth regiments, who formed the escort of honor. This morning another regiment arrived. We are now fully equipped and ready to march at an hour's notice. From reliable authority, I learn that we are to leave this week. General health prevails and all the men are in good spirits. All express a desire to be led against the foe, and if *outward* appearance is an index, the stalwart sons of the North will meet and overcome any obstacle which may present itself. If the South does not recede from her present attitude, a force will be sent against her that will compel her to terms whether it is agreeable or not. More in my next.

Yours respectfully,
A. CALDWELL.

* * * * *

On July 6, the 8th Pennsylvania rejoined the brigade at Martinsburg, Virginia. Sporadic skirmishing with local Confederate forces occurred until July

---
30. *Sunbury Gazette*, June 8, 1861.

17, when the 8th Regiment joined in Patterson's general advance to Bunker Hill as part of a flanking movement on Charlestown, Virginia. The entire brigade pushed forward on the night of July 20 to occupy a position commanding the ford over the Shenandoah River. By then, however, the regiment was short on time, and so it was ordered to Harper's Ferry to turn over camp equipment, and then moved by way of Hagerstown back to Harrisburg, where the men were paid and mustered out of service on July 29.[31]

* * * * *

Letters from the Sunbury Guards
Company F, 11th Pennsylvania Volunteer Regiment

*F*ollowing *a public meeting in Sunbury on the evening of April 17, the Sunbury Guards organized in the Grand Jury room of the courthouse on the night of April 19, where John P. S. Gobin was elected first lieutenant and Charles J. Bruner as captain. They arrived at Harrisburg by train several days later and became Company F, 11th Pennsylvania Regiment, on April 26, 1861. The regiment remained at Camp Curtin until May 4, when it transferred by rail to Camp Wayne near West Chester, Pennsylvania. On May 27 the 11th moved to a position along the Philadelphia, Wilmington & Baltimore Railroad to guard the approaches to the federal capital after*

Period lithograph of Camp Curtin in Harrisburg, Pennsylvania. (Credit: *Harper's Weekly*, September 1, 1862)

---

31. Bates, *Pennsylvania Volunteers*, 1:77–78.

several railroad bridges had been destroyed. The regiment dispersed along the rail line, with Company F taking a position at North East, Maryland. After three weeks, the regiment was relieved by the 1st Delaware Volunteers, and ordered to concentrate at Havre de Grace, Maryland. Then, on June 18, they marched via Baltimore and Harrisburg to Chambersburg to join Patterson's Pennsylvania column.[32]

Of all the ninety-day volunteers from Northumberland County, the Sunbury Guards came the closest to experiencing actual combat. Now attached to Patterson's 2nd Division under Maj. Gen. William H. Keim[33] in the 6th Brigade along with the 1st Wisconsin, 4th Connecticut, and the Philadelphia (McMullen's) Independent Rangers, the 11th Pennsylvania moved to Downstown on June 28, and the next day to Williamsport, Maryland. On July 2 a scouting party from the 11th and McMullen's Rangers forded the Potomac into Virginia and advanced on the enemy stationed at Hoke's Run (Falling Waters). They put the enemy to flight just as the remainder of the brigade approached the ford. The 11th then advanced up the main pike and formed into line of battle on the right of the 1st Wisconsin to oppose elements of a brigade under Confederate Col. Thomas J. Jackson.[34] The enemy held strong positions "behind fences, and concealed in grain fields," while one regiment sheltered among a local farmhouse, outbuildings, and "a pile of cord wood along the turnpike."[35] The 11th encountered heavy musketry and artillery rounds but withheld their own fire until they advanced to within two hundred yards of the enemy front. While the brigade's artillery drove the Confederates from their shelter, the 11th opened fire and the engagement became general until Jackson's men were forced to withdraw, first in relatively good order, but then in great confusion. The brigade pursued the enemy about two miles before breaking off the fight.[36]

The next day the brigade resumed the march and proceeded to Martinsburg, where it went into camp. On July 16 it moved to Bunker Hill and occupied the abandoned Rebel camps. Two days later the 11th marched to Charlestown. Patterson had orders to block Gen. Joseph Johnston's forces

---

32. Bates, *Pennsylvania Volunteers*, 1:106–09.
33. William H. Keim (1813–1862) served first as a major general of Pennsylvania Volunteers, and then as a brigadier general of U.S. Volunteers (the latter commission dating from December 20, 1861). He died of typhus at Harrisburg on May 18, 1862.
34. Jackson's brigade included the 2nd, 4th, 5th, and 27th Virginia Regiments, and would shortly become known as the celebrated Stonewall Brigade.
35. Bates, *Pennsylvania Volunteers*, 1:108.
36. Bates, *Pennsylvania Volunteers*, 1:108.

in the Shenandoah Valley while Brig. Gen. Irvin McDowell moved against the main Confederate army under Gen. P. G. T. Beauregard at Manassas.[37] *Before that operation commenced, however, the regiment's term of service expired, although Patterson persuaded the men to remain on duty for an extra week until replacements arrived. The 11th Pennsylvania was then re-mustered into service as a three-year regiment and allowed to retain its original unit number (the only Pennsylvania regiment so honored during the war). The Sunbury Guards, however, did not participate in the reorganization. They moved to Harper's Ferry on July 21, forded the Potomac, and then returned to Harrisburg, where they were mustered out of service on July 31. Their future military endeavors lay elsewhere.*[38]

Camp Curtin,
Harrisburg, Pa.,
April 24, 1861.[39]

Dear John:—Your favor of yesterday was received. I have not time to send you a copy of our Muster Roll this week, but will do so in time for your next week's paper. Sitting in the straw of our quarters with a drum for a desk, is a new method of corresponding. I am unaccustomed to it, and am afraid you will be unable to decipher this. Our Company, the Sunbury Guards, are mustered into service, and are now ready to march. I think we will be Company A in the tenth regiment. Our men are in fine condition and excellent spirits, and are anxious to show their metal [mettle]. For raw recruits the proficiency they have acquired in marching and the manual is astonishing. We have had squad drills nearly all the time since we have been here, and last night a number were practicing the Zouave drill[40] until 10 o'clock—some of them in their bare feet. It is difficult to form a correct idea of camp life. Some day of leisure I may give you mine in

---

37. James M. McPherson, *Battle Cry of Freedom: The Civil War Era* (New York: Oxford University Press, 1988), 339.
38. Bates, *Pennsylvania Volunteers*, 1:106–09; Bell, *History of Northumberland County*, 403.
39. *Sunbury Gazette*, April 27, 1861.
40. The "Zouave drill" is likely a reference to a specific manual of arms published in 1861 by Elmer Ephraim Ellsworth, titled *The Zouave Drill: Being a Complete Manual of Arms for the Use of the Rifled Musket, With Either the Percussion Cap, or Maynard Primer; Containing also a Complete Manual of the Sword and Sabre.* The Zouave drill was also often associated with a specific form of bayonet drill.

full. There is one continual scene of excitement. Troops are arriving and departing continually. Squads are drilling in every direction, and the loud word of command and the sharp ring of the musket make things look extremely warlike. The Pittston, Williamsport and Muncy companies are loud in their praises of the citizens of Sunbury for the treatment they received at their hands yesterday. A member of the Danville Rifles was slightly injured last night by the premature explosion of his revolver. This has exercised a good influence on our men, and they are now more careful with their shooting irons. One of our men, L. T. Rohrbach, was yesterday taken to headquarters to clerk in the enrolling department. It is doubtful if he will get off with us, as the rumor has just come into camp that we are to march tonight—destination not known. Our First Sergeant took unto himself a wife on Monday at our old friend Miller's, his lady having come on from Sunbury at his request for that purpose. The boys wish the young couple all the happiness imaginable. May their shadows never grow less. More anon. My love to all friends.

Yours truly,
J. P. S. G.[41]

* * * * *

Camp Curtin,
Harrisburg, Pa.,
April 30, 1861.[42]

Dear John:—The aspect of things has not materially changed since my last. New Troops arriving continually and very few going off. The tents are all full, but a number of new ones are being erected which will accommodate 5 or 6000 men. We are attached to the Eleventh Regiment, and have elected Capt. Jarrett, of Lock Haven, Colonel of the Regiment. He is an able and experienced soldier, having graduated at West Point, and subsequently followed the starry flag through the Mexican campaign. We are ready to march at ten minutes notice, but cannot tell when or where we will be ordered. The Department

---

41. Lt. John Peter Shindel Gobin.
42. *Sunbury Gazette*, May 4, 1861.

here will answer no questions—and here we must remain in blissful ignorance.

It would do some of our old Sunbury friends good to see us enjoying our camp-life. A happier and jollier set of fellows you never saw. We get up in the morning before five o'clock, and make our toilet, which is done by brushing the straw off and shaking it out of our hair. We drill for an hour and then proceed to cook breakfast, and eat it. After this is done, our tents are put in order, parade ground cleaned up, etc, which with a pipe or two consumes the time until half past ten, when we have another drill of an hour. Then comes dinner, and after it the men loll around and smoke until four, when the whole Camp is in motion; every company is compelled to drill for an hour or longer, just giving the men time to get their suppers. The evenings are spent in squad drilling—sitting around the camp-fires, telling yarns, cracking jokes and singing songs. We have a banjo and a guitar in our crowd, and some excellent singers, while our neighbors have a violin that we are able to borrow once in a while. Those acquainted with our Company are aware that we have some boys not easily taken down in spinning yarns either, so that we have a good time generally. At nine o'clock the gun sounds and the tattoo is beat by each Company, when all must retire to their tents, but often not to sleep. It went pretty hard at first, but now your humble servant can roll himself in his blankets, lay down in the straw and sleep as comfortably as though upon a Sunbury bed.

On Sunday last we had a new phase in our experience. It rained here all day and the water came dripping through the roof wetting our beds completely. However, we shook them up and went in. On Saturday we were reviewed by the Governor who expressed himself highly gratified at the display. There were 5000 soldiers upon the ground, and since that time, at least 1000 more have arrived. We were compelled to dismiss one of our men this morning for disobedience and drunkenness. His name is Langan, an Irishman, who joined our Company at this place. He was drummed out of Camp. We have taken in his place a resident of Sunbury, to wit: —Elias Heddings, who was this morning sworn in as a member of the Company. The men are all enjoying reasonably good health, and beg to be remembered by their friends. They are "spoiling for a fight" and very anxious to go through Baltimore. My respects to all,

Yours
J. P. S. G.

* * * * *

Camp Wayne,
West Chester, Pa.,
May 6, 1861.[43]

DEAR WILVERT:—We arrived here on Saturday evening last, at 7 o'clock, after a hard ride. We left Harrisburg about 9½ o'clock, with our haversacks filled with—well if you would call it fit to eat, you "can't keep a hotel." We had regular sea-biscuit, hard crackers and salt pork, fatter than any hog Mr. Engle ever raised. We had nothing else to eat all day, but the next morning the *ladies* of West Chester, brought and sent us out more coffee than we could use—coffee with cream and sugar in—coffee without either, so fragrant that it would even have suited the editor's (H. B. M.)[44] taste. Our fellows feel so grateful that they can hardly find words to express themselves.

When we left Harrisburg, (as we were passing out,) a lady called out, "that is the finest looking Regiment that has left Camp Curtin yet;" and Governor Curtin paid us the compliment of calling our Regiment the "bloody eleventh," after a Regiment of that name who served so gallantly in Mexico. I hope if we are so lucky, (or unfortunate, as you please,) to get in an engagement, that we will be worthy of the name, and I do know that there will be no cruelty enacted on the part of our fellows unworthy of a soldier or civilized man.

The Rev. Mr. Moore, a Presbyterian minister, with a citizen of West Chester, just now called to see Capt. Bruner, if any of our men were in need of under clothing, it having been reported to the ladies of West Chester, that some of the men belonging to our regiment leaving home expecting to get their uniforms immediately on arriving in Camp, had left home ill-provided; the Captain being absent, Lieut. McCarty told the gentlemen that our ladies and citizens at home had

---

43. *Sunbury American*, May 11, 1861.
44. Henry B. Masser, publisher of the *Sunbury American* and the writer's former employer.

attended to all their wants. They seemed pleased, and said, "they were glad there was one company that needed no assistance in that way."

We are very nicely quartered, and if we need anything, our slightest wish is gratified. The people here seem to anticipate all our wants. The boys are all well and satisfied, with the exception of not being equipped; but that will soon be remedied, as we have heard our Lieutenant Colonel (Coulter) made a requisition this morning for our uniforms and we expect them on Wednesday, when all will be right.

Please send the "American" regularly, as the boys wait for it anxiously.

Yours sincerely,
HARRIE D WHARTON.

* * * * *

Camp Wayne,
West Chester, Pa.,
May 8, 1861.[45]

DEAR JOHN.—Here we are in the ancient and hospitable town above named. Our regiment, the 11th, left Harrisburg on Saturday last, at 9 o'clock, A. M., and arrived here about 7 P. M., on the same day. All along the route the citizens crowded to the cars, and overwhelmed us with their congratulations. Our regiment is made up, with the exception of one company[46], from the region of the Susquehanna. Our men were highly complimented on their appearance, they having been pronounced the best-looking Regiment that left Camp Curtin. We were provided with biscuit, boiled beef and pork in our haversacks, and on this we subsisted until Monday morning. On Sunday morning the citizens of West Chester brought out coffee to us in buckets, with all the condiments, which our boys enjoyed prodigiously. We attended church twice on Sunday, and in the afternoon had service on the ground.

---

45. *Sunbury Gazette*, May 11, 1861.
46. Companies I and K, in fact, were recruited from Greensburg, Westmoreland County, in western Pennsylvania, while the remaining companies came from counties along the North or West Branch of the Susquehanna River, including Williamsport, Lycoming County (Companies A and D); Lock Haven, Clinton County (Company B); Mill Hall, Clinton County (Company C); Pittston, Luzerne County (Company E); Sunbury, Northumberland County (Company F); Muncy, Lycoming County (Company G); and Danville, Montour County (Company H). See Bates, *Pennsylvania Volunteers*, 1:110–115.

Monday and Monday night were hard on the boys. The rain fell in torrents, and the wind blew it through every crevice and nail hole in the quarters. However, they stood it manfully, not one of them wincing, but keeping up the laugh and joke all night. Nine of our boys were on guard all night, and came into camp in the morning thoroughly drenched. It appeared to do them good, for they were in the best of spirits.

Our accommodations are better than those at Camp Curtin. We have good straw and good quarters, and a double blanket apiece, while the colored individual who waits on the officers has more than he can carry. Of course where he obtained them does not concern us. For a pillow a carpet-bag is desirable, a cartridge box does remarkably well, while in an extremity a pair of boots answers every purpose. The boys rill into the straw at night as naturally as though they were accustomed to it all their lives.

We have easy times here at present, not drilling much, but the men are busy mending their clothes, washing, &c. Some of our men are good washers, only the shirts look as if the starch in them was of an inferior quality. The ironing is dispensed with. We hope in a short time to get our uniforms, when we will be soldiers in every sense of the word. The citizens of West Chester are very kind to us, doing all in their power to render us comfortable. It is the more welcome being in such decided contrast to the conduct of the citizens of Harrisburg. There almost every one conspires to rob men of all they have, by charging them three prices for all they need—here they would rather give us than take from us. We will all remember both places, but with different feelings altogether.

But I must close. They boys are all well, and in excellent spirits. They are prepared to do their duty. There is a report that the bridge at Conowingo is in possession of some 400 rebels. It is about 35 miles below us, and we hope we will be ordered to take it. I think Company F could do it in about half an hour. We are the color company of the Regiment, being the next company to the music and colors. We will defend it to the last, or die in the last breach.

Yours,

J. P. S. G.

* * * * *

Camp Wayne,
West Chester, Pa.,
May 14, 1861.[47]

DEAR JOHN:—This is an extremely dull day, and very unfavorable for drilling. It commenced raining last night about ten o'clock, and continued without cessation, all night. Some of our tents leaked badly, but the men were in the best of spirits and managed to keep dry, a number of them being provided with gum blankets. I paid a visit to Philadelphia last week, and purchased one for myself, and last night found it to be quite an institution. About three o'clock this morning, I awoke and found a small stream of water trickling down my neck. I moved to one side and was soon sound asleep again.

The people of West Chester continue their kindly offices to us. Last Friday the ladies brought out to the Camp over 2000 pies and about 15 barrels of milk, which were distributed among the men by companies. We all came in for a good share. They were contributed by the citizens of West Chester and vicinity. And also, on Saturday the ladies of ------ Valley sent our company a lot of woolen shirts, socks, towels and, as a present to us, they came very acceptable to all of our men.

Mess No. 1, composed of Messrs. Wharton, Irwin, S. P. and Joseph Bright, Weiser and Feig[48], had a grand dinner on Sunday last, to which I had the honor of being an invited guest. The eatables were gotten up in the best style, and tasted quite naturally, most of them having been brought from Sunbury by one of the mess, Mr. Irwin. The dessert consisted of cake and peaches and cream. A number of ladies were spectators of our festivities, but it was difficult to make them believe that Corporal Wharton baked the fine Sponge cake that decked the table, or that Corporal Bright churned the fine Sunbury butter in a patent wash-machine upon which he sat. Corporal Bright has become quite a favorite in town, and rarely returns to Camp without a bucket of milk, or some such luxury, presented by the citizens. We enjoy ourselves here the best we can, and I assure you we get up some good impromptu festivities.

---

47. *Sunbury Gazette*, May 18, 1861.
48. Henry D. or Charles D. Wharton, Jared C. Irwin, Samuel P. and Joseph Bright, Jacob Weiser, and Jacob Feig.

One night, last week, companies F and G gave a grand ball in lieu of the one most of our company attended at Georgetown about this time; or in other words, we celebrated "Pinkster." The music was furnished by our own orchestra. We kept it up until tattoo reminded us that it was bedtime. We had a fine time, only it don't seem altogether natural to dance with pantalooned feminines who are distinguished by a handkerchief tied to their coats. I could not help thinking of some familiar faces I had been accustomed to see at those festivities. For particulars inquire of our friend, the foreman of the *American* office.

One of our men arrived from Sunbury last night with a load of the niceties of this life. They were welcomely received. A number of the officers of the Eleventh regiment visited us, and we had a merry time, which was kept up until a late hour, notwithstanding the rain.

Our Colonel has arrived and taken command of the Regiment. We have a regimental drill every other day. Yesterday one half of the regiment had a sham battle, and it gave us uninitiated some idea of what we may expect. They were formed into two divisions, and ordered to charge bayonets. They rushed at each other with a wild yell and although the drums beat a retreat they never stopped until their bayonets were interlocked. Quite a number, to complete the act, fell down, and were carried off by their comrades. It was a very exciting sight, and the soldiers felt like going it in earnest. The second division, in which we are, intend trying it to-day.

Our Captain has obtained a furlough, and started for home this morning, where he intends spending several days.

The boys all send their respects, and desire to thank their friends for the many kind remembrances. I return my sincere thanks for the very acceptable presents sent me with Private Starkloff[49], and shall ever remember them with the utmost gratitude. Nothing is more gratifying to us than these testimonials of our citizens. May Heaven protect you all.

Yours truly,
J. P. S. G.

* * * * *

---

49. Earnest Starkloff.

Camp Wayne,
West Chester, Pa.,
May 14, 1861.[50]

DEAR WILVERT:—We are truly in the "garden of Pennsylvania." A county where noble deeds have been enacted, and greater chivalry shown than Jeff. Davis can boast of. Our boys feel proud that they are encamped on "sacred ground," and hope they will prove as successful and brave as did the hero of "Stony Point"—Mad Anthony Wayne.

Our fellows are in cheerful spirits; they stand the rain and cold without a murmur. If we only had our uniforms we would be satisfied, but as "Uncle Sam" is so derelict in his duty, I suppose we must put up with it.

You should have seen the excitement yesterday when Earnest Starkloff arrived—he proved himself (with the PRESENTS sent from our friends at home) to be a regular commissary. When his big box was opened, each one in our company stood anxiously awaiting for something from home. As each soldier received his parcel, you could hear them in a restrained voice murmur, "God bless them." You have no idea of the emotions one feels on receiving something from Sunbury. The liberality of Sunbury to the soldiers is the talk of the whole regiment, and I have heard some say, if they lived to return through Sunbury they would stop and thank the LADIES for their kindness. Sunbury can only be equaled by West Chester. On last Friday each Company, in rotation, was marched in front of the Quarter Master's Department and each man received the half of a large pie, with plenty of rich milk. The ladies of West Chester furnished them—they brought to the two Regiments about 2000 pies. After our boys had partaken of their bounty, they gave the ladies of West Chester "three cheers" with a will, and then such a "Tiger" with the "Big Indian" whoop (as Company F only can give,) it fairly startled them, and one could see by the ladies' smiles they knew we were sincere.

Our "mess" on last Sabbath had a dinner at our Hotel, the Continental, (such is the name we have given to the quarters of our "mess"). We sent out two invitations—one to Lieut. Gobin, who is a

---

50. *Sunbury American*, May 18, 1861.

great favorite in our company, and the other to Mr. Helbing[51], our 3d Sergeant.

Our "bill of fare" was roast beef, mashed potatoes with milk and cream, pickles, boiled corn, peaches and cream, (the cream was furnished by H. B. M's friend, Henry S. Evans,) and pound cake. A large bouquet decorated the table, and the pound cake was covered with flowers. Several ladies passed while we were eating, and expressed themselves by saying "THAT dinner was good enough for the most fastidious." Had it not been for the Captain of our "mess," Jared Irwin, our table would have been vacant of the delicacies.

I must close, as the Band is playing for Regimental parade.

Yours, truly,
HARRIE D. WHARTON.

* * * * *

[The following letter was received by a young lady in Sunbury from her brother, a member of the Sunbury Guards at Camp Wayne. The scenes so graphically described are much to be deplored, but not half so much as that the soldiers have been driven to insubordination and violence to protect themselves against the impositions of a dishonest commissariat:][52]

Camp Wayne,
May 19, 1861.[53]

Dear Sister. —I received your letter and your cakes—also the chicken, and flowers, for which I am very thankful indeed. You do not know how happy it makes me feel to know that you think of me once in a while. I was on the hospital list from last Tuesday until yesterday when I again resumed my duties. I had a cold, diarrhea and sore eyes.

We had quite a time here last Thursday night in consequence of the officer of the day putting a guard in the guard-house for smoking a pipe while on duty. The Captain of the Company to which the

---

51. S. Herman Helbing.
52. The paragraph in brackets is an editorial comment by the publishers of the Sunbury Gazette.
53. *Sunbury Gazette*, May 25, 1861.

guard belonged, brought out his company for the purpose of taking him out, when a row ensued between him and the Officer of the Day, and before the thing was ended about half of the Camp was under arms; but about that time the Colonel made his appearance, who, after a great deal of trouble and swearing, got the fuss settled.

Next morning we had another exciting time when they issued the rations. Instead of bread they gave us crackers about the size of a common plate, and as hard as a brick. When these were dealt out to the men they began to swear and throw them away, and soon the camp was flying full of crackers. The men made wagons and used the crackers for wheels—they made necklaces of them and strung them around their necks, and used them for epaulets and every other imaginable way that they could be used to show their indignation. At length the excitement became so great that the officers became alarmed, and attempted to stop them, but it was of no use. The men only howled, hooted, yelled and groaned at them, and pelted them with crackers; but at length they became quieted down, and went to their quarters swearing that they would kill the first man they caught hauling crackers or bad meat into the camp.

On Saturday morning the crackers and bad meat made their appearance again, but no sooner did the men see it than they made a break for the gates, forced the guards away, and away they went for town. About eight o'clock the town was full of squads of soldiers, headed by officers, scouring the town from one end to the other, driving the runaways to camp; but it took until sometime in the afternoon to get them in, and after they did get them in they were not in a condition to drill; therefore there was but little drilling done that day. This morning we got good beef and good bread, and everything went off first rate.[54]

We expect to get our uniforms this week, and there is a rumor in the camp that we will then be sent to Maryland.

Your affectionate Brother,
B. F. B.[55]

* * * * *

---

54. See the letter by Henry D. Wharton from May 21 (page 68) and Lt. John P. S. Gobin's letter of May 22, 1861 (page 69), for similar accounts of the ration problem.
55. The author is possibly Pvt. Benjamin F. Bright.

Camp Wayne,
West Chester, Pa.,
May 21, 1861.[56]

DEAR WILVERT:—We are still encamped in this valley of "noble deeds," but it is impossible for us to form any idea of our stay. There was a rumor this morning of our being ordered to Fort McHenry, opposite Baltimore, in a day or two, but the orders, like the promises of our uniforms, are to keep us in good humor and from grumbling; as for grumbling, there has been enough of it in this camp, because of the meanness of the Commissary and higher officers.

Up to last Thursday night all was fun and frolic. Friday morning came and the provisions we drew were not fit, as Nig Weitzel says, "for a South Sea Cannibal to eat." The rations consisted of pickled beef, salt pork, with the fat six inches thick, and hard sea biscuit—having actual *worms* in them. This was too much, the boys would not put up with such treatment. About four hundred men mutinied—and if you ever saw fun it was here. The men formed in procession, with a man carrying, in advance, a long piece of board for a flag staff—a piece of pork and beef made the flag, and a biscuit, on top, for spear. The procession marched through the camp, and on being ordered back to quarters, the Colonel was pelted with sea biscuit. The Commissary received three groans for his share, and his horse was completely covered with the biscuit—a string of biscuit around his (the horse's) neck, (pity it hadn't been a rope around the Commissary's,) biscuit for a saddle girth—biscuit to the tail, and biscuit on the foot of each leg.

After the men had fully expressed their indignation they went to their quarters quietly, and were satisfied. A tree in front of the "Guards" quarters was turned into a "Christmas Bush," the boys having literally made the boughs bend by the quantity of beef, pork and crackers hanging to them.

Do you think soldiers can sit quietly, with their arms folded, and receive such treatment and "grub?" No sir. And I tell you the 11th Regiment, for one, will not submit—they are the right stuff, and will

---

56. *Sunbury American*, May 25, 1861.

have their rights, and the next time will prove themselves to be, as Gov. Curtin called them, the "Bloody 11th."

If we are to have such food, and can't get any other, the citizens at home will have to stop the "supplies" on the soldiers passing through Sunbury, and send them to us. We have received things from home, and after having satisfied our wants, the emotions and gratitude cannot be expressed. Jared Irwin wishes me to say that the "Continental Hotel" of our "mess," is completely renovated, and is enjoying a big run of custom.

Yours, respectfully,
H. D. W.[57]

* * * * *

Camp Wayne,
West Chester, Pa.,
May 22, 1861.[58]

Dear John:—After nearly two hours drilling, it is rather difficult to guide a pen, or get your mind off of "By the right flank march," "charge bayonets," &c.

We have had exciting time in camp for the last few days. In place of soft bread we were supplied with crackers that looked and tasted as if they had been baked for the Mexican war. In place of fresh beef they gave us salt junk, strong and salty enough to bear an iron wedge. The crackers, or some of them at least, were mouldy and full of skippers. The men refused to eat them, and used them for various purposes, some of them making epaulets out of them, and not a few using them to cover the rents in the back part of their breeches. In this condition on Saturday they paraded around the Camp, groaning every person connected with the Quartermaster's Department. A number of them went to town where the citizens opened their houses to them, and gave them their breakfasts. The Colonel ordered out a squad to bring those in town to Camp, and at one time I feared that a collision

---

57. Musician Henry D. Wharton. His remaining correspondence would be signed consistently with these initials.
58. *Sunbury Gazette*, May 25, 1861.

would ensue. It was quieted, however, and on Sunday and Monday we received bread again. This morning they offered us crackers again, but our Company would not take them, and we have subsisted to-day on bread that we had on hand. To-morrow I understand they intend giving us flour. While I write[,] a crowd passed with an effigy of the Quartermaster on a pole. It was burned in front of the quarters of the Danville Rifles. A guard went to arrest the ringleaders, but only got one, and he was the wrong man. The men say that if it was necessary no objections would be made to eating crackers, but they will not allow the commissary to speculate off of their stomachs. In this I think they are right, and I will stick to them until "the crack of doom."

We have very ugly weather, and plenty of it. Rain is a great institution, but a man standing picket guard in it for two hours, or lying on his back in his quarters, covered with nothing but his blanket, and the rain dropping upon him through every crevice, comes to the conclusion that it is a decided nuisance. The men bear it all, however, without a murmur, and only insist upon receiving proper food. On Sunday it was my turn to stand for twenty-four hours as officer of the guard. We have one hundred and sixty men detailed every morning for guard purposes. They are divided into three reliefs, one of which is placed on duty every two hours. It is the duty of the officer to see that all is attended to. It rained all night, which gave me a correct idea of a soldier's life; I, however, was provided with a gutta percha cap and blanket, and kept perfectly dry all night. Most of the men were provided with the same articles, and those that were not were given sheltered positions. Notwithstanding these drawbacks, which we all expected, the life of a soldier has its interesting and attractive features, and I like it.

Our men are all well, but need their uniforms badly. We are to get them to-morrow, and from the sample shown us to-day they will be a good article. They are light blue, pants, roundabouts, and overcoats. We have undress parade every day, but it looks more like a parade of Falstaff's ragged regiment than anything else. However, our next one we expect to have in uniform.

We are all tired of camp life, and want active service. It is rumored to-day that we will be ordered to Fort McHenry this week. I hope this is so, for then we will have some prospect of a fight.

John W. Bucher paid us a visit this week, and we were all very glad to see him. The men listened to his budget of news with intense interest, and were sorry he could not stay longer with us. Charles Gass also visited us yesterday. He is a member of the Philadelphia Cavalry, Capt. Savage. He looked very well, and was in excellent health. My respects to all.

Yours,
J. P. S. G.

* * * * *

Camp Wayne,
West Chester, Pa.,
May 24, 1861.[59]

Dear John:—It is to be regretted that parties having control of an ultra-partisan sheet, in Sunbury, cannot leave politics out of the question when speaking of the volunteers.[60] The oft-repeated assertion that those who formerly acted with the Democratic party are the most active and anxious to volunteer, comes with a bad grace from those who sit in their comfortable chairs, and are only deterred from openly expressing their sympathies with the traitors from the fear of public opinion. Even the articles they do write seek to distract those engaged in the service by their endeavors to revive old and almost forgotten political animosities. If they are so zealous, why do they not shoulder the musket in the cause, or at least act as patriots, and for once be true to the teachings of the fathers of the Republic? The volunteers despise them for their efforts to divide them, and they may as well cease. We recognize no party but the party of the Union and the Constitution, which we have sworn to defend with our lives, and those who are acting as partisans at home will be remembered by every man in the service. I will, with the simple view of confuting their partisan articles, on first opportunity, send you a statement of the former political predilections of the men in our regiment.

---

59. *Sunbury Gazette*, June 1, 1861.
60. The opening sentence is a reference to the *Northumberland County Democrat*, a staunchly anti-administration newspaper started in Sunbury in March 1861. It's publisher, Truman H. Purdy, would become anathema to Northumberland County soldiers in the field.

A member of Company A, of the 9th Regiment, was buried to-day with the honors of war. It was an effecting sight.

The difficulty in regard to our rations has been arranged. We now receive flour, which we trade to the bakers of West Chester for bread, pound for pound. We also secure fresh beef.

Yours,
J. P. S. G.

* * * * *

[The following letter was handed to us for publication by a lady of this place.]

North East, Md.,
May 27, 1861.[61]

Dear Mother.—
We left Camp Wayne at 4 o'clock this morning, having received our breakfasts from the hotel proprietors of West Chester. After having eaten, some of us sang a hymn of which the chorus was, "Say brothers will you meet me on Canaan's Happy shore." With some difficulty we reached the cars, owing to the streets and platform being filled with spectators. After we had secured our seats one of the Sunbury Guards proposed three cheers for the people of West Chester for their kind attention to the Regiment, which was quickly executed. Another proposed three cheers in honor of the ladies of West Chester, which was followed by a volley of applause from the cars which greatly exceeded the first.

We reached West Philadelphia at 8½ o'clock A. M. From there we marched across Market Street bridge down to 23d street, down 23d to Chestnut, and on to Broad, and down Broad to Prime, and halted opposite the depot of the Philadelphia and Baltimore railroad. A rain then commenced to pour down in torrents, and the streets being literally jammed with people to see our departure, they got a severe drenching. We were hastily marched into the mammoth depot, escaping what would have made us uncomfortable for the remaining

---

61. *Sunbury Gazette*, June 1, 1861.

part of the day. We left the depot at 11 o'clock, A. M., the sun shining brilliantly, and we went on rejoicing.

It is said that we made a more beautiful display in marching through Philadelphia than any preceding regiment. We did not know where we were going until we arrived here. We thought we were going to Harper's Ferry. I have nothing to write in regard to the war, only should the rebels come in contact with the 11th Regiment, they will meet with a warm reception.

Your affectionate Son,
F. A. C.[62]

* * * * *

North East, Cecil Co., Md.,
May 28, 1861.[63]

Dear John.—Our Regiment left Camp Wayne on Monday morning, at 4 o'clock, A. M. After getting our breakfast in West Chester, the gift of her kind citizens, we were put into the cars, and started for our present encampment. We got out of the cars at West Philadelphia, and marched to Broad and Prime streets, where after a little delay, we again took the cars, and were off.

Our Regiment is scattered along the Philadelphia, Wilmington and Baltimore Railroad, between Elkton and Perryville. Our Company is the only one stationed here. We have to guard two bridges on the railroad, one about a mile below us, and the other a short distance above us. The nearest Company to us is E, from Pittston, which is about three miles below us at Charlestown. The Muncy company is at Chesapeake City, six miles above us. The Danville boys are at Elkton, about the same distance from us. The 6th Regiment, Col. Nagle,[64] which we relieved, have been ordered to Fort McHenry.

North East is a small village containing about 800 inhabitants, the majority of whom profess to be Union men, but we place very

---

62. The author's identity has not been determined, but the initials may possibly belong to Pvt. Francis Carr.
63. *Sunbury Gazette,* June 1, 1861.
64. James Nagle (1822–1866), of Pottsville, Schuylkill County. He later commanded the 48th Pennsylvania Volunteers before obtaining the rank of brigadier general of U.S. Volunteers on September 10, 1862.

little confidence in any one. It is situated on the North East River, about 12 miles from Chesapeake Bay. Shad and herring abound, and several squads are already out this morning trying their luck. Fresh fish will be quite a rarity to us.

We have received our uniforms and equipments, with the exception of overcoats and cartridge boxes. The uniform consists of gray pantaloons and light blue roundabouts, trimmed with dark blue, and a blue cap. They are well made and of good material, being much preferable to any I have yet seen. We have plenty of ammunition and are prepared to give all invaders a warm welcome. We are provided with excellent quarters in a large warehouse, which our boys have fixed up on apple pie order. The officers have quarters in a house adjoining, where we bunk upon the floor, wrapped up in blankets, with a coat for a pillow. I never slept sounder in my life than I did last night in that style. Even the passing of the trains, or the snoring of *Henry*, the colored individual, failed to awaken me.

At Wilmington we were received with every demonstration of pleasure. The station was crowded with people who cheered and shouted as we passed, and such a waving of hats, bonnets, and handkerchiefs as has not been witnessed for some time. Our boys cheered lustily for the "Blue Hen's Chickens."

It was with feelings of regret that we parted with the citizens of West Chester. The many kindnesses we received at their hands have endeared them to us, and I assure you never will be forgotten. Among those to whom Company F are particularly indebted are Henry S. Evans and his estimable lady whose hospitable mansion was ever open to us. But our friends were so numerous, that we cannot mention them. May God remember them all.

Our boys are all well and in excellent spirits. They look very well in uniform, and our regiment was pronounced the finest looking one that had passed through Philadelphia. I am not able to say how long we will stay here but probably not long.

Yours,
J. P. S. G.

* * * * *

North East, Cecil County, Md.,
May 28, 1861.[65]

MR. EDITOR,
We arrived at this place yesterday. It is a small town, situated about two hundred yards from the Philadelphia, Wilmington & Baltimore Railroad. We are, however, quartered at the railroad—the men in a large warehouse, and the officers at the depot. The quarters are very comfortable, both for officers and men—a great deal better than any we have had yet. The people here appear to be very kind, and are nearly all Union men. The Stars and Stripes is floating over a house right below our quarters. My company is the only one posted here. Captain Siegfried[66], of Col. Nagle's regiment, whom I relieved, told me that he and his command had been treated very kindly by the citizens. They were here three weeks. I think we have the best location of any of the regiment. We must act with a great deal of caution, however.

The Muncy company are posted at Chesapeake City, about six miles from the railroad. They had to march that distance last evening. The nearest company to me is Captain Johnson's from Pittston. He is about three miles below us. We have two sentinels posted about three quarters of a mile below the quarters, and two a couple of hundred yards above, along the railroad, to watch the bridges and culverts. At night we increase the number. We have plenty of ammunition. It is forty-eight miles from here to Philadelphia.

We were received with more enthusiasm at Wilmington, in the little State of Delaware, than in any other place we passed through since we left home. We all tho't of Captain Van Gaskin, of the town of Shamokin, when passing through the city of Wilmington. The "Blue Hen's Chickens" are all right.

The boys are all well and doing well, but hate the idea of being a railroad guard. Orders, however, must be obeyed, whether we like it

---

65. *Sunbury American*, June 1, 1861.
66. Captain James K. Siegfried, Company C, 6th Pennsylvania Infantry (three months). When the 6th reorganized as the three-year 48th Pennsylvania Volunteer Infantry on October 1, 1861, Siegfried was promoted to major, then to lieutenant colonel on November 30, 1861, and then to colonel on September 20, 1862. He became a brigadier general on August 1, 1864, and mustered out of service on October 11 that year at the expiration of his term. See Bates, *Pennsylvania Volunteers*, 1:62, 1203.

or not. We can get plenty of fish—shad, herring, pike, perch, &c. It is said you can catch as many with a dip net as a person can carry (not the pike however). Some of the boys are going a fishing this morning. I can hardly resist the temptation on going, but having business on hand, must stay at home. I cannot say how long we will be here.

Direct all letters to "Co. F, 11th Regiment, North East, Cecil County, Md."

C. J. B.[67]

* * * * *

North East, Md.,
May 28, 1861.[68]

Dear Wilvert:—After a tedious ride and march, we are at last in the enemy's country. The people seem friendly, but by the advice of Captain Bruner, and the good sense of our boys, the strictest vigilance is kept, knowing that discretion is the "better part of valor." There is a great difference in the feeling, seemingly, of the citizens of Pennsylvania, Delaware and Maryland. On the route from West Chester to Philadelphia, there was one continual shout, cheering us on our way, and what most warmed our boys was on passing Mrs. Eastwick's Seminary, in Chester County, Pa., the windows of the building were completely filled with young ladies, and the waving of their "kerchiefs"—the smiles and kisses thrown to us—was enough to urge a soldier on to duty. All the way through Delaware there were similar demonstrations of enthusiasm. When we got to Elkton, Md., a cloud gathered over us which dampened our good humor considerably. The people looked daggers at us, and one of our boys not having the chance of a *pop* at a secessionist, took revenge by shooting a dog, saying that he would not even "allow a Secessionist's dog to bark at him."

This is a small town about ten miles from Havre de Grace. There are two nice Rolling Mills about a mile east of this place, the business of the town is not increased by the Mills. The principal occupation of the citizens is fishing. A gentleman told me at his fishery, that he

---

67. The author is Capt. Charles J. Bruner, commanding officer of Company F.
68. *Sunbury American*, June 8, 1861.

had taken four hundred barrels of herring at one haul. This may seem a *big fish* story, but I am assured by others it is actually true. There is a Church here (Episcopal) one hundred and thirty years old. The brick[s] in it were brought from England, and in the church-yard is [a] grave-stone dated 1734. The walls of the building are three feet thick.

An election is being held here to-day for the Member of Debate, (the same thing as our Assembly). I saw a hand-bill in town urging all good men to go to the polls and vote for McIntire, to prove that the "old 5th district was unconditionally for the Union."

Our Regiment is distributed along the Philadelphia, Wilmington and Baltimore Railroad, from Elkton to Havre de Grace.—How long we will stay I cannot tell, but the impression is we will very shortly move to Washington.

In speaking of the election to-day, I should have mentioned a wise precaution of Captain Bruner,—knowing the feeling the people hereabouts, he requested his men not to visit the town or go to the polls, as the presence of military might influence them. I am happy to say the Captain's request, to a man, was lived up to.

The boys are all well—in fine spirits. I will write to you again as soon as anything of importance transpires.

Respectfully, Yours,
H. D. W.

* * * * *

North East, Cecil Co., Md.
June 4, 1861.[69]

Dear John: —We are still encamped here, guarding the railroad, all newspaper accounts to the contrary notwithstanding. We have been much pleased to read the accounts of the arrival of the Eleventh Regiment at Chambersburg, and they were so positive, that we almost concluded that it was a case of mistaken identity on our part. I think, however, that it all arose from the following facts: Gen. Patterson arrived at Chambersburg several days ago, and it is rumored that he was to march immediately for Harper's Ferry. Before he left Philadelphia, he

---

69. *Sunbury Gazette*, June 8, 1861.

told our Lieut. Colonel that our marching orders had been out for three days. Up to this date, however, we have not received them, although we are hourly expecting them, and I have no doubt by the time you receive this we will be off. If so I will telegraph to you. We are getting tired of this monotonous life, and a fight would be a luxury to us.

There was a special election held in this county, last Wednesday, to elect a member of the Legislature. McIntyre, the unconditional Union candidate, was elected by a large majority. In the district we were in, (North East,) there were seven secession votes cast, and nearly four hundred for McIntyre. The seven secession votes are all known, and will be carefully watched. None of our men were allowed to go to town during the day of the election, nor interfere with it in the slightest. In order that no stories of undue influence upon our part might be circulated, we even abstained from drilling during the day. We were prepared, however, for any difficulty that might occur.

One day last week we were informed that a secession flag was floating on a house about three miles above us. Next morning at three o'clock a squad started up to take it down. We found the house and flag, but the owner of it declared that he was a Union man, and that the flag was intended for a Union flag, that it had been made by his own family, who had an eye more to economy in material than anything else. As it was not quite a secession flag, but a mongrel between the two, we "faced about" and returned home, with an excellent appetite for breakfast. The boys were much disappointed that no resistance was made, as they anticipated a brush, and delivered up the cartridges with which they were provided, with reluctance.

The fish market continues brisk, while lobsters and frogs are above par. We catch any quantity of them, and they go very nice. Eels abound, and when the tide ebbs[,] our boys repair to the creek, and search among the rocks for the fish left there. They have had excellent success this far.

On Saturday last, several of us chartered a sail boat and took a trip down to Chesapeake Bay. The scenery is very fine, although I do not think it equals that along our own Susquehanna. We had a fine breeze, and returned in fine style with no mishap save a ducking which [P]rivate Rodrigue received. But that adventure I must reserve for a leisure hour. It was the richest sight I ever saw. It has furnished food for laughter for Sergeant Pleasants and myself ever since.

We have received our overcoats, and it improves the appearance of the boys wonderfully. Our rations have also improved and are delivered to us more regularly. We are well situated in every respect now, except that the pantaloons furnished us are not of as good material as we had supposed.

Trains containing soldiers pass us every day. The Highland Regiment[70], from New York, went down yesterday. They are a fine body of men, and look as if they were made of fighting material. I have no doubt they will give a good account of themselves. There is a general feeling of indignation expressed by all the soldiers at the cowardly assassination of Col. Ellsworth[71], and his death will be dearly atoned for by the traitors.

Ere next week I hope to be able to give you an account of the capture of Harper's Ferry by Gen. William's Brigade, of which the "Bloody Eleventh" form a part. It is a noticeable feature that every commissioned officer but three in the Regiment has red whiskers, and we intend having [theirs] painted. But I must close, as the mail is about leaving. My respects to all.

Yours, &c.
J. P. S. G.

* * * * *

North East, Md.,
June 4, 1861.[72]

Dear Wilvert:—We are now lying "becalmed," but like the crew of a good ship, from present indications, we will soon be moved to where there will be something to do for a "yankee ship, and a yankee crew," and the citizen soldier.—From the feeling and actions of our Regiment, I feel pretty certain that if they ever get into an engagement, they will prove themselves good and true men—not, I hope, like the fourteen hundred Southrons, at Fairfax Court House, Va., who were frightened

---

70. 79th New York State Militia (Cameron Highlanders).
71. In one of the early outrages of the war, Union Col. Elmer Ephraim Ellsworth, of the New York Fire Zouaves, was shot to death on May 24, 1861, by the proprietor of the Marshal House in Alexandria, Virginia, while attempting to remove a Confederate flag from the hotel's roof.
72. *Sunbury American*, June 8, 1861.

and made to retreat by forty-seven regular yankees. Pity for the South, her boasted chivalry is gone. Not that she is cowardly, but the miserable cause in which she is engaged. As for news here, there is nothing that would interest you but the condition and doings of our boys. They are well—in first rate spirits—to show it, neither the Principal nor Assistant Surgeon have been to see us since we have been quartered here. We have considerable sport among ourselves. In the evening we have music by our "string band," composed of Sergeants Heilbing and Pleasants, and Corporal Wharton, (by the way, Corporal S. Bright puts in a few interludes by his jokes,) and it is highly appreciated by the ladies and citizens of North East.—At all our entertainments we are so crowded that we can't keep the "front seats reserved for ladies and small children." Private Rizer has charge of the Menagerie. In his collection there is an Elephant, an Ostrich, a Cameleopard and a Giant. The animals are made by one or two of the boys, with the aid of blankets, and the Giant by one of the fellows sitting on the shoulders of another—with a blanket covering them.—They make a first-rate representation. On a visit to the town you can hear called by one citizen to another, "are you going out tonight to hear the music and see the Elephant?" I mention this to show how well the thing is made up, and the liking of the citizens for the amusement. You know Rizer's love of the ridiculous, and can imagine how well he acts his part.—There is very little dissension or quarreling in our Company, and you can almost call us a "band of brothers." The officers of the Company are very well liked, especially Capt. Bruner and Lieut. Gobin, and from my own knowledge, if any act of the enemy were done to them, as 'twas to Col. Ellsworth, our boys would act the part of the Zouaves, and avenge the death of either—such is the love of the men for them.

In last week's "Gazette," I saw a note of the arrival of our "big box," and the mention of crackers in it. I wish it distinctly understood that the crackers sent were picked from those that were covered with mould and worms. If he, the Editor, thinks they are "good enough," he should have some to eat that were left behind. We are in good quarters and are well satisfied.

Yours Fraternally,
H. D. W.

* * * * *

Camp of 11th Regiment, P.V.
Havre de Grace, Md.,
June 11, 1861.[73]

Dear John:—Our Company left North East on Sunday afternoon at 3 o'clock, and arrived here in the evening. We found our tents all up and ready for us to occupy. Our encampment is situated on Light House Point, facing the Bay. It is a beautiful location, and has the best parade ground attached that we have yet had. Our entire Regiment is here, together with three companies of the first Regiment of Delaware. The place of our Regiment along the railroad was supplied by the Delaware Regiment.

Some of us left North East with no slight feelings of regret which were only appeased by the thought that we were going into active and fighting service. We formed a number of very pleasant acquaintances while there, and the tears that fell from bright eyes, and the hearty "God bless you" that was uttered by ruby lips, would have thrown into the "melting mood," hearts less stout than ours. However, when we have won our laurels, and peace once more dawns upon us, we hope to have the pleasure of assuring them that we still live.

On our route hither we noticed quite a number of flags floating, upon the azure field of which still glittered thirty-four stars, and at several points the citizens gave evidence of their patriotism by waving of hats, bonnets, and handkerchiefs. Our reception here, however, and at Perryville, which is directly opposite, was rather ominous. Not a cheer was heard, nor scarcely a smiling face seen, and we were forcibly reminded of the Deserted Village.

Havre de Grace is one of the most poorly laid out towns I ever saw. It is strung along the bank for more than a mile, while back from the river you find a few straggling houses only. The streets are laid out after the order of a worm fence. You walk along very contentedly, and the next move you are square against a house standing away out in the street. After climbing around that, you find the way obstructed by a pump, and so on through the whole street. I have very little confidence in the loyalty of at least a majority of the citizens. Should it be occupied by a secession force, I am satisfied they would receive more

---

73. *Sunbury Gazette*, June 17, 1861.

aid and comfort than we do. Last night a detachment of the Delaware Regiment captured a secession flag about one and a half miles below town. They intend sending it to Wilmington. Our boys were very anxious to send it to Sunbury, but the fates were against them.

Our cartridge boxes have just arrived, and we leave to-morrow (Wednesday) morning for Chambersburg. How long we will remain there I cannot say—but a short time I think, as the movement of troops indicates that an attack will be made ere long on Harper's Ferry. For the present, those wishing to write to any of our men had better direct their letters to Chambersburg in care of Col. Jarret, and if we have left before they arrive they will be forwarded to us.

Our encampment here is fraught with historical reminiscences. It is upon the ground where it was intended to make a stand against the attack of the British in 1814. The embankment thrown up is yet to be seen, and the tents of messes Nos. 1 and 10 are pitched upon the spot where the soldiers should have awaited their approach just behind the breast-work. Southern chivalry, however, could not stand British courage, and yesterday I was shown the Brick church behind which they ran for shelter.

The facilities here for writing are about the same as those we had at Camp Curtin. To sit upon the ground and use a trunk for a desk, is not a position for a man to occupy who wishes to write a long communication. He finds his lower extremities somewhat in the way, and, not being a tailor, it is decidedly uncomfortable.

Our boys are all well and hearty, and send their respects to all friends. They were much pleased with the visit of Rev. Rizer and John B. Packer, at North East. Here we have met Captains Rhinehart, Lyons and Hoover, and their crews. Quite a hand shaking ensued, and they were objects of attention for some time. My love to all.

Yours,
J. P. S. G.

* * * * *

Havre de Grace, Md.,
June 11, 1861.[74]

DEAR WILVERT:—
We left North East on last sabbath, our passage from there to Perryville, was very quick, and the only "Patriotic" expressions exhibited was by some half dozen young ladies, and a whole regiment of "niggers," which our fellows did not like—not the ladies, but the niggers. Indeed the colored people here think that the entire army of the North have come to liberate them, so much so that they have become impudent. If that is their style, and keep on in the manner they are doing, we will have to "pop" them instead of the people of the "Confederate States."

Havre de Grace is most beautifully located,—the Susquehanna empties into the Chesapeake Bay at this place, and the scenery is most exquisite—not I think equal to ours around Sunbury. Leaving Sunbury out of the question, we all acknowledge "nature's beauty" around Havre de Grace.

You should have seen our boys get up this morning with their clothes damp, the rain oozing through the tents, particularly myself. After tattoo, not liking the heat, took my blankets to take a quiet snooze on "mother earth," and about 3 o'clock, A. M., if you ever saw a boy of five feet six, completely drenched it was me.

We are now under marching orders. The Colonel told us last evening, on Regimental review to be prepared to leave on a moment's warning. Our destination is Chambersburg; when we get there we expect to be forwarded to active life—not "playing soldier," guarding railroad bridges, (made out of stone,) to keep the rebels from burning them. Wherever, and whenever our regiment meets the enemy you may expect to hear a favorable account of Company F. The Sunbury Guards are composed of small men, but they are made of the right grit. Corporal Bright expects to get the reward that was offered by some Philadelphians for Jeff. Davis' head, and in the expectation of

---

74. *Sunbury American*, June 15, 1861. This letter contains the first usage of racist language that is now considered unacceptable, but which was commonly employed in the nineteenth century. It must be remembered that, despite specific opposition to slavery as an institution, most Northerners held generally racist attitudes toward African Americans. The offensive language occurs on several more occasions throughout this publication.

it he is quite jubilant. Our fellows are all well and send their "most pious regards" to all the "good folks" at home.

In my next I expect to give you the experience of a skirmish. I hope we will be successful—this war between "brothers" will be ended and our beloved country at peace. Excuse the imperfectness of this letter as I have a large crowd around me and my desk is a water bucket.

Yours fraternally,
H. D. W.

* * * * *

Camp of 11th Regiment, P. V.
Hagerstown, Md.,
June 17, 1861.[75]

Dear John:—Here we are at length encamped about a mile south of the above named place. We struck our tents this morning at 3 o'clock, and took the cars for this place where we arrived about 8 o'clock. At Greencastle the citizens were just about taking breakfast as we came into town, and it was with delight we beheld them coming from their houses, and sharing it with the men. We were hastily greeted, and well fed, for which we gave them our loudest cheers together, with a new yell, which company F calls her own. Our entrance into Hagerstown was unmarked by any incident of special interest. The Union feeling must be largely in the ascendency, judging from the number of flags flying. We have encamped with us here, besides the regiments that were with us at Camp McClure, the 14th and 15th Pennsylvania Regiments. The headquarters of Gen. Patterson and Gen. Negley[76] are also here. Capt. Doubleday and his command lay just below us. The 1st Rhode Island Regiment, which was at Williamsport, passed here this morning, headed by Gov. Sprague. They are a fine-looking body of men, well equipped, and on a forced march of thirty-two miles. They were present at the crossing of the Potomac, yesterday, of

---

75. *Sunbury Gazette*, June 22, 1861.
76. Brig. Gen. James Scott Negley (1826–1901). In October 1861 he was placed in command of the 7th Brigade in the Department of the Ohio and is mentioned again in the letter of William A. Fetter, 7th Pennsylvania Cavalry (page 269).

Cadwallader's division, and covered it with their field pieces. There are several other camps here, making in the neighborhood of ten thousand troops in the vicinity. McMullin's Rangers[77] are in the town. They are a fine-looking body of men, and excellently equipped.

To-day, while sitting in my marquee, I was surprised to hear someone inquiring for Mr. Gobin of Sunbury. On his coming in, I was pleased to see Rev. Coleman Savidge, formerly of our place, who is now stationed a short distance from here. With him was a gentleman from Lovettsville, Loudon co., Va., who left there, on account of an attempt being made to press him into the Secession army. He informed me that two thirds of the inhabitants of that region were in favor of the Union, but were afraid to express their sentiments, and that they were anxiously awaiting the approach of the Federal army. He states that at Harper's Ferry there were about 10,000 troops when he left, and that they had pressed into their service all the teams in the neighborhood. Boys of sixteen years of age were compelled to enter the army, but desertions were very numerous. He also stated that many of the soldiers were Union men, who could not be relied upon, nor would they fire upon the flag under which they were nurtured, and which they had been taught to revere and honor.

While writing to-night I heard a great cheering along the outposts, and on repairing to the spot I was edified by a view of the Second U. S. Cavalry, on their march south. They had just returned from Virginia where they were with Gen. Cadwallader.

I met Theodore Kiehl to-day, who is in the 14th Regiment. He is in excellent health and spirits, and looks better than I have seen him for some time.

I cannot say how long we will remain here. The probability now is that we will be ordered on to Washington. Our whole regiment is together, and all are enjoying excellent health. We have not had a single death in the Regiment from disease since we left, and have had no sickness save a few cases of diarrhea, caused no doubt by a change of water and diet.

I suppose you have received the news of the evacuation of Harper's Ferry by the rebels, and the occupancy of Martinsburg and

---

77. McMullen's Independent Rangers was a three-month unit raised in Philadelphia at the beginning of the war.

Leesburg by our troops. The rebels burned all the bridges, and our men were compelled to wade the Potomac waist deep. An eye-witness informed me they went over with a regular wild Pennsylvania yell.

I have neglected hitherto to express through you the thanks of the Company to Mrs. Elizabeth Hutter, wife of Rev. Edwin Hutter, of Philadelphia, for the box of havelocks furnished us by her. They come very acceptable, and she has our most sincere thanks.

For the next twenty-four hours I am to be officer of the guard, so I will need some rest. Therefore, wishing you and old friends a hearty good night, I remain

Yours, &c.,
J. P. S. G.

* * * * *

Camp, 5th Brigade, P. V.,
Hagerstown, Md.,
June 19, 1861.[78]

DEAR WILVERT:—On last Wednesday morning, about 2 o'clock, we struck our tents at Camp Susquehanna, Havre de Grace.—After waiting until 7 o'clock we were marched to the cars and embarked for Camp McClure, via Baltimore and Harrisburg. In marching through Baltimore we had no trouble, they supposing from our dress we were regulars. There was one expression of hostility, however, and that was by an old termagant, who opened her door, displaying a Secession flag, and making mouths at us, but our boys paid no attention to her. Happily no one saw her but our company, or there would have been trouble. In passing through the city I saw something that done a soldier good—a *quilt* made to resemble the American flag, and on it the "proud bird of liberty," besides the Maryland coat of arms. It was the prettiest piece of work, of the kind, I ever saw. When our boys saw it they could not restrain their feelings, and gave to that proud emblem such hearty cheers as to fairly make the streets ring and Secessionists tremble. When we arrived at Bolton station there was some delay, and a gentleman, a strong Union man, showed his

---

78. *Sunbury American*, June 29, 1861.

bounty by liberally supplying our regiment with fresh bread and good butter, that is, as many as could get into the house. It was, after a pretty hard march, very acceptable, and our boys, to use the expression of an old friend, were "too full for expression"—not *spirits*, but thanks. When we arrived at Harrisburg we changed engines, and after a tedious ride arrived at Chambersburg at 2 o'clock next morning. You have heard of the fellow, in sleeping, "hunting for the soft side of a plank," so it was with us. Our cars were those used for the transportation of cattle, and being too late to march to camp, made the best of it, and slept very soundly, so much so that your humble servant, in sleeping, dreaming of home, gave a kick, and for his pains fell off the bench and received a black eye. At breakfast time there was nothing for us to eat, and some of our boys, getting used to the "tricks of trade," strayed about town, and in their walk were invited in and hospitably entertained by some of the citizens—for myself I had the extreme pleasure of breakfasting with W. G. Reed, Esq., cashier of the Chambersburg Bank, a very fine gentleman, who has my heartiest thanks and warmest wishes.

We were then marched into camp, fixed our tents, and after four days hard drilling were ordered to Hagerstown. On last Monday, 3 A. M., we again struck our tents and arrived here about 8 o'clock. On our way down we were agreeably surprised at a small place, Greencastle, eleven miles below Chambersburg. It is a place to take in water, we stopped about five minutes, when we were completely stormed with eatables, supplied by the ladies of that place. One could hear the rest of our regiment shouting "a second Sunbury," "three cheers for the ladies of Greencastle," besides a "tiger" for those of our place. I tell you the ladies of Sunbury and Greencastle are held in high estimation by the "bloody 11th."

Yesterday morning, at 3 o'clock, our Brigade, under command of Gen. Nagle, were hurriedly marched to Williamsport, Md., about seven miles below, a messenger having arrived with a dispatch stating that the rebels, some 15,000 strong, were about to attack the Federal forces stationed there. There was considerable excitement in our Brigade, and if the rebels could have seen the steady step and determined eye of our soldiers, they would at once put an end to their foolish enterprise, cease to be traitors, and learn to be decent citizens. When we arrived we marched into a field adjoining the Brigade composed of the Pennsylvania Sixth, Eighth, Tenth, Twenty-first, (Scott Legion,) regiments, and a large force of cavalry from Carlisle and Philadelphia. The Ninth (Pa.) was stationed opposite Williamsport, and part of the Fourth Brigade was also back of the town. We were kept eleven hours in the broiling sun, lying on our arms, with one day's rations—one-half pound of pork and six crackers. About 5 o'clock, the enemy not approaching, each regiment in the Brigade were ordered on review, after which we took up march and arrived at this camp at 10 o'clock, P. M. The soldiers were very much disappointed that they didn't meet the enemy and engage in a fight, if they had, I think you would have heard a good account of the bravery and deeds of the Pennsylvania volunteers.

We are under orders to prepare for any emergency, and I think, if alive, you may shortly hear of me from the city of "magnificent distances," Washington.

I see Mr. Youngman gives me a "slap" in his last issue.[79] What I said I meant out of no ill will, and merely told the truth. If he thinks there is no "necessity," in speaking of the crackers, there is less in a journalist, who professes to be so great a lover of the Union and the volunteers (and I suppose he is) in speaking of the matter at all, for expressions the least disheartening worries the soldier, and almost makes him unfit for duty, particularly when coming from friends at home.

Yours, fraternally,
H. D. W.

* * * * *

[The following letter from a private in Company F, 11th Regiment, may be of interest to our readers:]

---

79. In the June 17, 1861, edition of the *Sunbury Gazette*, editor Youngman noted that "Week before last we published the following in regard to the crackers with which our soldiers had been supplied: 'If those sent home were a fair specimen, the boys had not much reason to make a fuss about them. They were good.'" Responding to Wharton's negative comment about the editorial's assessment of the crackers in his letter to the *American* (see June 4, 1861 on page 79, final paragraph), Youngman stated: "By reading what we said it will be seen that the latter part of the remarks of the American's correspondent was perfectly unnecessary."

Hagerstown, Md.,
June 20, 1861.[80]

DEAR SISTER.—We are encamped about three quarters of a mile from Hagerstown, in a clover field, but there is very little clover in it at the present time. A great deal of it was mowed by the soldiers with case knives for beds, and the rest is tramped so flat that you can scarcely see there had ever been any clover on it.

Last Monday night the Colonel received a dispatch to march to Williamsport immediately, as it was thought there would be a collision between the Federal and Confederate troops at that place, on that day. Five regiments left the camp immediately—the 14th, 15th and 11th Pennsylvania, the 1st Wisconsin, and 4th Connecticut. When we arrived there we found the troops were coming in from all quarters, but no Secessionists were to be seen. There were supposed to be from fifteen to twenty thousand U.S. troops within two miles of Williamsport. When we found the Secessionists were not about, we stacked our arms, and laid down to rest. At half past 5 o'clock, P. M., we had dress parade, after which we again took up our line of march to return from whence we started, where we arrived at about 9 o'clock, about as tired as men could well get. You had better believe we were sleepy, tired, and sore, after marching 14 miles, with about fifty pounds of baggage to carry. I had a blister on the sole of each foot about the size of a shilling. You never saw a set of fellows in a better humor than we were when we started, as all hands thought we would certainly have a brush with the enemy; but we were not quite so well pleased when we got the order to return.

Wilson Covert and Lloyd Rohrbach have again joined our company. I rather think they will be brought to their fighting weight in a short time. We are all well, and in good spirits, except a few who have the diarrhea.

We came near having another difficulty last night about the provisions. The Quartermaster had been cheating us from the time we left Harrisburg. Last night when we went to draw our rations he wanted to cheat us out of 56 lbs. of beef, about 30 lbs. of pork, 1 barrel crackers, 17 candles and 8 lbs. soap, &c.; but our Orderly

---

80. *Sunbury Gazette*, June 29, 1861.

Sergeant just told him that he had been playing that game about long enough, and that it was now time to stop it. The Quartermaster did not feel disposed to do so; therefore the Sergeant was under the painful necessity of kicking up a fuss, which having the desired effect, the provisions came forth, our Orderly was satisfied, and the difficulty ended.

We have now got as poor as there is any use of being. I do not believe that five dollars could be raised in our whole company. The Connecticut boys each got ten dollars yesterday, and they are going it high. Three of them just passed, each with a sheep on his back. Answer immediately, for I cannot tell how soon we may leave here.

Your Brother,
B.[81]

* * * * *

Camp Negley,
Hagerstown, Md.,
June 24, 1861.[82]

Dear John:—Our regiment is still quartered here, although for the last week we have been under orders to be ready for immediate march. It is a fine location for a camp, it being in a large clover field with plenty of good water close at hand. The Brigade to which we were attached has been changed, and a new one formed, comprising Magruder's Battery, the 11th Pa. Regiment, 1st Wisconsin, and 4th Connecticut. It will be the Sixth Brigade, and will be commanded by Col. Abercrombie, late of the 7th U. S. Infantry.[83] He is reported to be an excellent officer.

Last Monday night about 12 m., we were aroused from our slumbers, and directed to prepare to start on a forced march, taking nothing along but what we could carry. About 1 o'clock the 1st

---

81. The author has not been identified. There were only two men on the company roster with the first initial "B": Benjamin F. Bright and Benjamin W. Giddes.

82. *Sunbury Gazette*, June 29, 1861.

83. John Joseph Abercrombie (1798–1877). He would be promoted to brigadier general of Volunteers on August 31, 1861, and serve as commander of the 2nd Brigade in the 1st Division, 5th Corps, of the Army of the Potomac during the Peninsula Campaign.

Wisconsin Regiment started, and threw out an advance guard. The 14th and 15th Pennsylvania followed, and about 4 o'clock, A. M., the "Bloody Eleventh" filed silently out of the gate, and started on a quick march for Williamsport. Each man was provided with a chunk of fat pork, and a half dozen crackers, and the most Important item, 40 rounds of buck and ball cartridge. Nothing was heard save the dull heavy tramp of the men, or an occasional bark of a watch dog as we hurried along the road. After marching about a mile the regiment was ordered to halt, and every man load his gun—most of our boys, however, had taken the precaution to do that before we left camp. The farmers along the road, as they came to their doors, were somewhat surprised to see us passing, but not a word was spoken. It had been known in camp that the 9th Regiment, which had crossed the Potomac, had been encamped within five miles of eighteen thousand secessionists under Gen. Johnson,[84] and we felt satisfied we were going to relieve them. Here then was a time for thought, and the mind was busy, I assure you. We all felt confident of having a fight, yet as I gazed along the ranks, I could not see a pale face. Each man hurried along as though the salvation of the country depended upon his efforts, and all seemed eager for the fray. About 6 o'clock, the spires of a village appeared in view, and "Williamsport—Williamsport"—"Potomac" ran along the line in a hushed whisper. Before reaching the town[,] we filed off into a field, and were ordered to be ready for immediate action. On looking at the time we found we had marched 8 miles in two hours and ten minutes. We lay there all day expecting to be ordered to cross the river and "at them," but as the day wore on and no orders arrived, you could hear the muttered curses of the men in every direction. Johnson and his crew had left and the 9th was safe.

After sitting exposed to the broiling sun, I began to realize the fact that I had had no breakfast, so, in company with privates Irwin, W. B. Martin, and Christ, I started for town, about half a mile off. The hotels were all shut up, so we began inquiring at private houses for something to eat. After some search we obtained some pies, and it would have done our friends good to see us sitting on a cellar-door in the streets of Williamsport, stowing them away. We had considerable

---

84. This is likely a misspelled reference to Brig. Gen. Joseph E. Johnston, who was then in command of Confederate forces at Harper's Ferry.

fun over it. Up the street farther, I observed a young man from Lycoming County, accustomed at home to all the luxuries of life, contentedly sitting on a door step, eating a piece of bread and butter.

Williamsport, like most other towns we have visited in Maryland, looks like an ancient, "played-out" village. The houses are mostly frame, squatty buildings—remnants of the last century. A high bluff is between the town and the Potomac, which was occupied by the Home Guard at the time of the attack by the Virginians on the ferry. The firing must have been pretty severe, as quite a number of flattened balls were picked up by our boys. Some of them waded across to the Virginia side, and visited the deserted camp of the Secessionists a short distance from the shore. About 7 o'clock our Brigade was ordered to return to our camp, which we reached before 10 o'clock.

While at Williamsport we had the pleasure of visiting the 8th Regiment, and taking by the hand our friends of Shamokin, also, John H. Arnold and Jacob Keefer, of Company ----- 2d Regiment. They were all well, and in the best of spirits.

Last week, Lieut. Col. Bowman, and a man named Chase, crossed into Virginia at Williamsport, and were captured by a secession scouting party. What has been done with them we have not learned. This satisfies us that some of the rebels have returned.

On Thursday night the 14th and 15th Pennsylvania Regiments marched to Cumberland, where Col. Wallace was almost surrounded. On their approach the rebels retired.

Last night two sentinels of the 3d Regiment stationed along the railroad were shot at their posts—one of them fatally. This is the style of the warfare practiced by the Southern chivalry. They go sneaking among the grass like cowardly skunks, and shoot sentinels, but as soon as a Regiment appears none are to be found. They retreat before one fourth their number. We have arrested several in our camp, and on Saturday, we compelled one of them to take the oath of allegiance in presence of about half a Regiment of boys. The fellow was "orefully" frightened.

The weather is awful hot here, but we manage it very well. We drill here three or four times a day, and are getting along finely. Our boys are well with the exception of a few cases of diarrhea, none of which are serious. J. W. Covert and L. T. Rohrbach have joined us, but will be detailed for special service, I think, the remainder of their term. My respects to all.

Yours,
J. P. S. G.

* * * * *

Camp, 6th Brigade, 11th Reg't, P. V.,
Hagerstown, Md.,
June 24, 1861.[85]

DEAR WILVERT:—You can see by the heading of this note that we have again been put in another brigade. It seems that for our Regiment there is nothing to be done but being driven from one Brigade to another; how often it has been done I have not taken time to count. There is some consolation to the boys, however, to know that we are near the enemy and may have a chance for a fracas, and that they are to be commanded by so noble a man as Gen. Abercrombie, late Colonel of the 9th U. S. Infantry. We are lying in Camp in a perfect state of laziness as regards fighting—since our march on Williamsport the enemy have let us alone, our fellows have had a pretty good chance for drill, and they have been kept steadily at it too. It is mighty hard work, with the thermometer at 103° in the sun. The boys stand it well, perfectly satisfied, and are getting fat, particularly on the *pork* and *crackers*.

The Wisconsin Regiment, in the same Brigade with us, is a crack one, splendidly drilled, and by the way are kept harder at work than ours. Their Colonel is a gentleman, a well drilled soldier, and I believe a graduate of West Point. To show the love of his men for him, on leaving Camp McClure, Chambersburg, the Regiment being in full line, preparatory to leaving, he asked if they would fight for the "Star Spangled Banner," and die for it and him, the whole Regiment to a men fell on their knees and swore they would fight for the flag, protect him and die if necessary. In the action of such men, headed by Col. Starkweather, there need be no apprehensions as to the success of our cause.

---

85. *Sunbury American*, June 29, 1861.

Yesterday (Sabbath) about 4 o'clock in the afternoon, I heard some sweet sounds of music—thought the air familiar, went out of my tent to listen to it and was most agreeably surprised to hear that good old tune "Coronation" being played by the Wisconsin Band. If it wasn't foolish I would acknowledge that I felt a little something resembling a tear running down my cheek; but you know nature must have its way. The next piece was "Old Hundred," ending with "Auld Lang Syne," and I tell you there were tears ran down the cheeks of "braver hearts and stouter frames" than mine, on hearing those good old airs.

On Saturday last, Lieutenant Gobin, while talking with some ladies, was shown a supposed spy. The Lieutenant, with his usual gallantry, excused himself from the ladies and started after the fellow. He caught him, and after propounding a few questions, which he answered, the Lieutenant, not being satisfied, asked for a Bible—made the fellow take the strongest kind of an oath to support the Constitution and the Union—and then let him depart in peace. The fellow was most awfully frightened. Yesterday there was one taken with better grit—the Corporal of the Guard took him to the guard house. When asked his business he gave saucy and very imperfect answers, and swore awfully he would never take the oath of allegiance to the United States. He was then taken to Gen. Patterson's quarters, under guard, but what was done with him I have not heard. If I had the sentence to pass on him it would be "to dance on nothing, with a rope around his neck, and no fiddler to play the tune," hanging.

There was considerable fun in our company on last Saturday night. A fire occurred in the town right opposite our quarters. The boys couldn't get out, and they had an impromptu running of their own. They cry was "down on her Goodie," "hi, hi" "pass the Washy," "now she brings her," "that's the way, old boy," and then put her back in "the house." I tell you we had a high old time, and Col. Jarret thought we were a regular set of Firemen Zouaves.

Yours, fraternally,
H. D. W.

* * * * *

Camp of 11th Reg't, P. V.
Below Downsville, Md.,
June 30, 1861.[86]

Dear John:—I hope you will pardon me for writing this to-day (Sunday,) but as the day is not very strictly observed in this locality, and the rain confines me to the tent, I will while away an hour in chronicling the events of the day.

Yesterday the First Wisconsin, and our Regiment were ordered to strike our tents and prepare to march. This order occasioned great rejoicing among the men, as we knew, or rather thought we were going into Virginia. Our tents fell at two o'clock, P. M., and in fifteen minutes we were ready to start. We did not get off, however, until about four. At that time we bid adieu to Camp Negley, and the citizens of Hagerstown, and took up our line of march in a Southerly direction. Each company was provided with a baggage wagon, which, with the baggage guard, brought up the rear. The road over which we passed was one of the most uneven and rocky I ever encountered, winding hither and thither as though to oblige every farmer on the route. The dust was about four inches deep, it appearing as though all the ground within a hundred yards of the road had been taken from the fields and conveyed there for the express purpose of being wafted into our eyes, hair, and every part of the body. However, our knapsacks being on the wagon we trudged along in the best of humor, singing, shouting, and occasionally mounting a cherry tree that happened to stand along the road. About 8 o'clock we arrived at this place, and selecting a fine clover field, the Colonel ordered us to pitch our tents, but be ready to march early this morning. We soon had our tents up and our supper eaten, and in a short time all but the guards were [illegible phrase]. This morning, however, the General, Abercrombie, [illegible word] to send forward a scouting party before advancing, and accordingly four men were selected from each company, who about ten o'clock started off with one day's rations. The men selected from our company were Heddings, Kiehl, Brosious and McClusky. All the boys were anxious for the honor, but of course all could not go. Lieut. W. A. Bruner is with them; the whole under

---

86. *Sunbury Gazette*, July 6, 1861.

command of Lieut. Col. Coulter. As soon as they return I think we will move forward.

We are about one mile from the Potomac, over twelve miles above Harper's Ferry. The Rebels are in considerable force over the river opposite to us, and our pickets, who are extended to the banks, observe them jumping around over there quite promiscuously. This morning, some of our boys went down and took a look at them, and happily for one of the parties, "Jordan rolled between." This morning a scouting party of the 6th Regiment brought into camp five, whom they captured last night. They are reported as quite docile. They report that their head-quarters are at Martinsburg, which is directly South of us, and about seven miles distant. In less than forty-eight hours the Eleventh Regiment *will be there*. Mark the prediction.

There are encamped around us here the U. S. Second Cavalry, the 1st Wisconsin Regiment, the Philadelphia City troop, the 6th, 21st, and 23d Pennsylvania Regiments. McMullin's Rangers who have been attached to our Brigade, we expect to-day, and probably the 4th Connecticut. But there are enough here now to do the requisite amount of work, and all are anxious to begin forthwith.

I received a handbill from some kind friend calling on the patriotic citizens of Sunbury and vicinity to assemble and celebrate the 4th of July in a proper manner. We have made no arrangements here yet to celebrate the day, but I am of the opinion that some part of Virginia will hold us upon that day, and in all probability witness our efforts to sustain that time honored institution, and the associations connected therewith. Therefore, dear John, while you are listening to some stirring orations, occasionally give an ear to Southern breezes, and observe whether you cannot hear an occasional rattle of musketry, and discern the smell of powder. It will be a glorious day to fight, and an entirely new method of celebrating it—much preferable to us than any amusement I know of.

It is amusing to hear of the rumors in circulation at home about us. In order to quiet these I may as well state that at present writing every man in the company is well and fit for duty. While at Hagerstown some of us were attacked with diarrhea, but all are again sound, and none are killed, taken prisoners, or anything of the kind. Rest assured that if any calamity of this kind should befall any of us, it will be promptly communicated to our friends at home.

The land in this vicinity is of a rocky, rolling nature, although they raise splendid grain. Quite a number of fields are in our vicinity, some of which have already been cut. The farm houses, or most of them, are low, antique, log buildings, while the barns are as much unlike the snug, painted barns of our farmers as can well be imagined. I would like to see either of my old friends, George Conrad, or John Cooper, stowing their produce away in such tumble-down buildings as they call barns in this region. We are encamped upon the land of a man named Beckley (no relative of yours, Squire, I inquired) who says he has 200 acres of wheat out, and yet his barn is an old, unpainted, rickety building, only fit to harbor bats. The farmer just called at the General's quarters, and complained that sundry chickens, a hog, bee-hive, &c., had disappeared last night. Of course the Eleventh did it—they do everything in that line; but from certain indications, I am inclined to believe the Wisconsin boys dined on pork steaks to-day. There is a saw mill on the place that the boys have been examining, and Messrs. Fecht, Weiser and Joe Bright say it runs very well. The owner however, does not appear to appreciate their efforts, notwithstanding they informed him they had a large contract to fill.

The Battery attached to our Brigade has just arrived, and quartered near us. It is under command of Major Perkins.

I cannot tell where letters should be directed to us, as we are not aware of our destination, and it is doubtful whether they will reach us anyhow. In the meantime I will keep you informed of our movements if opportunity offers, and I am spared to do it.

But I am summoned for supper, which is a little extra to-day, thanks to our old friend Rigby, whom we employed at Chambersburg. It consists of beef steak, short cake, butter and honey. If we do not march I may send you another letter to-morrow. My best respects to all.

Yours,
J. P. S. G.

* * * * *

The 11th Pennsylvania experienced its baptism of fire at the Battle of Falling Waters on July 2, 1861. (Credit: *Harper's Weekly*, July 27, 1861)

Martinsburg, Va.,
July 3, 1861.[87]

Dear John:—Here we are on the eve of our national birth-day in the place above named, rendered famous since the rebellion by the gross acts of vandalism committed here by the rebels. The 11th Pa. regiment left Downsville on Monday morning, and marched to Williamsport, where we remained until Tuesday at 4 o'clock a. m., when we started for the "Old Dominion," the Wisconsin Regiment and the Eleventh Pennsylvania in the lead. It was a cold morning, but the boys plunged into the Potomac like old water dogs, all anxious to reach the other side. The water reached above the knees, but our clothes soon dried after we started on. About ten o'clock our scouts, McMullin's Rangers, came back and informed us that the secessionists in large numbers, were approaching us. We were immediately thrown into a wood, and formed into line of battle. After waiting some time we were ordered forward. Just as we arrived at Falling Waters, a volley of musketry informed us that our scouts had engaged the enemy. We were immediately ordered forward; the Wisconsin regiment took the

---

87. *Sunbury Gazette*, July 13, 1861.

left flank, and deploying as skirmishers, while we filed to the right into a woods, and formed again in line. The enemy consisting of four regiments of infantry, four pieces of artillery, and five hundred cavalry, were strongly posted in an orchard commanding the country for some distance, their right resting on the edge of a thick wood. The firing had become general on the left by this time, and we were ordered forward on a double quick. We had formed in a ravine, and as we rushed up the hill and over the fence, we were greeted with a volley that went whistling over our heads at a beautiful rate; yet not a man flinched, but pushed forward through a grain field to a fence skirting the field in which the enemy were. Here we delivered our first fire, when they opened upon us with a six pounder. Several six-pound shots came flying among us and about us that caused considerable "dodging" along our line. One struck about fifteen feet in front of our company, and were bounding over our heads, the wind of it knocking down one of Company K's men, who was in the rear. In the meantime we were pouring the buck and ball into them, and in the midst of this terrible fire formed in line to charge on them. Just at this juncture they opened on us with grape and cannister, when a number of our men were hit. We rushed for them, and they broke and fled, but not until our cannon had sent several shot and shell into their midst. One of our shells went through a barn behind which they were sheltered, which was soon in a blaze. We followed them for three miles, but they were too well acquainted with the country and escaped. The number of their killed and wounded we were unable to learn, but we were informed that they took three wagon loads along with them in their retreat, and a gentleman in Martinsburg informed us that he saw seventy of them buried in that place. We found two dead bodies on the field, and two more in a dying condition this morning, lying in the woods on our road to this place. Their route was covered with over-coats, blankets, canteens, haversacks, &c., and some of them even threw away their revolvers in their hurry to escape. The two were picked up by privates Snyder and Drieslinger of our Company.

Our victory was complete, and considering that it was the first time our boys stood fire, I think we have just reason to feel proud of our success. We were highly complimented by General Patterson who witnessed our charge. The secessionists told it in Martinsburg that they could have whipped the Wisconsin volunteers, but when *them regulars* charged on them they had to retreat. Our loss was one killed and nine wounded. The killed was a member of company H, from Danville, named Amos Zuppinger. He was shot right through the head. One of our company named Christian Shall fell near me, a grape shot grazing the left side of his head, and taking off part of his ear. I thought he was gone, but [he] had it dressed and joined us shortly after. Not a man of company F flinched, but they acted with the coolness of veterans, each man at last loading and firing as fast as he could, taking deliberate aim.

We slept on our arms all night, and next morning moved to this place. The chivalry had all departed some time before we arrived. But an alarm is sounded; we are ordered to fall in. The whole camp is in commotion, and the rattle of musketry is heard from our pickets. There is a prospect of another brush. I will write again.

Yours,
J. P. S. G.

* * * * *

Camp_____,
Martinsburg, Va.,
July 3, 1861.[88]

DEAR WILVERT—

Gen. Patterson's Army have at last advanced this far on the "sacred soil of Old Virginia." The Eleventh boys, first Wisconsin regiment, a few Cavalry and a portion of Captain Perkins' Artillery met with a most CORDIAL reception on their first visit to the hospitable State of the F. F. V's.[89] Yesterday morning (Tuesday,) preparatory to the moving of the entire force, a scouting party of thirteen men,

---

88. *Sunbury American*, July 13, 1861.
89. F. F. V. generally stands for First Families of Virginia. The reference here is likely being used in a derogatory way to malign the planter class of Virginia society, whom most Northerners held responsible for causing the war.

with a corporal, were detailed from the Eleventh and the Wisconsin regiments, under command of Lieut. Colonel Coulter, to visit the country on the Virginia side of the Potomac, opposite Williamsport, to discover the whereabouts of the rebels—our party met with a reception they had not bargained for. The scouts started at 2 o'clock in the morning; it was very dark and the boys having reached the opposite shore were moving along noiselessly, as they supposed, when, bang! bang! came the fire of 150 rebels right in the midst of our scouts which confused them some, they immediately returned their fire with double interest; making the rebels retreat without saying "with your leave" or giving our boys a chance to find out what damage they had done to them. Our fellows fired twice and had a third load ready for them, but the rebels thinking "discretion the better part of valor," left so abruptly that the boys kept the last load for another fight. Not one of the party was injured. How they escaped is beyond my comprehension.

About 4 o'clock of the same morning all the regiments in and near Williamsport—in fact all of Gen. Patterson's Division, were ordered to march into Virginia. We forded the river, and everything passed off pleasantly until we reached Falling Waters, four miles below Williamsport, when we heard of the rebels and it was not long 'till we had a smell of Jeff. Davis' "southern powder." There was a regular fight then—some may call it a skirmish, but from the way in which the cannon and the Minnie[90] rifle balls flew, I should call it, well a regular battle. The Wisconsin boys took the left of the line, acting principally as scouts and sharp-shooters, while our regiment took the right, the post of honor, and the battery, with the cavalry, the centre. If ever a pretty move and a display of bravery was enacted it was shown by the 11th regiment. The command was given (after the enemy commenced the fight) by Col. Jarrett to charge, away went the boys on a run, cheering at every jump, with the balls of the enemy flying around and about them, and repeatedly an eight-pound cannon ball striking in front and sometimes a ball bounding over

---

90. The correct spelling of the projectile that Wharton refers to here is Minié. The bullet was named after its French inventor, Claude-Etienne Minié (1804–1879). The bullet's design—cylindrical in shape with a conical hollow at the base that expanded to engage the barrel rifling when fired, causing the bullet to spin—greatly improved the accuracy and range of the firearm. The improvement suddenly made the muzzle-loading rifled musket a much more reliable weapon over its traditional smoothed-bore musket counterpart.

their heads. One of our drum corps picked up an eight pounder that flew over the right of our company and passed over the heads of our Charlie and Capt. Bruner. I was frightened then, supposing they and others were killed, but Capt. Bruner seeing the ball strike before them, cried "fall," which they did and thus escaped unharmed. It was when they fell I thought they were gone, but I was soon relieved, for up came a cheer, and I saw our brave fellows rush into the fight and pour a volley into the enemy that made them scatter. It was the evident intention of the gunners of the rebels' battery to break the centre of our column, thinking by doing so they would be confused and they (the rebels) have an easy victory, but they calculated wide of their mark, the steady and determined charge of our regiment, the continued throwing of shell and ball by the battery, with sharp-shooting of the Wisconsin boys, made them retreat and the first victory gained on Virginia soil was by a portion of the 6th Brigade.

The battle lasted about one hour and a half, and the length of ground on which it was fought was three miles.

The force of the enemy was four regiments with five hundred cavalry, about double our number. The loss of the enemy was over one hundred killed, fifty wounded, besides several prisoners, while our loss was two killed, one in our regiment and one in the Wisconsin, and about twelve wounded—two severely. The one killed in our regiment was a member of Company H (Danville Rifles). The enemy, on their retreat, said if it had not been for the d----d regulars they would have whipped us—the idea of them taking such raw recruits as us for regulars is laughable—they took us for U. S. Troops, from the fact of our wearing the undress uniform of the regulars, the coat being the same as that worn by the Dewart Guards.

The enemy have retreated toward Winchester, further down in Virginia, where we soon expect to have another engagement. Our whole force, by Friday, at Martinsburg will be about twenty-five thousand, with Doubleday's heavy battery, the Rhode Island battery and Perkins' battery besides some Cavalry, part of which [includes] the First City Troops of Philadelphia. When we do meet they will have more to remember than the recollections of the battle of Falling Waters. I should have stated that McMullin's Rangers took an active part in the fight, did good service and that with great credit. Our boys, Sunbury Guards, were in the hottest of the fight, they being in the centre, and strange to say no one was killed, and but one slightly wounded. The name of the wounded man is Christ Shall, from Cincinnati. I was at the Hospital assisting, when he came in, after the wound was dressed he turned to me and said, "Harry, where is my gun, I must go help the boys fight it out," and he went, and after returning helped Bill Christ to kill two beeves. That is what I call cool and shows considerable bravery. When the man fell, Capt. Bruner, seeing him, shouted, "boys, avenge the death of Shall," the Captain supposing him dead, away went the boys with a yell and made some pretty good work All our boys returned from the fight in good humor, and the "knife and fork game" played at supper, gave evidence that the day's work did not spoil their appetite.

I commenced this last night, the 3d, at Martinsburg and finish it on the 4th of July, opposite Williamsport, twelve miles above. The reason of my doing so, is, that the Wisconsin and our regiment have been sent here as guards to a train of two hundred wagons after a three' months supply of provision, and as escort to the Rhode Island regiment. Pretty work for the 4th, and as Sergeant Heilbing says, "not a glass of lager to drink." You have your fun today—we expect ours soon in a fight and a great deal more pleasure on our return home, if we are lucky enough to get there.

Yours, Fraternally,
H. D. W.

* * * * *

Hedgeville, Berkeley County, Va.,
July 3, 1861.[91]

DEAR MOTHER:—After writing you from Hagerstown, we were ordered to a little town named Downsville, 6 miles from Hedgesville. At the latter place I took the initiatory step in active service, having been ordered to take 30 men and proceed to the Potomac for the purpose of finding a ford. After going five miles down the river the traitors commenced firing on us from the Virginia side. We returned

---

91. *Sunbury American*, July 13, 1861.

the fire and they soon disappeared.—I think it was the hardest night I ever experienced. We were up to our necks in water, and a rain pouring down on us, but we reached the Virginia side about 12 o'clock at night. We returned to the Maryland side and laid down the rest of the night on top of a mountain. The next morning we crossed at Lock No. 4, in broad day light, into Virginia, for the second time. The Marylanders thought we would all be killed, but we returned safe, without finding a suitable ford.

But yesterday we crossed the river at Williamsport—that is, our Regiment, the 1st Wisconsin, Bill McMullin's Company, and a Battery of two guns, under command of Colonel Abercrombie. After proceeding about 4 miles, we were attacked by 4000 of the traitors (we had about 1800). We had pretty hard work for about two hours, when they began to retreat, and took back with them 3,000 more men that were coming to aid them. The left wing of the Regiment (to which the Sunbury Company and our own are attached) had the brunt of the battle. The Sunbury Company had one man wounded, and we had two, one severely. Charley[92] faced the music like a man, and in fact every man in the Regiment stood up like an old soldier.

To-day, at 9 o'clock, we march for Martinsburg. We have 20,000 men here now. I think we will run the traitors out of the country.

I must close, as we have new orders to march immediately. Direct your letters to Williamsport, Md., as we will probably have an expressman here occasionally.

WILLIAM A. BRUNER.

P. S.—The left wing had 1 killed and 10 wounded.

* * * * *

[We have been permitted to make the following extracts from the letter of Captain Bruner, to his wife, in this place:—]

Williamsport, Md.,
July 3, 1861.[93]

---

92. This likely is a reference to the author's brother, Capt. Charles J. Bruner of Company F.
93. *Sunbury American*, July 13, 1861.

We had quite a fight yesterday with the rebels, about 7 miles from this place, on the road to Martinsburg. Our Regiment was in the thickest of the fight. My Company stood like veterans, notwithstanding the six pounders and rifle balls rattled like hail about us. I had one man wounded slightly—a German by the name of Scholl. We were opposed by about 4,000 rebels. Our force consisted of our Regiment, two companies of the Wisconsin Regiment, who acted as skirmishers, McMullin's Rangers and Perkins' Battery, consisting of 2 cannon. There were about seventy-five or one hundred secessionists killed and wounded. We had one man from Danville killed and 6 wounded in the regiment. The Wisconsin Regiment had one man killed and one wounded. To-day we advanced to Martinsburg without meeting with any opposition. We expect to have a fight to-morrow on the road to Winchester at a place called "Bunker's Hill." I have no time to write any more.

You may think it strange that I am in Williamsport.—My baggage for the Company was all left behind, and I had to bring down two wagons and a guard of fifteen men with me to get it. We start from here at daylight, and may have to fight our way through. Charley Warton is with me.

CHARLES J. BRUNER.

* * * * *

Martinsburg, Va.,
July 7, 1861.[94]

Dear John:—My last letter to you was suddenly brought to a close by the sound of musketry. The "long roll" was beat, and in less than five minutes the whole regiment was in line, ready for action. Capt. Bruner having gone to Williamsport after our tents and baggage, which had been left behind, I was in command, and at the time of the alarm, was seated on the ground, with a bayonet for a candlestick, writing upon a drum. Of course out went the light, and this finished my writing. After waiting some time and nothing further being heard, the men were dismissed and cautioned to lay on their arms to be

---

94. *Sunbury Gazette*, July 13, 1861.

ready at a moment's notice. However the night passed and nothing further occurred.

The next morning, the 1st Wisconsin and our Regiment were ordered to Williamsport to bring up the Rhode Island Battery and a train of provisions and ammunition. We started about 6 o'clock A. M., but it was 12 before we reached the Potomac. We encamped on the Virginia side while the wagons were sent over and loaded. The whole day was consumed in this, so that we were enabled to get a little rest and celebrate the 4th in our own way. The most of us did it by taking a bath, and at one time at least five hundred of us were bathing our wearied limbs in its blue waters. It was a picturesque sight I assure you. The remainder of the day we strolled among the groves that lined its banks—congregating in groups, discussing the scenes of our late conflict—speculating as to what was going on at home, &c. Some of our boys were seated around writing to their friends and sweethearts, informing them, no doubt, of the deeds of valor performed by the Eleventh the day before.

We slept that night on the bank, and the next morning, being joined by the Eighth regiment, started for this place. We had 432 wagons loaded with provisions and ammunition. We expected that the rebels would make an attempt to capture this rich prize, and we were prepared to give them a warm reception. Our company was in the rear—the last company. The day passed, however, and we landed our train safely. Since then we have been quartered here with nothing of importance to note save being routed out and formed into line every night by attacks being made on our pickets. The enemy are encamped about 8 miles below us on Bunker Hill. Deserters are coming in every day who say they have 12,000 men, 16 pieces of artillery, and 800 cavalry. We have about 15,000 men here, and I think before the week is out it will be in our possession.

This place presents a sad spectacle, and gives us a proper idea of the "chivalry" of the rebels. The once splendid bridge over the road of the Baltimore and Ohio railroad, 48 locomotives, over 500 cars, the contents of the large shops, &c., are one grand mass of ruins, burned and broken completely up. Even the gas works of the town were destroyed. It is a sight calculated to steel the heart of any man against the authors of the work. The citizens appear very glad to see us, and are profuse in their professions of attachment to the Union. I took a walk through town this evening, and observed the ladies (good looking ones, too) promenading the streets chatting with the soldiers—citizens sitting at the doors, and all appearing perfectly at home.

The accounts of our fight differ so much from the facts, that without going into particulars I wish to correct a few of the many false reports. The scouting party that crossed the night before, was under command of Lieutenant Col. Coulter, and was composed of McMullin's Rangers, and details from the Eleventh regiment. Thirteen men headed by Corporal Oyster, were from our company. They were fired upon just as we were crossing the river, and that caused us to rush over to their rescue. The enemy, however, beat a hasty retreat.

At the time of the attack the Rangers and three companies of the Wisconsin Regiment were deployed as skirmishers. The rest of the Wisconsin Regiment were sent to prevent the enemy turning our left flank, and did not get a shot. The three first companies of our Regiment, A, B and C, under Col. Jarret, were filed off to protect our right flank against their cavalry, but a sight of them was sufficient, and the chivalrous sons of thunder, finding themselves flanked, were discomfited in the start. The balance of our Regiment was formed in line of battle, and fired upon the enemy, the artillery at the same time opening upon them. After firing several rounds we charged upon them, when they started off and we followed. Not another Regiment fired a gun. They only arrived on the ground after we had possession of it. The enemy lost about 80 killed, and how many wounded we could not learn as they were carried off. Among the killed of the enemy was one who I think was Kramer, formerly employed on the Northern Central Rail Road, and well known in Sunbury.

But it is time for turning in, which means lying down and going to sleep—going to bed is taking off your boots. If fortunate enough I hope to see you about the 25th inst., when the period of our enlistment will expire. How long I will remain at home depends upon circumstances. Remember me to all friends.

Yours,
J. P. S. G.

* * * * *

[The following letter was found on the battle ground at Falling Waters, by [P]rivate J. C. Irwin, of the Sunbury company, and sent home by him to his friends. It is signed "Elizabeth," and was written by a lady to her brother in the rebel army, by whom it was dropped, in the hurried flight of the secessionists. We give merely the first part of the letter, the balance being of no special interest to the reader:]

Sharpsburg, Md.,
April 27, 1861.[95]

Dear Brother:—I once more take up my pen as a safety-valve to the over-charged feelings of my sad heart. It may be the last time. Life if always uncertain, but now, indeed, it may be said truthfully, dangers stand thick to hurry us to the grave. May we be ready for it. *I*, as your sister beloved, may write freely to you; I think no one, save your own wife, has, or could have, more influence over you. O, if only I could persuade my dear brother to look at things as I do. I am no politician, you know. I love my country. I know no North, no South, no East, no West—it is all my country. O, how dear it is, and it seems now more dear than ever; God save her from ruin. *Now, my dear, my own dear brother*, stop and think *upon your knees*, does God require of you to leave the wife of your bosom, the children God has given you? You say you must defend your rights. I believe you think it your duty; but stop and think, my brother. Is it not, in the first place, the disappointed politicians of the South, who are too proud to work, and look down upon those who do, with disdain? They have roused up the feelings of the slaveholders to think their property in danger. Thus, many innocent ones have been dragged into it by sympathy, and they would be the first to *crush* down the poor, honest men, who are now ready to leave their homes and families to carry out their plans, laid in their unholy ambition. I do not justify the North, but the President was bound to keep his oath, and try at least to preserve the Constitution—not to mend it, but keep it. But they were not willing to give the man time for any of us to see what he would or could do. Why have you changed your views since last winter? They were then just *right*—just as a sensible, Christian man should talk

---

95. *Sunbury Gazette*, July 20, 1861.

and think, and as you will think if God should spare your life until the excitement is over, when you will look at things more calmly. I see the folly of both sides, and pray God to open the eyes of both to see their wrong. I can never think it your duty to go to war under the circumstances you are placed. No one can make you go; you have a certificate from the Doctor, and you need not go at all, and it is not your duty to fight for the institution of slavery when those who love it make a war. If you look carefully into the deep, deep, dark pool, you will see it is this that is at the bottom.

* * * * *

Camp—6th Brigade, 11th Reg't., P. V.,
Martinsburg, Va.,
July 12, 1861.[96]

DEAR WILVERT:—"After a storm there is always a calm." So it is with us. Inactivity, as regards fighting, is now our style—but from the great number of troops daily arriving at this point you may soon expect to hear of a grand battle, unless the valiant descendants of RANDOLPH will do as they did to us at Falling Waters, show the "nails in the heels of their boots," and that at double quick time. The soldiers are getting tired of lying idle, and think the life they now lead too monotonous, but I presume Gen. Scott[97] understands his business, and when the proper time arrives, all things fixed to his liking, this most unnatural strife of the Rebels will be crushed at one decisive blow. The force of Gen. Johns[t]on, the rebel leader, is now about nine miles below us, at Bunker Hill, but he is placed in a trap not easily to be released.—His provision is almost exhausted, and what is worse, he is completely surrounded, so that if he does not soon surrender[,] starvation must be the result. It is the general opinion here, that if those high in authority wished it, Johns[t]on's command would be forced to give up in a short time, without a blow being struck. I will not prophesy, but let time bring forth the verification of the above opinion.

On the day after the fight at Falling Waters, as we were marching on Martinsburg, several farmers who had been driven from their

---

96. *Sunbury American*, July 20, 1861.
97. A reference to Lt. Gen. Winfield Scott, general-in-chief of the Union Army.

homes, (leaving their families behind,) because they loved the Union, and would not join the Confederate army, returned with us:—in one instance it was really affecting—an old gentleman left us in front of a very comfortable looking house; but scarcely had he quit our ranks, when an old lady rushed thro' the gate, threw her arms around his neck, and exclaimed, "My God! Husband, have you returned safe?" the other members of the family standing in the yard, crying and alternately laughing and crying—it was a happy sight, but so affecting that our soldiers turned their faces aside, so as not to disturb the (then) happy family; after marching a short distance, the feelings of the soldiers changed, and Jeff Davis, with his infernal crew, got cursed in a manner fit to be applied to such outlaws as himself and hirelings who have made the "sacred soil of Virginia," the scene of bloodshed and carnage.

To give you an estimate of the amount of property destroyed by the Rebels at this place is beyond my calculation. There were about sixty locomotives entirely destroyed, fit for nothing except to be used as old iron, bridges destroyed, railroad track torn up, coal cars, (made of iron,) scattered for miles along the railroad, rendered worthless by the damage done to them by the Rebels—plenty of coal is scattered along the road, and some of it has been sold by the "Secesh" fellows to make a raise. One fellow, calling himself an agent of the Confederate Army caught in the act of selling, is now in *limbo*, and will, I think, be severely dealt with. The bridge destroyed at this place was a most beautiful one, and cost a great deal of money; instead of piers, the bridge was supported by large round pillars made of heavy granite, beautifully dressed; in fact, from the description I have had of it from the citizens here, I should think it had been the most costly railroad bridge, of its kind and size in the country.

Don't you think that where one party does the fighting and obtains the victory, they should have the credit? It seems, from the claimants, that our Regiment is to be robbed of its laurels won at Falling Waters, but when the official report of General Patterson is published, these aspirants for military fame, (without fighting,) will hang their heads in shame. The 15th and 23d Pennsylvania claim that they were in the battle and did the fighting, when, in fact, they were not within three miles of the scene of action. What makes the matter worse, some of the citizens, true to the Union, made two American flags, one for the 1st Wisconsin Regiment, and the other for the Pennsylvania Regiment that was in the battle—that regiment being the 11th and none other. When we entered this town the 15th and 23d, being in advance, claimed the honor and got the proud flag that was honestly intended for us.—Let them have it and much good may it do them, but my opinion is that men who will act in that way, will not make very good soldiers, and won't care much to *show the white feather.*

I think, from what I have learned, you may expect us at home by the 20th inst., that is if we live, and fate is not against us. The boys are all well and in good spirits in anticipation of going, (and the fun to be had at,) HOME.

Yours, fraternally,
H. D. W.

* * * * *

Camp—6th Brigade, 11th Reg't., P. V.,
Martinsburg, Va.,
July 13, 1861.[98]

DEAR WILVERT:—The 15th and 23d Regiments have been caught in their dirty tricks, and are made to blush for the ill manner in which they treated us. The citizens of the now loyal town found out the deception that had been played upon them and have taught these Regiments a lesson not soon to be forgotten. Last evening, at our dress parade, a gentleman came into our camp carrying a flag, behind him were some fifteen young ladies, one of whom presented said flag to our Regiment in the following neat address—

To the 11th Regiment of Pennsylvania Volunteers,

GENTLEMEN:
In behalf of the ladies of this neighborhood, I am delegated to present to you this FLAG as a token of their high appreciation of your

---

98. *Sunbury American,* July 20, 1861.

courage and gallantry in leaving your quiet homes, facing danger and death, to march to the succor of those, whom the rebels, the enemies of our glorious government, had placed under the reign of terrorism. My God bless you, preserve your health and lead you honorably and triumphantly through this contest for liberty and rights; and when the "Star Spangled Banner" shall in triumph wave over all sections of our once happy country, when it may be said, and repeated of Gen. Washington, that he was the Father and founder of our glorious republic, then may you be guided safely to your homes, and posterity will rise up and call you blessed, that you sacrificed comforts and pleasures and endangered your lives to perpetuate our glorious Union and handing it down to them unimpaired.

Again, God bless you, and aid you to preserve the honor of THIS FLAG, which I now present.

Col. Jarrett received the flag and made a very appropriate speech, assuring the young ladies that the whole object of the "Army of the North" was to protect them from all harm, to place the citizens in a situation to follow their usual avocations, and make traitors and rebels respect the proud emblem of Liberty and be subservient to the Constitution and the Laws. He assured them that as long as the 11th was a Regiment[,] that flag would be carried and never allowed to be dishonored. Cheers were given with a will for the young ladies, citizens of Martinsburg, and the "Star Spangled Banner," with a big Tiger that echoed through the woods and made the welkin ring.

Yours, &c.,
H. D. W.

* * * * *

Martinsburg, Va.,
July 14, 1861.[99]

Dear John:—One accustomed to the quiet peaceful Sabbath of a country village could hardly realize that to-day is that sacred day of rest. To us it is no day of rest. We have the usual routine of guard-mounting, dress parade, foraging, and every other of the incidents of

---

99. *Sunbury Gazette,* July 27, 1861.

a day in camp. Besides, to-day we have had a general court martial, at which Capt. Bruner sat, and the men are busily engaged in washing their clothes, and cooking provisions for a march. We were ordered last night to draw five days['] rations and as much more as we could carry, and be ready to march on Monday morning early. Where we are going is a question the men have been discussing all day, but without coming to any conclusion. Some say Winchester, while others say part of the division is to be moved to Harper's Ferry where they say the principal depot for supplies is to be located. However, we will go and see.

News was received here yesterday by a courier, of Gen. McClellan's victory near Beverley. It is a glorious affair. Considerable rivalry exists among the different regiments here, each one being anxious to be first on the field of battle. If the enemy stand long enough I feel assured some valiant fighting will be done by Patterson's division. The 23d regiment are endeavoring to write themselves into notice by stating that they took part in the battle at Falling Waters, when the fact is, in consequence of their taking off their clothes to wade the river, stopping to dress, &c, on the opposite side, they were so far behind, that they never reached the scene of action until the enemy had disappeared, and they did not get sight at a single rebel, unless he was a prisoner. In their letters they speak of Perkins' Battery as "our battery" when it was attached to our Brigade, and was with us the entire day. This is a small business, and while I do not like to impute cowardice to any one, I cannot conceive that a man who would set down and willfully pen falsehoods, such as have been published, would fight.

Quite a number of new regiments have arrived here since my last. We must have over 30,000 men here at present. Among the recent arrivals is the 11th Indiana regiment of Col. Wallace, which has been attached to our Brigade. Col. Starkweather of the 1st Wisconsin, on being informed of this addition, exclaimed, "Well, now we can lick all hell," and that is the general opinion. The 1st Wisconsin, 11th Pennsylvania, 4th Connecticut, 11th Indiana, and Perkins' Battery, is certainly a strong brigade, while our Commander, Col. Abercrombie, is in every sense worthy of the position he occupies. I do not think his superior is in the division.

There are no news of importance in camp that I am aware of. Deserters continue to come in every day, bringing statements of the force and condition of the rebel army, which are not very flattering to the friends of J. Davis, Esq. In the meantime, our scouts are busy, and scarcely a day passes without them sending one or more rebels to "Kingdom Come." On Friday, however, they killed one member of the New York 9th, but not until he had settled two of them. They will not stand more than one fire, no matter how small the force.

[Our correspondent gives the speech of the lady who presented the flag to the 11th Regiment, which we published last week.]

The flag was received by Col. Jarret, who, making a profound courtesy, replied:

"Madam: it is with profound respect, and feeling of the deepest gratitude, that I accept from the ladies of Martinsburg, this token [illegible phrase]—their patriotism and generosity.

I see upon that flag that all the stars are there—not one has been erased, and should a hostile hand attempt to obliterate one from that glorious galaxy, I am not mistaken when I say that every member of the 11th Regiment is ready and willing to risk life and limb in its defense.

Ladies, we come not to the fair State of Virginia to lay waste your fields, or plunder your towns; we come for no such purpose. Neither do we come to wage war against peaceable and law abiding citizens—all such we are ready to protect—but we do come to enforce the laws of our common country, and chastise those who are found against us.

Ladies, in behalf of the 11th Regiment I tender you our sincere thanks for this noble token of your patriotism."

I tell you we did some tall shouting for the ladies, the Union, the flag, Col. Jarret, &c.

The only objects of admiration in Virginia, that I have seen, are the ladies and the turnpikes. The latter are the best I have ever seen, and kept in the most excellent repair, while the former almost equal our own Pennsylvania fair ones.

The Third, Fourteenth and Fifteen Regiments have just started off in the direction of Harper's Ferry, or Dam No. 4, but they are under sealed orders. I suppose we will leave under similar orders tomorrow, and probably will not know our destination until we arrive at it. I don't care where it is, but hope it will be where we will have another dash at them.

The best of health prevails in our regiment. We have not a single sick man in the company. The men are in the best of spirits, and anxious to get out of this place. My respects to old friends.

Yours, &c.,
J. P. S. G.

P. S.—News has just been received of another victory of McClellan. In consequence the 14th and 15th have returned, and it is said the whole program has been changed. Whether it will effect our orders to march I cannot say. At 9 P. M. we are still under orders.

* * * * *

Camp—6th Brigade, 11th Regiment, P. V.,
Charleston, Va.,
July 19, 1861.[100]

DEAR WILVERT:—"There is many a slip 'twixt the cup and the lip." That saying was verified, in our case, yesterday. Numerous were the conjectures of the boys of the pleasure they calculated on when they got home—They were in great glee with the idea of being discharged so soon—their time expiring on next Tuesday, the 21st, at five o'clock, P. M., but as there is "a tide in the affairs of men" that can't be stopped, so it was with them, and their happy visions were, as the printers say, "knocked into PI." Six regiments of the three months Pennsylvania troops, whose time is soon up, were ordered on review by Gen. Patterson, and after having formed in column, ten companies deep, he, the General, addressed them, told them that they had acted well THEIR part, and he was proud of them, that they did the hard work, in fact we have been "wet-nurses" to the army at Washington, while those at Washington had marched but ten miles in the enemy's country, we had left the land of Pennsylvania, settled secession in

---

100. *Sunbury American*, July 27, 1861.

Maryland[,] had crossed the Potomac and trod on the "sacred soil" of Virginia—(in speaking that, he could not see that it was any more SACRED than our own)—had whipped them at Hoke's Run, Falling Waters, chased them through Martinsburg and again offered them fight at Bunker's Hill, a place of great notoriety, where the rebels would not stand, but showed us how well posted they were on a foot race. It had been his intention to have marched us immediately on Winchester, but from information gained from engineers and scouts he knew their exact position, how many troops they had, their number exceeding ours by two thousand, besides four thousand Virginia Militia, whose bravery was noted on paper, that they had masked batteries and had felled trees on the road we would march to reach there, for some six miles, knowing this and being responsible to his government for the lives of his men, besides the wives, children, mothers, sisters, relatives and sweethearts of his men looked to him for their protection, the enemy could not lure him onto destruction, so he abandoned the idea and marched us to this place. He then told the men their time would soon be up, and he was ready to discharge them, but that he could not hold this place if they would leave him before he was reinforced by the three-year men, he having that day received a dispatch from Gen. Scott requesting us to stay for a week or ten days longer until he could send in troops to take our place. Our boys had made up their minds not to stay a minute longer than their time, but when Patterson told them his situation, spoke of the honor of Pennsylvania, and then said that all who would stick to him and help him out of the scrape, should shoulder arms, our boys could not stand it, up went their muskets to a shoulder, and some, who were afraid that they wouldn't be counted in, stuck their caps on tops of the bayonets so that the General could have a fairer sight of them. Our regiment consented unanimously.—You should have seen the old General then, his eyes kindled, it seems with the fire of his younger days, his frame expanded and he exclaimed, "well done my brave bloody 11th," "you Jackson blue jackets." "Oh, you blue jacket rascals, I would not be afraid to meet four regiments of rebels if I had you boys of the 11th Pennsylvania alone." After considerable talk and coaxing[,] the other regiments, with the exception of the 2d

Pennsylvania, concluded to stay, the General assuring them that they should not be taken away from here into a fight, all he wanted was for them to help to keep this point until the reinforcements came, and then he would send them home to their families.

It was a proud day for our regiment, and reflects more credit on them than the victory of a half dozen battles. It takes men of considerable good humor and forbearance to do as our boys did after the treatment they received, half the time not having enough to eat, receiving no money, and even now some of the boys['] clothing won't hide their nakedness.

After marching into camp Col. Jarrett made a short speech to the boys of our regiment, he thanked them for giving so hearty a response to Gen. Patterson's request, called them the "idol of his heart," and "henceforth he would not call them any more hard names." His remarks aroused the boys, and they forgetting the bad treatment received, gave him three hearty cheers with a big tiger. All our boys are very well, and although they are determined to fight for and protect the "Star Spangled Banner," they have a great desire to see the "loved ones at home."

Yours, Fraternally,
H. D. W.

* * * * *

Harper's Ferry, Va.,
July 22, 1861.[101]

Dear John:—Contrary to all our expectations the entire column of Gen. Patterson is encamped in and around this place, where we arrived yesterday afternoon. On Monday morning last our column left Martinsburg en route for Winchester by way of Bunker Hill. It had been reported among the men that we might expect a brisk engagement there[,] as the enemy were there in large numbers and strongly entrenched. About 10 o'clock, A. M., the head of our column reached the place, and the second cavalry charged upon and drove the enemy before them. Almost the entire force had abandoned the position before we reached there, leaving but about 2000 men to hold the place.

---

101. *Sunbury Gazette*, August 3, 1861.

These fled precipitately on our approach, leaving a beef half skinned, a lot of corn, &c., and even their coffee warm on the fire. These soon became victims to the ravenous appetite of the men. The cavalry in their charge killed one and captured three persons. We encamped there that night where we remained until Wednesday. Bunker Hill, so called, is a high eminence, commanding the country for a great distance around, and is an excellent location to make a stand. Had the rebels courage enough to fight, no better position could have been chosen. I feel satisfied had we been attacked we would have defeated five times our number.

On Wednesday our scouts came in and reported that the road to Winchester was impassible in consequence of trees being felled, fences built and ditches dug across the road for about six miles. They also reported the reinforcement of Gen. Johns[t]on during the night, and a description of the fortifications. These are very heavy and command three sides of the town. Those on the side we expected to march in were heavy sand bag batteries formed in the shape of a V, the open end toward us, and in it were planted some twenty large navy guns, stolen from the Gosport Navy Yard. Had we advanced on that route, subjected to this heavy cross fire, we would have been cut to pieces. Gen. Patterson very prudently took up the line of march in a roundabout way. In the evening we arrived at Charlestown, where we lay encamped until yesterday.

This is the town rendered famous by the trial, confinement, and execution of John Brown,[102] and is one of the most violent secession holes in the State. It is, however, a very pretty little place, and contains some fine buildings. The residence of Senator Mason is a noble edifice.[103] A six-pound cannon, mounted, a lot of muskets, rifles, slugs, &c, were found secreted in the place.

On Thursday a number of the Pennsylvania Regiments, whose term of enlistment was about expiring, were formed in line and addressed by Gen. Patterson, who, after complimenting them and stating the reason that he had not marched on Winchester, he said he had a favor to ask, to wit: That he had received orders from Gen. Scott to hold that place, but if all the regiments whose term would expire in a

---

102. The trial of abolitionist John Brown was held at Charlestown from October 27–31, and his execution took place on December 2, 1859.

103. Gobin may be mistaken here, as the residence of Virginia Senator James M. Mason, known as "Selma," was located in Winchester rather than Charlestown.

few days left him he would be unable to do it. Therefore he asked, for the honor of Pennsylvania, and for his sake, that they would remain one week after their time, in order to allow other troops to come in. I am happy to say that the Eleventh Regiment, or a majority of them, responded to the call like men and consented to stay. Of our company nearly all agreed to remain a week longer. Only some eight or ten insist upon going home, and their places can easily be filled by men from other Regiments who desire to stay. Of all the three-month regiments here the 1st, 11th, 17th and 24th Pennsylvania, and 11th Indiana were the only ones patriotic enough to remain. This is gratifying to us, and is, I think, the crowing act of the Eleventh. It shows the material the Regiment is composed of. Our Colonel was very much pleased and declared we were the idols of his heart. Therefore we will in all probability not leave for home before to-day a week, (Monday next) when we will return with the pleasing consciousness of having done all that was asked of us in defense of our country and its government.

The cause of our march upon this place I am unable to state, probably it is in view of the operations of Gen. McDowell. The Secessionists must have been very strongly posted here. On a hill near where we are encamped were found four 34-pound cannon they had spiken[ed] and left, being unable to take them along. Capt. Doubleday now occupies their place and will be somewhat harder to frighten than the former possessors were.

Harper's Ferry is the most rugged, romantic place I ever beheld. The scenery is beyond description. As a stronghold, it is my opinion, in the hands of determined men it would be impregnable. The ruins of the rifle manufactory, the arsenal, and other shops, are living pictures of secession chivalry. The inhabitants are all Union and hurl the most bitter anathemas at the rebels. They evince the most bitter hatred, and express the hope that we will not leave one alive. I had intended exploring the country to-day, but we have just been ordered to prepare to go out on picket which will be very pleasant, considering that it commenced to rain. In all probability this will be the last letter I will write, hoping to see you soon.

Yours, &c.
J. P. S. G.

* * * * *

Letters from the Taggart Guards
Company B, 34th Pennsylvania Volunteer Infantry
(5th Reserves)

*T*he *final county militia company to report on the first phase of the war, the Taggart Guards, came from the borough of Northumberland. Named in honor of their elected leader, Capt. James Taggart, the company initially organized on April 28, but by the time they tendered their services to the governor, the state's three-month quotas under the initial call to arms had been filled and their offer was declined. Governor Curtin, however, determined not to waste the extra volunteers but instead retain them for state service as the Pennsylvania Reserve Volunteer Corps (Pennsylvania Reserves), a division of three-year regiments. (Although Curtin intended to use the Reserves solely for the defense of the Commonwealth, the War Department would soon formulate other plans.)[104] The Taggart Guards thus left for Harrisburg on May 27 and became Company B of the 34th Pennsylvania Volunteers (5th Pennsylvania Reserves).[105] On June 21 the 5th Reserves along with the 13th Reserves (42nd Regiment) and a battery of artillery moved to Cumberland, Maryland. On July 13 they took a position at Bridge No. 21 on the Baltimore & Ohio Railroad, and then on July 22 marched to Piedmont, Virginia, where they went into camp to await further military developments.[106]*

The actions of the Taggart Guards were reported to the Gazette *by a correspondent who only signed his letters as "Old Soldier." A later edition of the newspaper, however, referred to the author by the initials "J.D.S.," which pointed to Sergeant James D. Slater, Company B, as the letter-writer (the content of subsequent letters verified his identity as well).[107] At the time of his enlistment, Slater was a thirty-eight-year-old single boatman living*

---

104. The Pennsylvania Reserves included fifteen regiments (thirteen infantry, one artillery, and one cavalry) organized into three brigades. After the War Department only accepted the first fourteen of the twenty-five three-month regiments assembled for service, Governor Curtin organized the remaining regiments into the Reserves. After the Union defeat at Bull Run, the division was quickly rolled into the reorganized Army of the Potomac when more men were needed. For more information see Uzal W. Ent, *The Pennsylvania Reserves in the Civil War: A Comprehensive History* (Jefferson, NC: McFarland & Co., 2014).

105. Another local company from Milton, the Pollock Guards—named after former governor and Milton resident James Pollock—also mustered into service with the 5th Pennsylvania Reserves as Company H. They are only mentioned here in passing, since none of their members contributed any correspondence to the Sunbury newspapers.

106. Bell, *History of Northumberland County*, 406.

107. Bates, *Pennsylvania Volunteers*, 1:675. See also Old Soldier's letter of January 18, 1863.

in a Northumberland hotel. His pen name "Old Soldier" was likely derived from the fact that Slater had previous military experience, having served as a sergeant in Company C, 2nd Pennsylvania Infantry, during the Mexican War (enlisting at Danville on December 26, 1846, for the duration of the war; he received a medical discharge at Vera Cruz on April 8, 1847).[108] His previous service likely allowed Slater to describe the activities of the Taggart Guards with relative ease and familiarity.

Camp Curtin,
June 5, 1861.[109]

MR. EDITOR.—Camp Curtin is nothing but a receiving ship for the troops, and a place for the wire-pullers. They form a regiment one day, and break the slate the next; but as a company the Northumberland boys are doing well. We were examined on Friday and sworn in on Saturday. Our men all passed but two, and when they were sworn in there were nine more men than we could take. Some of them went home with an honorable discharge from the Captain. Some joined other companies. Our boys stuck to the text like men, and are all contented and happy.

There are about three thousand men in camp here—good and true men who are all ready to learn the art of war, but their instructors are like the men, being able to do almost anything better than handle the sword. The wise ones of the camp say that we will be formed into a regiment this week, and we will be the first of the reserve under Col. Gregg.[110] They say that the Colonel has friends at Court, and we will be all right.

---

108. James D. Slater, Northumberland Borough, Northumberland County, Pennsylvania, 1860; *Eighth Census of the United States, 1860* (National Archives Microfilm Publication M653, roll 1149), "United States Census, 1860," *FamilySearch* (https://www.familysearch.org/ark:/61903/1:1:MX5J-29Z : Sat Mar 09 13:55:42 UTC 2024), Entry for James D. Slater, 1860 (accessed June 7, 2024); James D. Slater, Co. C, 2nd Pennsylvania Infantry; *Compiled Service Records of Volunteer Soldiers Who Served During the Mexican War in Organizations from the State of Pennsylvania* (National Archives Microfilm Publication M1028, roll 12); "United States Mexican War Index and Service Records, 1846-1848", , *FamilySearch* (https://www.family-search.org/ark:/61903/1:1:QLXQ-R414 : Fri Mar 08 23:47:15 UTC 2024), Entry for James D Slater, from 1846 to 1848 (accessed June 7, 2024).

109. *Sunbury Gazette*, June 8, 1861.

110. A reference to the Pennsylvania Reserve Corps.

Our feed is good and plenty, and our friends from home have not forgotten us. Last night we had tobacco distributed. This morning we breakfasted on some fine eels sent to us by some of the boys at home. May they prosper. The men in camp have nothing but good feeling towards each other, and everything goes on in kindness and good nature.

Our boys send their thanks for the visit of our old friend from home—the *Gazette*—and we hope its visits will continue weekly. As soon as we are formed into a regiment, we will move from here. All seem to prefer active service, and as the President will issue a proclamation for more troops, they will be called into action and have a hand in the fight. We have all the daily papers in camp, with sensation articles in them, to catch the loose pennies of the public, but the news of one day is contradicted the next.

I will conclude by saying that not one of our boys has been in the guard-house since we have been here. They seem determined to learn the drill, and do their duty to themselves and country.

OLD SOLDIER.

* * * *

Camp Curtin, Pa.,
June 12, 1861.[111]

MR. EDITOR.—We are getting along in the same good old way. There has been a good time at our quarters since my last letter. Our folks from home were down here on Friday and Saturday last, and some of them [stayed] until Monday. It seems now to us that the ladies of our good old town bake better cakes, make better pickles, better butter, and, in fact, are better looking, than we ever knew them before. Our old friends from Point [township] were here to see us and take us by the hand. They did not come with empty hands, and know how to prepare the relishables as well as the ladies of Northumberland, and then their butter can't be beat. In fact they are second to none, for I have a share of all the good things that come to camp, and I pretend to be a judge of good eating.

---

111. *Sunbury Gazette*, June 17, 1861.

On Friday evening four companies from Philadelphia came into camp here, and on Saturday the 2nd Michigan regiment came off the cars and encamped with us for the night. On Sunday morning they started for the Federal Capital. They were armed, equipped, and ready for fight. Having received a dispatch while *en route* from Pittsburg to this place, stating that they had better not come through Baltimore, the officers and men declared that Michigan would be found on a direct line south—her duty to the Union of States first, last, and forever. On starting from Camp Curtin on Sunday morning ten rounds of cartridges were distributed to the men, and their muskets loaded. They are a fine-looking body of men, and look and act the soldier. Eight of the companies have Harper's Ferry muskets, and the right and left companies of the regiment have Minie muskets. There are 101 men in each company, and three ladies.

On Saturday Camp Curtin looked more like a tented field than at any other time since our arrival here. The Michigan officers have a great advantage over the officers of the Pennsylvania Reserve Corps. They have their commissions and ours have not. It seems hard for a soldier to be sentenced by a Court Martial composed of officers without commissions, and sentenced to five days bread and water, and then drummed out of camp, up and down the lines where there are four thousand men on parade. The sentence was executed on a soldier on Monday evening at Camp Curtin for striking an officer who was no officer while he had no commission.

Our boys were on guard at the Arsenal on Sunday, twenty-nine in number, officers and men. They felt much pleased with the citizens of Harrisburg for a warm breakfast sent to them on Monday morning. The men of our company seem to understand how to be well used— the reason is, they behave properly.

Capt. Taggart was absent for five days, but returned from Philadelphia on Monday evening well and in good spirits, and when the officers are in good humor the men are ditto.

On Tuesday the Express wagon came into camp with two boxes of tobacco, one of smoking and one of chewing, which being distributed among our men amounted to one paper of smoking, and six plugs of chewing to each man. We are indebted for this supply of the weed to our old friend with a new title, Major David Taggart, and to Freshmuth & Brother, and Morris Marler, of Philadelphia. Our Captain finds and makes friends wherever he goes, and he deserves them.

I said something last week about forming a regiment, but it appears that the slate is not yet full. Col. Gregg is here and looks as if he could command a regiment with credit to the country. He looks like a man and that is saying a good deal these times, and when the slate gets full we will let you know. There is another company here, from Philadelphia, the name of whose Captain is Taggart, so our friends writing to the boys will direct in care of Capt. James Taggart, to avoid mistake.

The news from Fortress Monroe is in camp, and is freely commented upon. But all seem to regard the matter in the same light, and think that the next fit of absence of mind Pierce gets he will have to walk, and make room for some good man.

It seems that the boys have forgotten the good advice given them by their pastor. A few can be seen reading their Bibles, but the most of them have turned their attention to "history."

Our feed continues to be good. As it may be a satisfaction to some of the readers of the Gazette, I will give a full ration for seventy-seven men per day: Fresh Beef, 67 lbs.; Salt Pork, 18 lbs.; Bread, 36 lbs.; Potatoes, 3 pecks; Rice, 6 lbs.; Sugar, 8½ lbs.; Coffee, 4¼ lbs.; Vinegar, 1 qt.; Candles, ½ lb.; Soap, 2 lbs.; Salt, 3 lbs. So it can be seen that we have enough and to spare.

A young man of Capt. Campbell's command, died in the hospital last night, of brain fever. Our men in the hospital are getting along finely. I hear some talk in our quarters among the married men about the distribution of the fund raised for the benefit of their families. If you can get them a true statement of the facts, please let them know.

I hope I will be able to give a better account of Camp Curtin in my next letter. There are some men in camp offering to bet that we will move on to Chambersburg inside of twelve days, but they know there is no money among the men to take the bets. If we move in twelve days there will have to be more activity in the war department than there has been. Some of the members of the Legislature thought they would show their devotion to the Union by offering their services for the war, and the Governor showed his devotion to the Union by accepting them, but if they play the same give away game they did in the Legislature, God help the Stars and Stripes.

OLD SOLDIER.

* * * * *

Camp Curtin, Pa.,
June 20, 1861.[112]

Mr. Editor:—There is a change in camp. Col. Seiler has left, and his place is filled by Col. Charles J. Biddle, who has cleaned up things about here in earnest, so if our Northumberland friends come to see us they will find affairs changed for the better. The Colonel understands how things ought to be done, having seen service on the line between Vera Cruz and the City of Mexico, so that the volunteers can make up their minds to do their duty.[113] Our boys seem determined to do their duty wherever they are placed. One of the smart ones in camp attempted to pass one of them yesterday, but found out that there was no playing soldier, for he received a bayonet in his leg. The Captain of the Guard complimented him on doing his duty.

There are all kinds of stories in camp about clothing, pay, and the movement of regiments to Camp Freedom. I suppose we will see our uniforms when they come, receive our pay when the authorities are ready to pay us, march when and where the State or United States may direct, and eat our grub and be thankful that we have plenty to feed on. I would like to see the men look more like soldiers, but I suppose the man at the helm must have time to get his boat in the proper current. If the report is true that the soldiers in Camp Curtin are to celebrate the 4th of July in their new uniforms, they will not come too soon, for some of the men need them very much.

For the benefit of the readers of the *Gazette* who have not visited camp, I will give an account of a day's proceedings here, beginning

---

112. *Sunbury Gazette*, June 29, 1861.
113. Charles J. Biddle (1819–1873) served as an infantry captain during the Mexican War, eventually promoted to the rank of major. At the outbreak of the war, he was appointed a lieutenant colonel in the Pennsylvania Reserve Corps, and became colonel of the 42nd Pennsylvania. In October 1861 he was elected to the Thirty-Seventh U.S. Congress and resigned from the Army in February 1862.

at the firing of the gun at four o'clock in the morning. The reveille is then beat, and the boys turn out and fall in for roll call and guard detail. After roll then drill until breakfast—then the men that are detailed for guard duty are marched to the parade ground, reviewed, marching in front of the guard house, divided into three reliefs, and the guard of the previous day relieved. Then there are men detailed for cleaning quarters, some for police duty, and a sergeant and seven men from each company to go for rations. At nine o'clock the drums beat for drill. After drill some of the men exercise with muskets, some write, some read, and others sleep till dinner time. There are two passes allowed to a company per day, and we have it so arranged that they pass out six or eight men a day. After dinner there is some one of the boys sent down to Harrisburg for the mail. At about two o'clock we receive our mail, and those who get letters have work until dress parade at 5 o'clock. Then comes supper, and our day's work is done. Having now leisure, the fun begins.

The amusements of the evening commence with a grand exhibition of the "Wild Man of the Woods," the "Trained Elephant," and the "Man Monkey," followed by grand music, vocal and instrumental. A violin will start with "Old Zip Coon," while some vocalist will strike up with "William Reiley," or the Star Spangled Banner, variated with "It was the biggest Ram that was ever fed on Hay." It must be seen and heard to be appreciated. There is a crowd across from our quarters. The violin is playing, and you hear "Join hands and circle around." They are having a good time there. Opposite the Captain's quarters is a crowd, and our boys are trying their skill. We have a String Band composed of a violin, banjo, tambourine, bones and triangle. They make music that men listen to with order and quiet by the hour, in crowds of hundreds.

But tattoo puts an end to the gayeties, and the men turn in and take the soft side of the board. Quiet reigns around, and you hear nothing but the hail of the Guard, "Who comes there!" The answer may be "Friend, with the countersign," or "Friend with a bottle." If it is the former, the guard says, "Advance, friend, and give the countersign!" and if the latter, he is very apt to say, "Advance, friend, with the bottle and pull the cork!"

Girls at home, get out your handkerchiefs, for there is something happened here that should make you weep! Our drummer boy has went and got married. You may try to console yourselves with the idea that he has only married his beloved drum or banjo, and not a woman. But girls, delude not yourselves with such a hope! In the "Patriot and Union" you will find a notice in this wise: MARRIED: On a certain day in June, by the Rev So and So, Mr. Geo. Burkinbine, of Northumberland, to Miss Mary E. McWilliams, of Harrisburg.

So you see that the bold soldier boys will marry when they get a good chance.

OLD SOLDIER.

* * * * *

Bedford, Pa.,
June 25, 1861.[114]

Mr. Editor.—It being reported at Camp Curtin that Col. Wallace was being surrounded at Cumberland, Md, by the rebels, aid was sent to him from that Camp, via the Pennsylvania railroad, and then down through Bedford, of which aiding party we formed a part, which accounts for our being here. Our boys are all in camp except two, one being left at Huntingdon, and the other at Hopewell where we encamped the first night of our march.

We read in history of great warriors whose paths were strewed with flowers—ours was good feed first and the flowers afterwards. The good people of Huntingdon treated us with good warm provisions, and they will have a warm place in the hearts of our boys. We traveled to Hopewell on the cars, and then the tug commenced. We started off with seventy-five boys who did not boast of what they could do, for they had not yet tried. We marched on with our Captain at our head, giving us words of encouragement, with the understanding that we were to halt at Bloody Run, the place were so many gallant men of the Indian wars were slain. Our teamster, who was from the neighborhood, pointed out the spot to our men. We halted to the Bloody Run Spring, drank, and then marched on to the town, where

---

114. *Sunbury Gazette*, June 29, 1861.

we eat our dinner prepared by the patriotic citizens. The drum then beat to fall in, and we took up our line of march for Bedford Springs. The Bedford folks had prepared for us, and intended to keep us over night, but we marched three miles and a half further on. There was not one of our boys that did not come into camp with the company, and that in truth, is something that not many companies can say. The Bedford folks sent us our supper, and then we took our blankets and hunted a soft spot on the ground for the night, having no tents to cover us.

The boys think the State marched them here to the Bedford Springs for the benefit of their health, but I think it was for the health of Virginia, and especially for Gov. Wise. If Bedford Springs water won't cure the rebels *blue pills* will effect a cure. The boys are all ready to march into the Old Dominion, and had not Col. Wallace been reinforced you would have heard more from us.

We are getting our uniforms and tents this morning; also a lot of fresh beef, and altogether are doing first rate.

OLD SOLDIER.

* * * * *

[We received our last letter from "Old Soldier" on Friday of last week, and give the following portion of it. When the Northumberland soldiers once get into the enemy's country we may expect more exciting incidents from them.]

Camp Mason and Dixon,
July 1, 1861.[115]

Dear Friends—I appear once again from a strange part of our State, about half a mile from the Maryland line, and seven miles from Cumberland. We are encamped in a small valley, and as I write[,] the men are turning out for drill. The country around us is very poor, and we don't fare as well as we did at Camp Curtin, nor as well as on our march here. We have not received our uniforms yet, but have been provided each with one pair of shoes, one pair linen pants, two

---

115. *Sunbury Gazette*, July 13, 1861.

pairs of woolen socks, muskets, and canteens. The boys handle their muskets very well.

We had a visit to our camp yesterday from Col. Wallace, and some ten or fifteen of his men on horseback. The Colonel is a good-looking man, and his men are fine looking fellows. I suppose you have heard of their fight on Friday last, when the Minie rifles and saber bayonets of the Wallace Zouaves dealt death to the traitors. There were fifty rebels and nineteen Union men, and the latter slew them hip and thigh. There were thirty rebels killed and wounded, and of Wallace's men there were one killed and one wounded. Col. Wallace told our officers that he had sent some of his men out on a scout, and a dispatch came which called him home to Cumberland, stating that his men had taken forty head of cattle and two prisoners. We told Wallace to stir them up as much as possible, so that we shall have to come to his assistance, for we are getting anxious to try what we can do. We do not wish to be like the French king, who marched on the hill, and then marched down again. The desire of this camp is to do or die.

I received the *Gazette* yesterday, and it was the center of attraction for some time. Those at home who have time should write often to the boys, and not wait for a letter from them, for their facilities for writing are few. We would like to take our friends by the hand again, not forgetting our good friends in Point township, but we cannot do so at present. The will must be taken for the deed. We are still in good health, except two men, who are at Bedford, and are as well taken care of as can be under the circumstances. Our Captain is going to Cumberland to-day to see how he may like the place, and perhaps my next letter will be from there.

* * * * *

Camp Simmons,
Near Piedmont, Va.,
July 15, 1861.[116]

Dear Gazette:—We left Camp Mason and Dixon on Monday last, and arrived at Cumberland the afternoon of the same day, after a very fatiguing march over high mountains and through deep ravines. The

---

116. *Sunbury Gazette*, July 27, 1861.

road was exceedingly rough and the day hot and sultry. We came here by order of Gen. Scott to take the place of the Indiana Zouaves who were ordered to join Gen. Patterson at Martinsburg.

Our encampment was on a high eminence immediately back of town and in every way well fitted for the purpose. The town has a few months ago near nine thousand inhabitants, but it now presents the appearance of an almost deserted village, business of all kinds is paralyzed, and the citizens generally look upon affairs with the greatest apathy and indifference, not knowing what position to assume. Indeed it reminds one of the cities of Palmyra and Thebes, its gorgeous temples and magnificent public and private buildings being viewed as objects of idle curiosity, and specimens of her ancient splendor and glory.

We remained at Cumberland until yesterday, when we were ordered to this place, where we are now encamped, waiting for means of transportation to carry our baggage, provision, &c. We are on the line of the Baltimore and Ohio Railroad, one of the most important links of communication and magnificent structures on this continent, but like all other institutions that might possibly benefit the Government, it has fallen a prey to the accursed policy of those who dared to plot the destruction of this "land of the free and home of the brave."

At this place the bridge crossing the Potomac lies in complete ruins, and the track torn up for miles. Nearly all their property, machine shops, engines, &c., have been destroyed. The original cost of this road was twenty-eight millions of dollars. Maryland and Virginia each contributing fourteen millions. It will certainly cost from five to ten millions to put it in the condition it was before the present excitement sprung up. But this is not all: everything along the line is ruined; the crops neglected and stock poorly cared for, and those who have dared to show their loyalty have been driven from their homes, and their property confiscated. Though many have, for fear of this result, joined them, or allowed themselves to be impressed, they exchange the former for the *endearing consolation* of paying tax which will not fail to render them bankrupt.

Why men of so much intelligence as those at the head of this rebellion, allow themselves to be gulled by the false dogma of secession,

I cannot possibly conceive—certain it is they know of our strength, numerically, pecuniarily, as proven by statistics that do not lie. They contend their men are better commanded, disciplined and equipped, but is this correct? If so, where springs the unbounded charity that compensates their officers and men, and furnishes them with clothing? Are their men all nabobs? A striking evidence of their liberality we find in the avidity with which the confederate loan was sought. Of their bravery, think of the Potter and Pryer exhibition.[117] But true it is they are well armed. That Great High Priest in the Sanhedrim of Secession, Jno. B. Floyd, well cared for them on this point.[118]

We will leave here to-morrow morning for Romney to join Gen. McClellan's division, and engage in the battle against Gen. H. A. Wise. It is said that he has over twenty thousand men within 48 hours' march of this place, though at different points. One of our scouting parties captured last night a body of Secession Cavalry, eight horses and a lot of baggage, &c., but, unfortunately, through the negligence of our guard it was retaken, with the loss of their guide. His name was Kelly, and formerly a Secesh. When found, his head was completely cut open. To-day two companies left here for Piedmont for the purpose of driving out the Secesh there. It is thought they would have a scrimmage[,] as there were yesterday nigh four hundred Secesh cavalry there. They are said to be a fine body of men, well-armed and equipped. Two of our companies are awaiting orders to march every minute. Scouting parties of rebels can be seen a mile or so from here.

Of the twenty companies composing the two Regiments, but eleven are here, the others being out on picket and scouting duty. The Milton company, Captain McCleery, is under orders to march to New Creek to drive back some seventy Rebels that are said to be there. The men are all anxious to leave here, and think if thrown into

---

117. This passage may be a reference to an aborted duel in 1860 between Congressmen John Fox Potter of Wisconsin and Roger Atkinson Pryor of Virginia. Pryor, the aggrieved party, called off the affair after Potter elected to fight with bowie knives, a choice which Pryor deemed "uncivilized." The Northern press hailed the incident as a coup over Southern chivalry. For more details, see William B. Hesseltine, "The Pryor-Potter Duel," *The Wisconsin Magazine of History* 27:4 (June 1944): 400–409.

118. The last sentence refers to a widely held suspicion that John B. Floyd (1806–1863), Secretary of War under James Buchanan, had deliberately sent large stores of government arms and supplies to federal arsenals throughout the South in anticipation of open rebellion. Resigning from the War Department on December 29, 1860, he professed to oppose secession but joined the Confederate Army after Virginia withdrew from the Union.

an engagement, would make a good report of themselves. They have great confidence in the abilities of Cols. Biddle and Simmons. The latter is a graduate of West Point, and is no doubt eminently well qualified to conduct operations with credit, not only to himself, but to those under him. He served with distinction in the Mexican war. The two Northumberland County companies are in his regiment, and I am glad to say are getting along well. Captains Taggart and McCleery enjoy both the esteem and confidence of their men. Capt. Taggart's company has the most important position in the regiment, being on the left flank. The flanking companies always carry rifles, and are used for skirmishing.

The men generally are in the enjoyment of very good health. Two deaths have occurred in the above companies, resulting, I believe from brain fever. Their bodies have been sent home. We are getting along finely now. All we want is a little money and news occasionally, and a pass at the secessionists to sharpen our appetites.

Yours Respectfully,
S. M. BUOY.

* * * * *

Letters from Former Northumberland County Residents

As the Sunbury newspapers chronicled the activities of these local companies, they also occasionally published letters from former residents of Northumberland County who wrote home to share their wartime experiences with friends and former neighbors. During the early months of the war, the Sunbury Gazette shared several letters written by former residents of the city who were then living in Indiana and Ohio, as well as an unidentified individual who was in Baltimore at the time (it is not evident that he was attached to a specific regiment, or even in the service, although he offered various observations about the activities of the 1st Pennsylvania Infantry). The transplanted Hoosier, William P. Welker, may not have actually made it into the ranks of the Indiana volunteers as well, but his Buckeye counterpart,

Richard W. Druckemiller, did in fact enlist on April 20, 1861, at Upper Sandusky, Ohio—under the alias Richard W. De Miller—and then mustered into Company I, 15th Ohio Infantry, one of that state's three-month regiments, at Camp Jackson near Columbus on April 27. The regiment remained in camp until its service ended on August 28. Druckemiller then apparently returned to his hometown and joined the Sunbury Guards when it reorganized as part of the 47th Pennsylvania.[119]

Fort Wayne City, In.,
May 4, 1861.[120]

Friend John:—I received a copy of your paper yesterday, and the first thing that met my eye was the list of names of the Sunbury boys who left for "Camp Curtin." I felt rejoiced, indeed, when I heard that Sunbury was one of the first towns that sent on volunteers; and the only regret I have to make is that I was not there myself to go with the boys. When I heard that Sunbury had made up one of the first companies[,] I concluded to start on for Harrisburg and join them; but with the next mail came the news that there were more men at Camp Curtin than accommodations could be obtained for. I then abandoned that idea and determined to go with the "Hoosier Guards," a company from this city. The Hoosier boys are not behind hand when the time comes for them to fight for their country and their flag. As soon as the news reached this city that Fort Sumter had surrendered, the citizens called a meeting, and a company was raised and started on for headquarters at Camp Morton, Indianapolis. From there they expect to be sent on to Cairo, an important point on the Mississippi [R]iver. Since the above company has left three more have been started, two of which have been accepted and expect to march by Monday or Tuesday. The Hoosier Guards number about one hundred rank and file. If they are accepted and I am not among the number that are rejected, I will be happy to write to you from Camp Morton next week. The reason I speak of some being rejected is this:

---

119. Richard W. Druckemiller, 15th Ohio Infantry; Compiled Military Service Records; Records of the Adjutant General's Office, Record Group 94; National Archives Building, Washington, DC.
120. *Sunbury Gazette*, May 11, 1861.

In the other company that left they had too many men for one company, and I expect it will be the same way with the companies that leave next week. I received a letter from R. W. Druckemiller when I first arrived in this State. He has gone with a company from Upper Sandusky, Ohio, and is now laying at Cleveland, Ohio. I see by the *Gazette* that his brother is one of the noble crowd that left Sunbury. My wish for the Sunbury boys is, that if the conflict comes and they are marched out to the field of action, that they may fight to the last and, if need be, die for their country. And the Ladies of Sunbury—"God bless them"—I see have not been behind hand in their duty. May they live many years yet and see the country again united together *never to be again divided by Southern traitors.*

I must close this letter in time to get it in the morning's mail. I have written it on a place just large enough to hold a sheet of paper and an ink stand. If I get to Camp Morton I will write to you again.

Truly Your Friend,
WM. P. WELKER.

* * * * *

Baltimore, Md.,
May 27, 1861.[121]

Friend Youngman.—Being now in Baltimore, I thought that a letter from a city which has become so notorious might be of interest to you.

In regard to the Union feeling here I would state briefly that from what I have observed in Baltimore and Harford counties, there is at least twenty to one in favor of the Union.

A friend of mine who arrived in Baltimore on Saturday night, who has been working in Gatesville, N. C., and had just made his escape when he arrived here, told me he had a very hard time of it getting through. He came *via* Norfolk, Richmond, and Harper's Ferry. He said he could not get a ticket at Richmond unless he had an order from the Governor, and so he wrote a recommendation from the mayor of an assumed place, and signed the mayor's name to it

---

121. *Sunbury Gazette*, June 1, 1861.

himself, and then took it to the Governor, and got an order from him to the ticket agent to sell him a ticket on the railroad. He states that there are large forces at Richmond and Norfolk, that they have the niggers at work throwing up fortifications, and have a large number of very heavy guns mounted. At Harper's Ferry the train was stopped and searched.

The 1st Regiment of Pennsylvania Volunteers, who were stationed along the line of the Northern Central railroad, made a great many friends by their gentlemanly conduct while in the discharge of their duties. They were relieved by the arrival of the 12th Regiment of Pennsylvania Volunteers who were ordered to take charge of it on Saturday. The people generally were very sorry to see the 1st leave. They came as far as Woodbury and Melvale, two and three miles from Baltimore, and encamped for the night there. On Sunday morning they were brought into Baltimore by two extra trains, and marched up Howard Street, and around to the Baltimore and Ohio railroad Depot, when they were taken on to Washington. They were all in good spirits and very jubilant over the prospect of seeing immediate service.

Two very large cannon from Pittsburg, were taken to Fort McHenry yesterday. They were of about 10-inch bore, about 10 feet long, and 2½ feet in diameter at the butt. They are intended for throwing shell. They took 10 eight-wheel car loads of shell to the fort on Saturday.

I was along with a detachment of troops from Company D, 1st Regiment, that marched from the Relay House to Cockeysville to take John Merryman[122] prisoner. Mr. Merryman was one of the leaders of the bridge burning party that burned the bridges on the Northern Central Railroad. The detachment marched up to Mr.

---

122. John Merryman (1824–1881), the post-war state treasurer of Maryland (1870–1872), became the subject of a famous *habeas corpus* case, *Ex parte Merryman* [17 F. Cas. 144 (C.C.D. Md. 1861) No. 9487], at the start of the Civil War. Aiding in the destruction of several bridges north of Baltimore to prevent Pennsylvania troops from marching through Baltimore and inciting riots, Merryman on May 25, 1861, was arrested by U.S. troops, indicted for treason, and confined in Fort McHenry. Through his lawyers, Merryman petitioned Supreme Court Chief Justice Roger B. Taney for a writ of habeas corpus. The writ was disobeyed by Maj. Gen. George Cadwallader, the military commander in Maryland, under orders from President Lincoln even though Taney cited Cadwallader for contempt. Taney then ordered that Merryman was "improperly held" and had him released. Merryman was never tried for treason, and Taney vindicated the writ of habeas corpus. John Merryman Biography, *Archives of Maryland* (Biographical Series), https://msa.maryland.gov/megafile/msa/speccol/sc3500/sc3520/001500/001543/html/1543bio.html (accessed October 6, 2024).

Merryman's residence about two miles above Cockeysville, and surrounded the house. The Lieutenant who commanded the detachment then went to the door and knocked. An old darkey made his appearance and was told that we wanted to see Mr. M. The old fellow said he was not at home. The Lieutenant told him that that story would not take, and drawing a revolver, told him to show him to Mr. Merryman, and so the old darkey had nothing to do but lead the way. The officer went upstairs and knocked at the door, and Mr. M. made his appearance. He was very much surprised to see an officer there. The Lieutenant told him he was his prisoner, and calling six men, he marched Mr. M. down to Cockeysville, with a body guard, two soldiers in front, one on each side, and two behind, with bayonets fixed. They brought him down on the Express train, and took him to Fort McHenry.

Should there be other news worthy of note during my stay here I will inform you of it.

Yours, &c.,
H. Y. F.

* * * * *

[The following letter written by a Sunbury boy in one of the Ohio regiments, was handed to us for publication:]

Phillippi, Va.,
June 10, 1861.[123]

Dear Friends.—I sit down to write you a few lines to let you know that I am well and in the land of secession. I suppose you heard that this place was attacked and taken without the loss of a man on our side. The Indiana 9th Regiment, the Ohio 14th, and the Regiment from Wheeling, were engaged in it. Our regiment did not get here until the next day. Col. Kelly, of the Wheeling Regiment, was wounded by a wagoner as he rode up to demand the surrender of the baggage. There were about fifteen of the secessionists killed, and one of their Colonels shot through the leg as he was getting his horse out

---

123. *Sunbury Gazette*, June 22, 1861.

of the stable to run. The cannon ball passed through the outside of the stable, and then through two stalls, before it hit him; and then through the other side of the stable, and lodged in a log.

There were about 2000 secessionists here, and were attacked about 5 o'clock in the morning, before the most of them were up. They never fired a gun, but ran as if old Nick was after them. Some of them did not have time to put on their pants, or take their guns with them. We captured seven prisoners, six hundred stand of arms, and sixty horses. All the inhabitants have left the town, and the boys are quartered in their houses. I am now writing on some secession paper which the boys got in a rebel printing office that they cleaned out. We have pretty good times now guarding this place, but we will have to move from this to-morrow, for a town called Buchanan, 30 miles farther south.

There is a funeral just moving up the hill. It is a grand sight. Drums are muffled and beating the dead march—one thousand soldiers are in procession. It is a Captain that was shot by the picket guard in mistake for an enemy. The coffin is hauled on a cannon wagon, with the Union flag wrapped around it, and six horses to haul it.

I think I shall enlist for the three years-service, after my three months are out, as most of our regiment is going to do so. Tell Dave he had better not go for the three years-service, for I am afraid he will see harder times than he can stand. You need not answer this, for if you do I don't think I will get your letter, as mails only come by chance in this country.

Yours with respect,
R. W. DRUCKEMILLER.[124]

* * * * *

---

124. Richard W. Druckemiller, later a member of Co. C, 47th Pennsylvania Volunteers.

Image by artist Winslow Homer of the 79th New York Highlanders on parade in 1861. (Credit: *Harper's Weekly*, May 25, 1861)

Letters from Chaplain Peter Rizer
79th New York State Militia
(Cameron Highlanders)

Aside from the foregoing letters printed by the Gazette, *the* Sunbury American *also ran a series of accounts from former Sunbury clergyman Rev. Peter Rizer. Appointed chaplain of the 79th New York (Highlanders) State Militia, Rizer immediately went to Washington, D.C., and was mustered into service by Adjutant General Lorenzo Thomas on June 20, 1861. The regiment had already been enrolled on May 29 in New York City. Rizer joined the 79th at Camp Lochiel near Alexandria, Virginia, in early July, when the regiment was organized into a brigade under Colonel William T. Sherman along with the 13th and 69th New York, 2nd Wisconsin, and a battery of the 3rd U.S. Artillery. As part of Brig. Gen. Daniel Tyler's 1st Division in Irvin McDowell's Army of Northeastern Virginia, the 79th New York participated in the first major military operation of the war that culminated in the Battle of Bull Run (First Manassas). After crossing the Potomac into Confederate territory on July 7, the 79th moved on July 16 toward the railroad junction at Manassas. On Sunday morning, July 21, McDowell began his general movement against the Confederate forces gathering at Manassas. Sherman's brigade remained in reserve until the afternoon, when they were sent to recapture lost Union guns on Henry House Hill at the southern end of the Confederate line. With Sherman sending his regiments into the fight in piecemeal fashion, the 79th advanced alone after an unsuccessful attack by the 2nd Wisconsin. Initially repulsed and taking severe fire, the 79th charged again until a barrage of musketry cut down Colonel Cameron.*[125]

Washington, D.C.,
July 8, 1861.[126]

H. B. MASSER,

DEAR SIR:—In company with our friends, the Highland Officers, I reached Camp Lochiel on Saturday evening last. It is a most beautiful situation, about three miles from this city, on the Heights above Georgetown. On Sunday morning, a little before sunrise, I stood gazing around, in full view of the Capitol and other magnificent buildings, Arlington Heights, Fairfax Court House, the winding Potomac studded with sails, and all other beauties of nature and art stretching out before the eye in this region. Just then I heard the band of our Regiment playing the Scotch air, "Scots wh'a hae," with so much solemnity, and in such plaintive strains, that my whole attention was absorbed. It seemed to me, that nothing more was needed to "lend enchantment to the view."

After spending one night in Camp, and just as the soldiers were assembling for divine service in the rear of the Staff Officers' tents, the baggage wagons came rattling into the enclosure, and we were summoned to pull up stakes and remove the encampment into Virginia, in the vicinity of Camp Corcoran. Accordingly, the 79th Regiment, N. Y. S. M., have now pitched their tents on the "SACRED SOIL," and may be found not far from the aqueduct opposite Georgetown. How long they may be left in their present quarters, depends upon

---

125. William Mark McKnight, *Blue Bonnets O'er the Border: The 79th New York Cameron Highlanders* (Shippensburg: White Mane Books, 1998), 26–29.
126. *Sunbury American*, July 13, 1861.

the "higher powers that be." Inasmuch as many troops have been ordered from this vicinity towards General Patterson's Division, which it is said needed reinforcements, it is plausible to infer that when the Highlanders will be ordered to move again, it will be in a southern direction.

Col. CAMERON has been quite sick for the last eight or ten days with Dysentery, but is now much better. He expects to go over to Camp to-morrow.

The general health of this region continues good, but of course among so many people as are here congregated, there are numerous cases of sickness.

It is not our province to know the designs of Government until they are expressed in orders. But from sundry movements, especially the ordering away of so many regiments, it is reasonable to suppose that a grand demonstration is soon to be made.

Capt. Ellis and Lieut. Elliott express themselves in glowing terms of pleasure concerning their recent visit to Sunbury. They entertain [e]specially grateful feelings towards the many fair friends with whom they met, and from whom they received so much patriotic attention.

Excuse haste, as several clergymen have just invited me to join their party, in discussing matters appertaining to the religious interests of our military. You may expect to hear from me again. I expect to go to Camp this evening.

Yours, Truly, R.

P.S. Rev. Mr. Gallagher, of the 24th N. Y. Regiment, entertains a very pleasant recollection of his passage through Sunbury, where the ladies entertained him with music, and desires his respects to be presented to all the kind people.

* * * * *

Camp Lochiel, Alexandria County, Va.,
3 miles S.E. of Georgetown,
July 16, 1861.[127]

H. B. MASSER, ESQ,—DEAR SIR.—Our present encampment is called by some, after Thurlow Weed. But many prefer retaining the name first given on Georgetown Heights, because it is historically dear to the Cameron clan. We are now on the "sacred soil of Virginia," getting ready for the grand march. In our vicinity are numerous other encampments, among which are the 13th and 69th New York and the 2d Wisconsin Regiments. The Highland Regiment has about one hundred tents erected, with streets and avenues between, like a regularly laid out town. The Staff Officers' tents are on the East, then a row for officers of the line, and next those for the soldiers generally. Good boarding can be had at the neighboring farmhouses, of which the officers generally avail themselves.—The men draw rations from the Quartermaster, and subsist themselves in messes of from eight to ten. Much social feeling prevails. A few evenings ago, a grand Concert of Band and vocal music was given at the Colonel's marquee, in compliment to some highly intelligent ladies, who made us a visit. The Cameron song, "Bonnets of blue," and "Bonnets on the border," elicited great applause. I am glad to say that Col. Cameron appears to be entirely convalescent, and in fine spirits. That Philadelphia Editor, to whom you referred in your last "American," was too fast. Col. Cameron is as brave a man as can be found in the army, and is now ready to lead his Regiment wherever the Government may choose to order them. We are now under marching orders, and may be off in the direction of Fairfax Court House in a few hours. Some of our baggage is to be sent to Alexandria, but our tents are not to be struck for the present. Everything indicates a speedy advance of the grand army.

Our Regiment, the 79th N. Y., is formed into a brigade, with the 69th N. Y., Col. Corcoran; 13th N. Y., Colonel Quimby; 2d Wisconsin Rifles, Lieut. Col. Peck; and Sherman's Battery, formerly Ringgold's Flying Artillery, Col. Sherman;—the whole to be under the command of Gen. Tyler, a splendid looking U.S. officer of the Regular Army. It will number about five thousand men, and

---

127. *Sunbury American*, July 13, 1861.

will constitute a part of the Central Column, to be led by Gen. McDowell.

Thus you may perceive that the grand Campaign embraces four divisions; viz: Gen. Butler in the East, at Fortress Monroe; Gen. Patterson on the Potomac; Gen. McClellan, now in Western Virginia; and ours in the centre, near which, it is said, will be the Commander-in-chief, LIEUT. GEN. SCOTT. I suppose the whole army will present a force of 300,000[128] men, marching towards Richmond, probably via Manassas Junction. The general impression here is, that the enemy will try to make a stand at Manassas Gap, which they call their Thermopylae—But the enemy has made so many "masterly evacuations," that it is very difficult to say, with any degree of certainty, where he will make a stand. At all events, our army, in the confident belief that we are doing the will of God in endeavoring to maintain our NATIONALITY, our UNITY, and the INTEGRITY OF THE BEST GOVERNMENT ON EARTH, will soon be on the way to Richmond, if the grand march has not already begun. This region of the Capital teems for miles around with armed and intensely eager troops. The country is white with tents, and the reveille and tattoo may be heard morning and night in every direction. The prancing of noble steeds, the bristling cannon, the sound of the bugle, and the long files of infantry, together with the thousands of baggage wagons, ambulances, &c., show the undreamed of power of this wonderful Republic of the United States. For weeks Regiment after Regiment, has been marched across the Potomac, until we are forced to conclude that the time must be very near, when such a demonstration is to be made, as the world has never seen. The only explanation on the conduct of the Rebels will admit of is, that they are under judicial blindness. That famous municipal institution, which Dr. Palmer, of New Orleans, proclaimed "DIVINE," has so demoralized the public sentiment of the South, that they call evil, good, and good, evil. But God says, "Pride goeth before destruction, and a haughty spirit before a fall."

---

128. The original article cited 300,000,000 men, but this was obviously a typo on the part of the newspaper editors. Even the estimate of 300,000 was a gross exaggeration on Rizer's part. At the time of the Battle of Bull Run on July 21, five days after this letter was written, McDowell's forces alone only totaled about 35,732 men.

In this vicinity, our soldiers are surprised to find so much impoverishment, where the natural advantages of soil, climate and situation are so striking. Neglected fields, indifferent buildings, NO SCHOOL HOUSES, and a people who depend upon others to do their work, show the necessity for a change. And I verily believe, that God will "make the wrath of man to praise him," by means of our army, in waking up the slumbering energies of Old Virginia, which by nature is second to no State in the Union in mineral and agricultural resources. After the war, many of these Northern young of the army, will return to marry Virginia girls and settle on the "sacred soil." They will bring with them, taste, industry and science, and thus demonstrate the onward progress of the Anglo-Saxon race.

R.

* * * * *

Washington, D.C.,
July 23, 1861.[129]

H. B. MASSER, ESQ.,—*Dear Sir:*—Our mutual friend, Col. Cameron, fell on the field of battle at Bull's Run, near Centreville, on the 21st inst., whilst bravely commanding his regiment. He had suffered much from an attack of dysentery, several weeks ago, but his strong constitution enabled him to lead his troops out of Camp Lochiel on Tuesday last, and take his position in the grand army. When he first reached the battle-ground he was somewhat unwell, but under the excitement of the occasion he soon rallied, and discharged his duties with high spirit. Col. Cameron was mounted during the battle on his splendid charger, lately sent him by his brother at Lewisburg, until about 10 o'clock, when he gave him in the care of his servant, taking an unmounted position. During the engagement Col. Cameron was perfectly cool and collected, proving the truth of what I heard him declare—that he was not afraid of bullets. During the action Capt. Laing, of the 76th, went up to him, and after giving him some refreshments, remonstrated against the exposedness of his situation. But the Colonel would not change, as he felt it his duty to be with

---

129. *Sunbury American*, July 27, 1861.

Colonel James Cameron, the first Union officer of that rank killed in the Civil War at the Battle of First Bull Run on July 21, 1861. (Credit: The Horse Soldier, Gettysburg, Pennsylvania)

his troops, though in the very midst of danger, where bullets whistled most fiercely. The gallant Captain, above mentioned, was soon after severely wounded in several places, and brought off the field in a carriage. He is now lying at the Infirmary in this city. About 5 o'clock in the afternoon a Minnie ball came whizzing from the enemy, which struck the Colonel in the breast and brought him to the ground. As he fell he raised his hand to his mouth, from which the blood gushed out, and he expired with a single groan. Thus fell one of the bravest officers in the service of our Government. He had conscientiously espoused the cause of his country. He had confidence in the triumph of government over anarchy—He believed that God has no sympathy with treason, and therefore freely offered his heart's blood on the altar of freedom.

Col. Cameron was over six feet high, and of an erect and commanding form. In uniform he appeared admirable to all observers, and bore a strong resemblance to Gen. Jackson. I had a long conversation with him a short time ago, on the subject of religion, and he expressed strong faith in God and in every word which the Bible contains, at the same time acknowledging his sins. His peculiar religious views were of the Presbyterian stamp, and I remember hearing him express his decided preference for the Convenanters. He was a man of noble impulses, and has placed many friends under obligations to his memory, who will never forget his generosity.

A sorrowing widow survives him at his residence, on the banks of the Susquehanna, in Northumberland County, Pennsylvania.

His brother, the Secretary of War, has sent a deputation for the recovery of the Colonel's body. I am now at his house, awaiting their return.

Yours, truly,
R., Chaplain 79th Reg., N. Y. S. M.

Having learned more definitely the particulars of Col. Cameron's death, I wish you to incorporate in my communication sent this morning, the following, viz:

Our troops had fought bravely and determinedly up to 5 o'clock, P. M., when it was concluded that the day was ours. The Fire Zouaves were now ordered to skirmish in the woods, but they were mostly cut up by the Rebel Infantry, and driven out. The 69th Regiment then made an effort to out-flank them on the right, and the 79th were marched up in front of a masked battery on the left, and here the 79th received a most galling fire from the battery, which mowed down their ranks like grass. Notwithstanding these embarrassing circumstances, Col. Cameron made a third effort to rally his men, raising his pistol (which had just been handed him by his orderly,) and waving it over his head, saying: "rally, Scotchmen, rally!" Seeing the impracticability of effecting a rally, Lieut. Elliott, of the 10th Company, approached and said: "Colonel, the Regiment is already gone, and all we can do, is to take off the wounded, many of whom may bleed to death if not speedily relieved. I will tie a white handkerchief to my sword, and carry it as a flag of truce in behalf of the wounded." The Col. said, "yes, do so," when he received a minnie rifle ball in his left breast, near the middle, and fell dead upon the spot. This happened between 5 and 6 o'clock, P. M.—His body was borne off the field by eight of his men, on muskets, four of whom were shot down in the performance of this melancholy duty. The Colonel's steed is now in this city.

Col. Cameron wore on the field, a plain grey coat, but retained his felt hat, with feather and eagle attached. It is supposed the feather attracted attention from the Rebels.

Intelligence reached here about an hour ago that the body had been recovered, but this is a mistake.

Furnished with a Government conveyance, I went over to-day to Fort Corcoran, to look after our baggage, and have just returned.—

On the way I heard that the Rebels have advanced as far as Fall's Church.

Yours in haste,
R.

* * * * *

The 79th Regiment, New York Highlanders—Col. Sherman's Brigade—Col. Cameron's Staff—Eagerness for the fray—Capt. Shillinglow—Capt. Laing—Col. Cameron's Sword.[130]

On Tuesday, the 16th inst., at 8 o'clock, P. M., the Grand Army of the United States, under Maj. Gen. McDowell, marched from the banks of the Potomac towards Manassas Junction. The 79th Regiment under Col. James Cameron, encamped at Lochiel about

---

130. *Sunbury Gazette*, August 3, 1861.

2½ miles S. E. of Georgetown in Alexandria County, Va., left their quarters in due time, and found themselves bivouacked that night at Vienna, on the spot, were a few weeks previously, Gen. Schenck's advance post of Ohio troops had been fired on by a masked battery. The 79th Regiment, New York Highlanders, numbered upwards of a thousand men; about 200 of whom were left in camp under command of Lieut. Morrison, of the 1st Company.

Col. Cameron's Staff consisted of the following officers, viz: Major McClellan, Adjutant Ireland, Aid[e]-de-Camp Lieut. Daviess, and Chaplain, P. Rizer. The names of the following Captains are familiar to me: Morrison, Manson, Shillinglow, Christie, Coulter, Brown, Ellis, Laing, Farrish, Barclay.

Our Brigade, which was placed under command of Gen. Tyler, consisted of the following, viz:

69th Reg. N. Y. S. M. under Col. Corcoran.

79th Reg. N. Y. S. M. under Col. Cameron.

13th Reg. N. Y. S. M. under Col. Quimby.

2nd Regiment Wisconsin Volunteers, Lieut. Col. Peck Commanding, and Sherman's Battery, under Col. Sherman.

I was present, in the council of officers, when after dress parade, a day or two before, our Colonel communicated the orders to be ready with three days cooked rations in their haversacks, for a march in eight hours. All were eager not to be left behind with the reserve, for the tents were not yet to be struck. And I well remember how Capt. Shillinglow's eye kindled with delight when he ascertained that his position was to be on the advance. Poor fellow! He fell on the battle field of Bull's Run, by a cannon ball, which cut off both his legs. I had often noticed him on parade, with his erect form, martial mien and peculiar Highland bearing; and I cannot but deeply regret the loss of one so young and full of life and courage.

After the battle, when the road to Fairfax Court House was lined with retreating soldiers and civilians for miles, I heard myself called to a carriage about 10 o'clock at night. I soon learned that Capt. Laing, of the 79th was there, dangerously wounded with bullet holes in his neck, side and left arm. He was supported by several men. As he wished to speak with me, I was obliged to mount up on the wheel, and by holding my ear close to his mouth, learned from him that he wished me to visit him next day at the Infirmary, in Washington city, and to inform Gen. Cameron[131] that he had brought with him off the battle field the sword of his brother, our lamented Colonel.

After a walk of about 40 miles in a round-about way, I found myself again at Camp Lochiel, by 5 o'clock next morning. More anon.

R------, Chaplain, 79th Reg. N. Y. S. M.
Sunbury, Pa.,
July 31, 1861.

---

131. A reference to Simon Cameron, Secretary of War. He was frequently referred to in the local media as General Cameron due to his former position as a general officer in the Pennsylvania militia.

2

The Army Reorganizes, August 1861–January 1862

The major Union defeat at Bull Run jolted the North into realizing it faced a potentially long, difficult, and costly war. Fortunately, the national mood did not devolve into despair but rather renewed determination. Right away it became clear that the ninety-day men, whose enlistments were dissolving just as the fight at Bull Run began in earnest, would hardly meet the urgent need the War Department now faced. President Lincoln therefore immediately signed into law a pair of bills, each authorizing the enlistment of 500,000 three-year volunteers. Pennsylvania's recruitment quota under the new measures, revised from earlier figures established by presidential proclamation on May 3 under the three-month system, was set at 82,825 men (the Commonwealth eventually furnished 85,160 soldiers). Lincoln then replaced Irvin McDowell with Maj. Gen. George B. McClellan, a capable administrator with a few minor but highly publicized victories in western Virginia to his credit, who set about reorganizing the Union military into a sustainable fighting force that could confront the enemy.[1]

When he took command on July 27, 1861, McClellan assumed control over approximately 50,000 men, some 1,000 cavalry, and about 650 artillerymen stationed in and around the national capital. As new regiments arrived, he organized them into provisional brigades of four regiments each and placed them in camps located around the Maryland suburbs, where they received armaments, equipment, and some rudimentary instruction. Brig.

---

1. McPherson, *Battle Cry of Freedom*, 348; *The War of the Rebellion: Official Records of the Union and Confederate Armies* (Washington: Government Printing Office, 1880–1901): Series III, Vol. 1, 380–83. Hereafter cited at *O.R.* The total number of men furnished by the two enlistment bills would eventually reach 700,680 men.

Major General George Brinton McClellan was appointed Commanding General of the U.S. Army on November 1, 1861. (Credit: Matthew Brady Collection, National Archives)

Gen. Fitz John Porter assumed charge of these provisional forces. After the brigades were "well established, and the troops somewhat disciplined and instructed," McClellan later noted in his official report to the War Department, they were organized into several divisions of three brigades each (the Army Corps structure that eventually came to characterize the Army of the Potomac, with each corps containing three divisions, would not be introduced until the following spring). Once the regiments were in fit condition, they were transferred to existing forces stationed on the Virginia side of the Potomac River.[2]

---

2. George B. McClellan, *Report on the Organization and Campaigns of the Army of the Potomac* (New York: Sheldon & Co., 1864), 50–53.

Letters from the Sunbury Guards Company C, 47th Pennsylvania Volunteer Infantry

One of the new three-year regiments that proceeded to Washington in the aftermath of Bull Run included a reconstituted version of the Sunbury Guards. Organized on August 5, 1861, and now led by Capt. John P. S. Gobin, the Guards became Company C of the 47th Pennsylvania Volunteer Regiment. The Guards rendezvoused at Camp Curtin on September 1, where the regiment was formally organized under the command of Colonel Tilghman H. Good. On September 20 the regiment left Harrisburg for Washington, arriving the following day. They went into camp at Kalorama Heights until September 27, and then moved across the Chain Bridge to join forces stationed in Virginia. Relocating to Camp Advance at Fort Ethan Allen, the 47th was attached to the 3rd Brigade under Gen. William F. "Baldy" Smith's Division, along with the 33rd, 49th, and 79th New York Regiments. Rather fortuitously, the presence of the latter unit brought the Sunbury Guards back into contact with their former townsman, Chaplain Rizer.[3]

Some minor skirmishing occurred in the vicinity of Falls Church at the end of September, during which the regiment was turned out but no major engagement ensued. The 47th then moved with Smith's Division to Camp Griffin, where they participated in a Grand Review at Bailey's Crossroads on October 11. It was during this time in camp that the Sunbury Guards suffered their first and perhaps most emotional loss, when their thirteen-year-old drummer boy, John Boulton Young, suddenly died from smallpox (the letters conveying the sad news home carried a particularly solemn and forlorn tone). Aside from a small diversion to Dranesville on December 20, where the regiment again expected a fight that did not materialize,[4] the 47th remained at Camp Griffin until January 22, 1862, when it was ordered to accompany Brig. Gen. John Milton Brannan to his new command at Key West, Florida. The regiment went immediately to Annapolis on January 23, quartering in the facilities of the U.S. Naval Academy until they boarded the Steamship Oriental on January 27 to head off to their next assignment.[5]

---

3. Bates, *Pennsylvania Volunteers*, 1:1150–51.
4. At the Battle of Dranesville (December 20, 1861) in Fairfax County, Virginia, the 3rd Brigade, Pennsylvania Reserve Corps under Brig. Gen. Edward O. C. Ord, routed the Confederate forces of Brig. Gen. James Ewell Brown (Jeb) Stuart before the 47th Pennsylvania could reach the field.
5. Bates, *Pennsylvania Volunteers*, 1:1150–51.

CAMP CURTIN,
Sept. 4, 1861.[6]

Dear Wilvert:—The *American* was received last week and eagerly read by the men. We have been mustered into the United States service, and have received our tents and uniforms. Our Regiment, Col. Good's, has removed to the field adjoining Camp Curtin, where our quarters are much superior to those in the old camp. The men are all in good health and spirits, and are learning very rapidly.

Our uniforms are dark, and of excellent material, as are all our accoutrements. I give you a list of the members of my company, as far as mustered in the service:

    Captain—J. P. Shindel Gobin.
    1st Lieutenant—James Vandyke.
      2d—William Rees.
    1st Sergeant—Daniel Oyster.
      2d do C. S. Beard.
      3d do Jared Brosious.
      4th do William Piers.
      5th do Peter Smelser.
    1st Corporal, Christ Schall.
      2d do Charles F. Stewart.
      3d do Jacob K. Keefer.
      4th do Isaac Kembel.
      5th do John H. Heim.
      6th do William Plant.
      7th do Samuel Eister.
      8th do D. W. Kembel.
    Musicians—Henry D. Wharton.
      Boulton Young.
    Wagoner—Jeremiah Gensemer.

[List of privates and officers up to this time, 90. The company, when full, will number 101, when the list will be published.]

Then men arrived last night for me, that will swell my company nearly up to the maximum. They are good men, and all of them, I am satisfied, will give a good account of themselves when an opportunity offers.

---

6. *Sunbury American*, September 7, 1861.

What has become of Smith Head, who borrowed money to buy articles for his family? He came to Harrisburg with us and returned the same night, leaving me to account for his blanket, besides minus the money he got of me. He is a precious scamp.

Yours,
J. P. S. G.

* * * * *

Camp Curtin, No. 2.
Harrisburg, Pa.,
September 10, 1861.[7]

DEAR WILVERT:—There is a scarcity of news here, but knowing our "folks at home" would like to hear from the boys, I concluded I would give you the state of their health and a *full* list of our members. The boys are all well and are enjoying themselves in the usual style of camp pleasure. The following is a complete copy of our muster roll:—

J. P. S. GOBIN, Captain.
James Vandyke, 1st Lieutenant.
William Rees, 2d do
Daniel Oyster, 1st Sergeant,
1 C. S. Beard,
2 Jared Brosious,
3 William Piers,
4 Peter Smelser.
1 Christ Schall, Corporal,
2 Charles F. Steward, Corporal,
3 Jacob K. Kieffer, Corporal,
4 Isaac Kembel, Corporal,
5 Samuel Eyster, Corporal,
6 John H. Heim, Corporal,
7 William Plant, Corporal,
8 Daniel W. Kembel, Corporal

---

7. *Sunbury American*, September 14, 1861.

Privates

John Bartlow,
David S. Beidler,
Martin Berger,
Henry Brown,
George Frity,
J. W. Firth,
George R. Good,
Jesse B. Green,
Jacob Grubb,
Samuel Haupt,
Freeman Haupt,
George Hepler,
George Horner,
Alfred Hunter,
Charles Harp,
Conrad Holman,
Cornelius Kramer,
Theodore Kiehl,
James Kennedy,
Stewart Kirk,
Thomas Lothard,
L. K. Landaw,
Warren McEwen,
Adam Maul,
Samuel Miller,
John McGrow,
B. F. Miller,
Eli Miller,
George Malick,
John W. McNew,
George Miller,
John Monsh,
Francis McNeal,
Robert C. McNeal,
Reuben Wilson.

George W. Bortle,
James Brown,
Wm. Brannen,
R. W. Druckemiller,
William Fry,
Levi Miller,
David Naylor,
John B. Otto,
Richard O'Bourke,
William Pfeil,
Alex. Ruffaner,
P. M. Randalls,
Samuel M. Reigel,
James R. Rine,
Joseph Smith,
Mark Shipman,
John C. Steiner,
Henry Senft,
Timothy Snyder,
Isaac Snyder,
John W. Smith,
John Sunker,
Ephraim Thatcher,
Henry W. Wolf,
Peter Wolf,
James Wolf,
Theodore Woodbridge,
David Weikel,
John E. Will,
George C. Watson,
John W. Walton,
James Whistler,
B. F. Walls,
Samuel Whistler,

We *have* enough men to fill our company, but they are not all sworn in. According to Col. Good's statement, however, we will have all our companies filled by to-morrow, Wednesday, and our Regiment perfected; that is, full complement of men, arms and equipments, and a finer looking Regiment you never saw—all of the "manor born."

I suppose you have heard that our 1st Lieutenant, James Vandyke, has received the appointment of Quarter Master to our Regiment. It is conceded, generally, to be an excellent choice, and that he will attend to his duties faithfully, and will act honestly with the Regiment.

Capt. Gobin has the confidence of all our boys for his gentlemanly manners and his kindness to them. *He* always attends to the *wants* of the men before his own are gratified. Our "little Zouave," or "Infant Drummer," is very well, and is still the "observed of all observers."[8] As soon as I can obtain any news of importance, or anything that would be of interest, I will send it to you.

Yours, fraternally,
H. D. W.

* * * * *

Camp Curtin,
September 17, 1861.[9]

Dear Friends:—While the rain is pattering upon my "house," and the boys are making the night hideous by their howlings, I will just write a few lines to inform you of our doings. My company is full, having the complement of one hundred and one men. We were furnished with our rifles and overcoats to-day, and the boys are much pleased. Both are excellent articles. We are now fully equipped, having everything necessary to go to work. We expect to leave to-night for Washington or Baltimore. Our company has been made the color company of the regiment, the letter being according to rotation used,

---

8. "Little Zouave" and "Infant Drummer" are references to John Boulton Young. Young was twelve years old when he was allowed to enlist as Company C's drummer. Young wore a special Zouave-style uniform made just for him. The uniform, as well as Young's drum, survived the war and are now on display at the Northumberland County Historical Society in Sunbury, Pennsylvania.

9. *Sunbury Gazette*, September 21, 1861.

C. It is the same as E. in the 11th. Wm. M. Hendricks has been appointed Sergeant Major, so that old Sunbury is pretty well represented in the regiment, having the Quartermaster, Sergeant Major and Color Company. The boys are all well, and in the best of spirits, notwithstanding the rain. Our tents however, are pretty good ones and protect us. Boulton is lying by me as I write, just about going to sleep. I will write again when we reach our destination.

Yours,
SHINDEL.

* * * * *

Camp Kalorama,
Washington City, D.C.,
September 22, 1861.[10]

DEAR WILVERT:—After a tedious ride we have, at last, safely arrived at the City of "magnificent distances." We left Harrisburg on Friday last at 1 o'clock A. M. and reached this camp yesterday (Saturday) at 4 P. M., as tired and worn out a set of mortals as can possibly exist. On arriving at Washington we were marched to the "Soldiers Retreat," a building purposely erected for the benefit of the soldier, where every comfort is extended to him and the wants of the "inner man" supplied.

After partaking of refreshments we were ordered into line and marched, about three miles, to this camp. So tired were the men, that on marching out, some gave out, and had to leave the ranks, but J. Boulton Young, our "little Zouave," stood it bravely, and acted like a veteran. So small a drummer is scarcely seen in the army, and on the march through Washington he was twice the recipient of three cheers.

We were reviewed by Gen. McClellan yesterday without our knowing it. All along the march we noticed a considerable number of officers, both mounted and on foot; the horse of one of the officers was so beautiful that he was noticed by the whole regiment, in fact, so wrapt up were they in the horse, the rider wasn't noticed, and the boys were considerably mortified this morning on discovering they

---

10. *Sunbury American*, September 28, 1861.

had missed the sight of, and the neglect of not saluting the soldier next in command to Gen. Scott.

Col. Good, who has command of our regiment, is an excellent man and a splendid soldier. He is a man of very few words, and is continually attending to his duties and the wants of the Regiment.

I am happy to inform you that our young townsman, Mr. William Hendricks, has received the appointment of Sergeant Major to our Regiment. He made his first appearance at guard mounting this morning; he looked well, done up his duties admirably, and, in time, will make an excellent officer. Our Regiment will now be put to hard work; such as drilling and the usual business of camp life, and the boys expect and hope an occasional "pop" at the enemy.

Our boys are all well, and as complimentary to H. B. M, are waiting anxiously for the *American*.

Yours fraternally,
H. D. W.

* * * * *

Camp Kalorama,
Washington, D.C.,
September 27, 1861.[11]

Dear John:—To-day is one of those dull, dreary ennui creating days that all who have any experience in camp deprecate. A drizzling, pattering rain compels you to remain in-*doors* as much as possible, and together with the mood which it creates prevents all drilling. Therefore most of us have nothing to do but lie in our tents and sleep, or indulge in day-dreams. Fortunately for us the kind Gift of the Presbyterian Congregation of Sunbury, a library of twenty-five volumes, gives us something with which to employ our time. To-day you will find one volume in almost every tent, while the best reader in the party is acquainting the balance with its contents. We thank them heartily, and particularly the excellent pastor, Rev. Reardon, for their remembrance of us in this shape.

---

11. *Sunbury Gazette*, October 5, 1861.

As you will perceive by the heading, our Regiment is encamped on the heights of Kalorama, close to Georgetown, and about two miles from the White House. It is a very fine location for a camp, only the rain of last night and this morning has made it somewhat muddy. Good water is handy, while Rock Creek, which skirts one side of us, affords an excellent place for washing and bathing.

We left Camp Curtin on Friday, the 20th, and got in Camp here on the following evening. Our trip was unattended by any incidents of note, everything passing off quietly and safely. We passed through Baltimore about 12 o'clock at night, but the lateness of the hour did not prevent the appearance, at a great many windows, of white robed fair ones, who had evidently risen from their beds to greet and cheer us as we passed. At the depot, where we took the cars for here, we found the Union Relief Association had provided ice water in abundance for us, while hot coffee could be obtained for three cents a cup. I indulged in *several* of the latter. We left Baltimore about one o'clock, P. M., but did not arrive at Washington until eleven, A. M., where, after taking breakfast, provided by the Government, we were marched to camp.

Yesterday, being thanksgiving, no drilling was allowed, so, having obtained a pass from the Colonel, and also one from the acting Brigadier General, I started on a tour of observation. In the morning I took a cab and drove to Tennelly town, where I had the pleasure of grasping by the hand Capt. Taggart, of Northumberland, Capt. McCleary, of Milton, Lieut. Colt and others. They looked well, and represent their commands to be in excellent condition and ready for action. They were then under orders to be ready to move at a minute's warning, and had two day's cooked rations on hand. Gen. McCall's division, comprising the entire reserve corps of Pennsylvania, are encamped around there and have thrown up quite a formidable fortification which commands the country and all the roads for a considerable distance around. When it is considered that this point is only about two miles from Chain Bridge its importance is readily seen. Should the rebels attack that point[,] I feel assured Fort Pennsylvania, as it has been named, will give them a warm reception. The Northumberland Band, which is to be attached to the Fifth Regiment, had just arrived the evening before. All were in good health.

In the afternoon I attended Professor McCoy's lecture on "The National Crisis," delivered in the Hall of the House of Representatives. It was an excellent address, and I was never more highly entertained. Among the audience were President Lincoln, Secretaries Seward, Wells, and other dignitaries. Gen. Pomeroy, of Kansas, presided over the meeting. The lecturer, in the course of his remarks, quoted from Washington's Farewell Address, and at the same time produced upon the stage Washington's favorite cane, and asked permission of the audience to hold it in his hand while reading. It produced quite a sensation I assure you.

We were highly pleased a few days ago to receive a visit from our mutual friend, John Buyers, of Sunbury. I would have liked to have gone to town with him, but the Colonel thought I had better remain in camp. They are very strict, and now if we wish to visit Washington our pass must be signed by the Brigadier General.

Our men are all in good health, with the exception of a few cases of diarrhea. We have an excellent Surgeon. And the fact is our entire staff is one of the best in the field.

We cannot forbear, in this connection, returning our thanks to Col. Welsh, commanding Camp Curtin, for the many kindnesses received at his hands. As a soldier and a gentleman[,] he has no superior. The improvement in Camp Curtin since under his command is the subject of general notice, he being without doubt the most efficient head it ever had. In all his acts he is most materially assisted by that Prince of good natured fellows, Major Unger, and his gentlemanly assistants. All will be gratefully remembered.

I cannot tell how long we will remain here. But until further notice direct all letters to Company C, 47th Regt., P. V., Camp Kalorama, Washington, D. C. My love to all friends.

Yours, &c.
J. P. S. G.

* * * * *

Camp Advance,
September 28, 1861.[12]

Dear John:—Yesterday I had hardly finished my letter to you when we received orders to pack up and move. Amid all the rain[,] we struck our tents and marched down to the Chain Bridge, across it, and once more trod the sacred soil. We marched about two miles in the direction of Fall's Church, where we are at present encamped. This morning we are at work throwing up entrenchments, so the probability is we shall remain here for some time. The rebels are about four miles from us. We have a large force here, enough for any emergency, and if we are attacked you will hear of the rifles of the 47th doing some execution, particularly if they give us time to get our *pits* finished.

The men stood the rain and march like old veterans, and after we had pitched our tents on a side hill, lay down and slept soundly. If anything occurs I will write again.

Yours, &c.
J. P. S. G.

* * * * *

Camp Advance,
Fort Ethan Allen,
September 29, 1861.[13]

DEAR WILVERT:—First of April or "moving day" seems to be the order with us: we have changed camps three times in as many days. On Friday last we left Camp Kalorama, and the same night encamped about one mile from the Chain Bridge on the opposite side of the Potomac from Washington. The next morning, Saturday, we were ordered to this Camp, one and a half miles from the one we occupied the night previous. I should have mentioned that we halted on a high hill (on our march here) at the Chain Bridge, called Camp Lyon, but were immediately ordered on this side of the river. On the route from Kalorama we were for two hours exposed to the hardest rain I ever experienced. Whew, it was a whopper; but the fellows stood it

---

12. *Sunbury Gazette*, October 5, 1861.
13. *Sunbury American*, October 12, 1861.

well—not a murmur—and they waited in their wet clothes until nine o'clock at night for their supper. Our Camp adjoins that of the N. Y. 79th (Highlanders), the one in which Mr. Rizer is Chaplain. The Reverend gentleman visited our Regiment last evening;—he seemed very much gratified to meet the Sunbury boys, and gave them all a hearty shake of the hand. Mr. Rizer has service every Sabbath at ten o'clock A. M., and prayer meeting at night. During the week, he has prayer meeting at dress parade (weather permitting,) and always before going to battle he addresses his Regiment, and concludes by exhorting them to "trust in God and keep their powder dry."

We had not been in this Camp more than six hours before our boys were supplied with twenty rounds of ball and cartridge, and ordered to march and meet the enemy; they were out all night and got back to Camp at nine o'clock this morning, without having a fight. They are now in their tents taking a snooze preparatory to another march this morning. From the hard breathing and the peculiar sound produced through the nasal organ, I should say the boys were pretty tired after their last night's march. I don't know how long the boys will be gone, but the orders are to cook two days' rations and take it with them in their haversacks, so, from that you can soon expect to hear from us, and mark me, no "Bull's Run" affair this time, but vice versa a general routing of the Rebels.

There was a nice little affair came off at Lavensville, a few miles from here, on Wednesday last; our troops surprised a party of rebels (much larger that our own,) killing ten, took a Major prisoner, and captured a large number of horses, sheep and cattle, besides a large quantity of corn and potatoes, and about ninety-six tons of hay. A very nice day's work. The boys are well, in fact, there is no sickness of any consequence at all in our Regiment, and my particular friend, the literary gentleman of our mess, Al. Hunter, is in perfect enjoyment of health, and as an old Doctor in our town used to say, "is now locked in the arms of Morpheus." If anything of importance transpires I will send it to you immediately.

Yours, fraternally,
H. D. W.

12 M.—Sunday, Sept. 29.

I open my letter to inform you of a very important affair that occurred yesterday afternoon. Munson's Hill, which is about eight miles from this Camp, was taken. Brig. Gen. Wadsworth's division was in advance, supported by Gen. Heye's command. The main body of the army advanced on the road to Ball's Cross Roads. Upton's Hill, where fortifications had been commenced by the rebels, had been evacuated when our forces arrived there. The army passed on and took possession of Munson's Hill, the enemy having beat a retreat. Our men took possession and will hold it, together with all the advanced possessions of the rebels.

A detachment of the Fourteenth N. Y. Volunteers, by a flank movement in the rear of Munson's Hill, cut off and captured a mounted officer, a lieutenant and six privates. The officer and men were brought to Fort Corcoran, and one of the men, being wounded, was sent to Georgetown Hospital. This is something very important to us, and it is from this cause our Regiment was called out last night. From what I hear now, the whole [A]rmy of the Potomac is in motion and, perhaps before you get this you may hear of something desperate.

H. D. W.

* * * * *

Camp Chestnut, Va.,
October 13, 1861.[14]

DEAR WILVERT:—As you perceive we have again moved and are now ten miles distant from Washington. The location of our camp is fine and the scenery *would* be splendid if the view was not obstructed by heavy thickets of pine and innumerable chestnut trees. The country around us is excellent for the Rebel scouts to display their bravery; that is, to lurk in the dense woods and pick off one of our unsuspecting pickets. Last night, however, they (the Rebels) calculated wide of their mark; some of the New York 33d boys were out on picket; some fourteen or fifteen shots were exchanged, when our side succeeded in

---

14. *Sunbury American*, October 19, 1861.

bringing to the dust, (or rather mud,) an officer and two privates of the enemy's mounted pickets. The officer was shot by a Lieutenant in company H, of the 33d.

Our own boys have seen hard service since we have been on the "sacred soil." One day and night on picket, next day working on entrenchments at the Fort, (Ethan Allen,) another on guard, next on march and so on continually, but the hardest was on picket from last Thursday morning 'till Saturday morning—all the time four miles from camp, and both of the nights the rain poured in torrents, so much so that their clothes were completely saturated with the rain. They stood it nobly—not one complaining; but from the size of their haversacks on their return, it is no wonder they were satisfied and are so eager to go again tomorrow. I heard one of them say "there was such nice cabbage, sweet and Irish potatoes, turnips, &c., out where their duty called them, and then there was a likelihood of a Rebel sheep or young porker advancing over our lines and then he could take them as 'contraband' and have them for his own use." When they were out they saw about a dozen of the Rebel cavalry and would have had a bout with them, had it not been for an unlucky circumstance—one of the men caught the hammer of his rifle in the strap of his knapsack and caused his gun to fire; the Rebels heard the report and scampered in quick time, much faster than they did at "Falling Waters" when the "Bloody 11th" was after them.

There was quite an excitement here yesterday; our whole division was called out—all expecting a fight. After supplying the regiments with ammunition the arms were stacked and the men were ordered to hold themselves in readiness, as an attack was momentarily expected. At night the men were ordered to sleep on their arms and have their ammunition buckled around them ready for action. Coffee was made and provisions cooked for any emergency, but the enemy kept out of danger and we were not molested, however, every precaution is taken and if we get in a fight with them they will be met with a warm reception.

I think it will not be long ere there will be a heavy engagement, if there is one I will write, that is if I don't get "popped," but as you have telegraph and newspaper facilities better than we have I suppose the news would be in the *American* before you could receive a letter from me. The boys are all well and as a jockey would say in "fine condition."

Yours, fraternally,
H. D. W.

* * * * *

Camp of the Big Chestnut,
October 19, 1861.[15]

MICHAEL YOUNG, ESQ.—*Dear Sir:*—It is with the most profound feelings of sorrow I ever experience that I am compelled to announce to you the death of our Pet, and your son, Boulton. He departed this life and took his departure for a better world on Thursday. I did not get the news until yesterday morning, when I immediately started for Georgetown, hoping the tidings would prove untrue. Alas! When I reached there I found that little form that I had so loved, prepared for the grave. Until a short time before he died[,] the symptoms were very favorable, and every hope was entertained of his recovery. But "he who doeth all things well" ordained otherwise, and has taken him to that bourne whence no traveler returns. He had endeared himself to every member of the Company and Regiment and to-day a thousand men mourn his loss. Never have I felt so heart stricken. He was the life and light of our Company, and his death has caused a blight and a sadness to prevail, that only the rude wheels of time can efface. He was truly a remarkable boy, and had he been spared would have reflected honor upon his connections.

It is the business of a soldier to die, and we should not mourn when we see one so young and pure leaving this world of trouble for one so much brighter and happier. Yet Boulton had so wound himself around the tendrils of my heart that I feel as if his place could never be supplied. A son or brother could not be dearer to me.

Every attention was paid him by the doctors and nurses, all being anxious to show their devotion to one so young. I have had him buried, and ordered a stone for his grave, and ere six months pass a handsome monument, the gift of Company C, will mark the spot where rests the idol of their hearts.

---

15. *Sunbury Gazette*, October 26, 1861.

I would have sent his body home but the nature of his disease prevented it.¹⁶ When we return, however, if we are so fortunate, the body will accompany us.

I returned from Georgetown late last night. Everything connected with Boulty shall be attended to, no matter what the cost is. His effects that can safely be sent home, together with his pay, will be forwarded to you. But I do not feel like writing—my heart is full; I miss the blithe form and light step of him I loved. I will console myself with the thought that he has merely preceded some of us, at least, a short time, to a better world. May we all die as happy, is my prayer. Hoping Mrs. Young and all friends will accept my sincere sympathies in this, their and our deep affliction, and lean upon the giver of all good for consolation,

I remain truly yours, &c.,
J. P. SHINDEL GOBIN.

* * * * *

Resolutions by Company C

Camp of the Big Chestnut, Va.,
Head Quarters, Co. C, 47th Regiment, P. V.,
October 21, 1861.¹⁷

At a meeting of Company C, 47th Reg., P. V., B. F. WALLS, ESQ., was chosen President and HARRY D. WHARTON, Secretary. The President stated the object of the meeting, and the following preamble and resolutions were unanimously adopted:

Whereas, By a stroke of Divine Providence, JOHN BOULTON YOUNG, our drummer, has been taken from our midst to dwell in the realms of bliss, with all as pure as he, Therefore be it

Resolved, That we deplore the loss of one who had wound himself around the tendrils of the hearts of all who knew him, and whom we loved and regarded as the *pride* of our Company and Regiment.

---

16. John Boulton Young died of smallpox.
17. *Sunbury Gazette*, October 26, 1861.

Resolved, That as long as life lasts the memory of BOULTIE will be revered among us, and while we will miss his light step and ringing laugh, we are consoled by the thought that he is now happy in the realms above, where his *reveille* will be listened to by all the spirits of the just,

Resolved, That feeling it is the business of soldiers to die, we regard his decease, so young, so pure, as teaching us all the necessity of being at all times prepared for that *march* we all must eventually take.

Resolved, That we present our sincere sympathies to the bereaved parents, and hope that they will be comforted by the thought that our mutual loss is the gain of their son and our *pet*.

Resolved, That Company C appropriate the sum of one hundred dollars for the purpose of erecting a suitable monument over his remains, and that a committee of eight be appointed to select a suitable one, and have it placed over his grave.

Resolved, That said committee consist of Capt., J. P. S. Gobin, Chairman and Treasurer, Lieut. William Reese, Daniel Oyster, H. D. Wharton, Peter Haupt, B. F. Walls, Esq., Wm. H. Hendricks, and Robert McNeal.

Resolved, That a copy of these resolutions be sent to the parents of the deceased, and that they be published in the *Sunbury American* and *Sunbury Gazette*.

BENJ. E. WALLS, *President*.
Harry D. Wharton, Sec'ry.

* * * * *

Camp of the Big Chestnut,
October 20, 1861.[18]

DEAR FRIENDS:—Your box and letter were duly received last night, although I did not get to see Mr. Rizer. His Regiment left here on Friday night and went to Annapolis, from where they are going on some secret expedition on the coast. Mr. Rizer just got to Washington in time. Hendricks is in Washington but I do not think

---

18. *Sunbury Gazette*, October 26, 1861.

he can get a pass to come out here, and if he does come, he will have to follow us up, as we expect to move to-night. Mrs. Vandyke came out this morning and is in camp to-night. She took supper with me. I tell you I had an extra supper. The grapes you sent by her were all spoiled. Everything else in the box was in fine order. The horse radish came nice, I tell you—Also the celery. Tell Mrs. Young I have been cracking it between my teeth all day. Bill don't like it, so I got the whole bunch. I have not tried that Brandy yet, but am very grateful for it. After being out on picket in the rain for 24 hours, a little of it is worth a fortune. Tell Mrs. Snyder I will think of her kindness every time I take a drink. You know I will not abuse it, or disgrace myself.

There is not much news, but before next Sunday I hope to be able to tell you of a glorious victory. On Tuesday night last the left wing of our Regiment was out on picket, and were driven in by the Rebels. The right wing was ordered out, and I was ordered to take my company to Stewart's house, drive the Rebels from it, and hold it at all hazards. It was about 3 o'clock in the morning, so waiting until it was just getting day, I marched 80 men up; but the Rebels had left after driving Capt. Racy's Company into the woods. I took possession of it, and stationed my men, and there we were for 24 hours with our hands on our Rifles, and without closing an eye. I took 10 men, and went out scouting within half a mile of the Rebels, but could not get a prisoner, and we did not dare fire on them first. Do not think I was rash, I merely obeyed orders, and had ten men with me who could whip a hundred—Brosious, Piers, Harp and McEwen were among the number. Every man in the company wanted to go. The Rebels did not attack us, and if they had they would have met with a warm reception, as I had my men posted in such a manner that I could have whipped a regiment. My men were all ready and anxious for a fight.

I suppose you have heard of the death of dear little boultie. I had him buried in the cemetery, and the men have raised over a hundred dollars for a monument for him. I went over to Georgetown to the hospital, and had everything attended to regardless of cost. The doctor there told me it was the worst case he ever saw. It was the regular black, confluent small-pox. I loved that boy as I would my child, and his death is mourned by the whole regiment. I had him vaccinated at

Harrisburg, but it would not take, and he must have got the disease from some of the old Rebel Camps we visited, as their army is full of it. There is only one more case in our regiment, and he is off in the same hospital. I had all my men vaccinated, and myself too. Mine took well, and my arm is getting very sore. Bill's (Hendricks) arm is very sore, and he is quite sick to-night from it. I think we have blocked it completely.

You must not get alarmed if you do not get a letter from me now for some time, but write often. We are going to make another advance, and I cannot tell when we will get our baggage and tents on so that we can write, probably not until we have driven the rebels some distance further on, which we will do without much trouble.

J. P. S. G.

* * * * *

To the Patriotic Citizens of Northumberland County.

Camp of the Big Chesnut,
October 20, 1861.[19]

I have an appeal to make to you which I hope you will respond to cheerfully and promptly. I have under my command in the advance of the army, now in Virginia, one hundred good and true men. They are here to battle for your rights and your liberties. Many of them are related to you by the ties of blood and friendship, and you feel an interest in their welfare. The Government has supplied them with one blanket apiece, which, as the cold weather approaches, is not sufficient. We are told that it is impossible to get a full supply manufactured, so that some must do without an additional one probably all winter. Some of my men have none, two of them, Theodore Kiehl and Robert McNeal, having given theirs to our lamented drummer boy when he was taken sick. Now what I want is this:—Cannot some of our patriotic citizens take the matter in hand and collect one hundred blankets for my company? I know the citizens of Sunbury

---

19. *Sunbury Gazette*, October 26, 1861.

and the Augustas[20] will not refuse to help keep us warm this winter. Each can give a least one blanket, (no matter what color, although we would prefer dark,) and never miss it, while it would add to the comfort of the soldiers tenfold. Very frequently while on picket duty their overcoats and blankets are both saturated by rain. They must then wait until they can dry them by the fire before they can take their rest. I hope this matter will receive your kind attention, and you will receive the thanks of all the men. If the full number is not raised, send what you can, and they will be divided among the men, in the different tents. All contributions sent to my care to Washington, D.C., for Company C., 47th Regiment, P. V., will be thankfully acknowledged in behalf of my company.

Yours Respectfully,
J. P. SHINDEL GOBIN,
Capt. Comp. C. 47th Regt. P. V.

* * * * *

Camp Griffin,
November 3, 1861.[21]

Dear John:—I have just finished my supper, and while I am enjoying my pipe, I think I can put in a half hour in chronicling what little news we may have in this region. I dislike apologies, but nevertheless I think one is due you for my silence. But the fact is, we are kept so constantly at work that my entire time is taken up. We have forced our way thus far into Virginia, mainly over roads and bridges of our own construction, levelling the forests as we proceeded. Then, in addition, we are compelled to spend twenty-four hours every six days on picket. The men have become almost as handy with the axe and shovel as with the rifle, and I assure you they handle the latter article well.

Friday night, yesterday, and last night were, I think, the most disagreeable times we have yet experienced. We were visited with a most terrific storm, accompanied by a drenching rain. Numbers of the tents were blown over, the stakes being pulled out by the force of

---

20. Upper and Lower Augusta, the two townships immediately bordering Sunbury.
21. *Sunbury Gazette*, November 9, 1861.

the wind. Mine stood, but I expected every minute to see it go over. As it was[,] most of us got a good ducking. However, to-day it has cleared off nicely, and we are all right again, not the least impaired by the storm. Last night the men took possession of a neighboring barn where they spent the night in preventing each other from sleeping. Not even the storm could dampen their spirits.

On Tuesday last I was field officer of the pickets, and in company of Lieut. Geety and Sergent Piers, took a scout beyond our lines about three miles. We visited the site of the house of Mrs. Childs, which was burned a short time ago by a shell from Minors hill. The destruction was complete, house, barn, corn-crib—all were burned to the ground. The rebels had been sheltering themselves behind these and firing upon our pickets for some time, and Gen. Smith took this method to rid us of them. The remedy was effectual. The citizens were hovering around the ruins as we came up, who professed strong Union sentiments. Striking the Leesburg turnpike a short distance above[,] we encountered a horseman whom we stopped and notified that he must come with us. After some faltering he produced *documents* informing us that he was Gen. McDowell's guide and scout. He informed us that the nearest Rebel pickets were at Hunter's Mill, which is about two miles south-east of Vienna. The country through which we passed presented a desolate appearance. The houses are nearly all deserted, and those occupied are by women, or men too aged to do military service. We entered one house and found an old white-haired man, eating his supper, which consisted of boiled potatoes and water. Not a particle of salt, bread, coffee, or anything else eatable could be seen. The furniture and clothing were of the most wretched character. As we had not our haversacks with us, we could not add anything to his repast. At the point where our most advanced post rested two ladies reside, mother and daughter. The husband of the younger, she informed me, was in the Southern army. They were completely destitute of the necessities of life, and have been living off the rations of the pickets for some time. I had taken some ham along out with me, and got them to cook it and help me to eat it. My men gave them the contents of their haversacks, for which they were very grateful, and in return, gave the men, about the only thing they had, a lot of honey. These are but fair samples of the condition of families generally. Our men relieve them wherever they go.

Our picket lines run along by the house and farm of a man named Steward, who is a Quartermaster in the Rebel army. His wife is a sister of Jackson, the murderer of Ellsworth. She was caught giving information to the rebels, and was arrested and sent to Washington. I took occasion to look through the house in search of evidence, and among other articles found the enclosed, which you may give your readers the benefit of:

Mrs. Stewart:—Please accept our most hearty thanks for the nice breakfast we have partaken of, and of the kindness manifested to Southern soldiers. May your sorrows be dreams, and your joys bright realities. Your friends,
    J. R. RAMBO,
    J. B. EDMUNDSON,

Sept. 10th, 1861.

[This was written on the back of an envelope directed to James Rambo, 1st Regiment Virginia Cavalry, in care of Capt. W. E. Jones, of the Washington Mounted Rifles.]

We found several slaves and two small children at Stewart's, who are all in a state of want, and dependent upon our army for their daily subsistence.

Quite a number of old acquaintances have visited us during the last few days. Among the rest was Isaiah Gossler, 1st Sergent of Company K, 3d Pennsylvania Reserve. He was in the best of health and spirits, and looks the soldier all over. To-day Messrs. Goodrich and Geist, attached to the Band of the 5th Reserve, came to see us. Both were enjoying excellent health.

We have been expecting an advance for some time. Nearly every day we received orders to cook rations, and be ready to march. Before we have used up these rations we receive similar orders. We are becoming tired of this section, and would like to get out of it. Gen. McCall's pickets, about a mile and a half to the right of us, were driven in on Friday night, which seems to indicate an advance of the rebels. They will be warmly received if they come, as there are mostly, if not quite, 26,000 Pennsylvanians [illegible phrase] to show their mettle. Having a little leisure time this morning I rode through the 6th, 9th, 11th, and Bucktail Regiments. The men all looked hardy and content and seem satisfied to give a good account of the old Keystone stock.

On Friday last the brigade was marched over to Gen. Smith's head-quarters, formed in line and an invitation given to all who wished to serve in Ayre's Battery to step to the [illegible word]. They were to remain members of the company, receive the same pay, bounty, &c., but be on detached service. I am happy to say not one of my men availed himself of this opportunity to change, and but seventeen in our entire regiment. Quite a number of the New York 33d volunteered.

On the 31st we were mustered out, and our rolls are now in the Paymaster's hands. We expect to be paid in the course of a few days. We are anxiously awaiting the result of the naval expedition, as we feel confident we will follow up any success it may meet with. My men are in good health with the exception of a few fever cases, not in the least serious. Colds are prevalent but we do not mind them. I will write again when anything worthy of note occurs. We give thanks, hearty thanks to friends for their [illegible word] remembrances. I remain.

Yours, &c.
J. P. S. G.

* * * * *

Camp Griffin, Va.,
November 17, 1861.[22]

DEAR WILVERT:—As you perceive we are still at our old encampment, "out in the wilderness." This morning our brigade was out for inspection; arms, accoutrements, clothing, knapsacks, etc, all were put through a thorough examination, and if I must say it myself, our company stood best, A No. 1, for cleanliness. We have a new

---

22. *Sunbury American*, November 23, 1861.

commander to our Brigade, Brigadier General Brannen,[23] of the U.S. Army, and if looks are any criterion, I think he is a strict disciplinarian and one who will be as able to get his men out of danger as he is willing to lead them to battle.

There is a great difference in the treatment now to what we had in the three months service. The boys have plenty of work to do, such as picket duty, standing guard, wood-chopping, police duty and day drill; but then they have the most substantial food; our rations consist of fresh beef (three times a week), pickled pork, pickled beef, smoked pork, fresh bread, daily, which is baked by our own bakers, the Quartermaster having procured portable ovens for that purpose, potatoes, split peas, beans, occasionally molasses and plenty of good coffee, so you see Uncle Sam supplies us plentifully, and if we had what we draw cooked in Sunbury style and by Sunbury cooks, we would like as an old landlord, not far from town, used to say "like fighting cocks," but as it is our cooks do very well, the boys are gaining flesh rapidly, and some are assuming the appearance of Joe, the fat boy from Pickwick.[24]

A few nights ago our Company was out on picket; it was a terrible night, raining very hard the whole night, and what made it worse, the boys had to stand well to their work and dare not leave to look for shelter. Some of them consider they are well paid for the exposure, as they captured two ancient muskets belonging to Secessia. One of them is of English manufacture, and the other has a Virginia militia mark on it. They are both in a dilapidated condition, but the boys hold them in high estimation as they are trophies from the enemy, and besides they were taken from the houses of Mrs. Stewart, sister to the rebel Jackson who assassinated the lamented Ellsworth at Alexandria. The honorable lady, Mrs. Stewart, is now a prisoner at Washington and her house is the headquarters of the command of the pickets.

On last Sunday night, the 10th of this month, Lieutenant Vandyke, with three officers, [led] by a Virginia guide, were out reconnoitering for the purpose of capturing two horses belonging to a noted rebel. They were out about five miles beyond our pickets and came on, as they supposed, the sought for "contrabands;" they

---

23. Brig. Gen. John Milton Brannan (1819–1892).
24. A literary reference to a character from *The Pickwick Papers* by Charles Dickens.

entered the barn and soon brought out a "blooded nag," which proved, on examination of the teeth, to be an old stager some forty years old. The "old one" was let loose and the Lieutenant's party, nothing put out by their failure, proceeded on their enterprise. After a short advance, Secesh Cavalry were heard and the party took refuge in the woods, when an exclamation came from the guide, "By Heavens boys, we are surrounded by the infernal rebels but no give up, let us fight our way out or die like men." There was some confusion then, and I guess a "little 'fraid," but they were soon relieved from suspense, as the Lieutenant's quick eye soon discovered the cause of their alarm, and his merry, laughing shout of "sheep as sure as Jupiter," made them feel comfortable and sent them on their way rejoicing. The party, after being out all night, returned to camp pretty well jaded but not in the least disheartened. The same party intend going out on another "hunting" expedition, when they expect to be more successful. Anyone who is aware of the Sheriff's character,[25] well knows he never says fail, and you can depend on it that he won't come back from his second trip without fulfilling his purpose—either something contraband or what would suit his purpose better, a rebel prisoner.

Since the success of the secret expedition, we have all kinds of rumors in camp. One is that our Brigade will be sent to the relief of Gen. Sherman, in South Carolina. The boys all desire it and the news of the "Press" is correct, that a large force is to be sent there, I think their wish will be gratified. Our boys are all well and I am happy to inform you that the small-pox is completely exterminated from our Regiment.

Yours, fraternally,
H. D. W.

* * * * *

Camp Griffin, Va.,
November 18, 1861.[26]

Dear John:—We have been having a series of "right smart" storms in this region, one of which is now in progress. The wind blows as

---

25. Lieut. Vandyke formerly served as the sheriff of Northumberland County before the war.
26. *Sunbury Gazette*, November 23, 1861.

though it was determined to uproot everything that opposed its course. The soil being of a very yielding nature, we find it extremely difficult to keep our tents up, and still more so to arrange our chimneys so as to prevent them from smoking. The inhabitants in this vicinity tell me these storms are not as severe this fall as they usually are, but if it blows any harder than it did last Saturday, I think it would be rather hard to navigate.

Yesterday we were inspected by our new Brigadier General, J. M. Brannen. The men passed an excellent inspection, and were highly complimented by the staff for the excellent condition and cleanliness of their arms and clothing. The inspection lasted until about one o'clock, after which a party of us started for Falls Church, with a view of seeing the country, and getting a view of Fairfax Courthouse. I found Falls Church to be a village containing about twenty-five houses, two churches, a tavern, &c. The residences, with but few exceptions, were deserted, and stand there as living monuments of the folly of secession. The most of the houses are of a superior character, proving the owners to be persons of more than ordinary wealth and taste. Rows of cedar trees adorn each side of the street, and the yards around different residences give it a most beautiful appearance. The Church that gives the place its name is an old fashioned structure, in which Washington used to worship. It is built of brick imported from England prior to the Revolution. In conversation with a gentleman who resides near, I learned that the minister last officiating, had left with the greater portion of his flock for Secessia some time ago. About the time we arrived there the Chaplain of the 22d N. Y., was in the midst of an excellent discourse, so we entered and took seats. In every direction the walls bear evidence of the desire of different individuals for immortality. They are literally covered with names. I frequently found myself wandering from the thread of the discourse, and engaged in reading the names thus prominently paraded before us. The congregation was composed of soldiers from Maine, Massachusetts, New York, and a small delegation from Pennsylvania. However I must not forget to mention that *one* lady graced the occasion with her presence. After church we continued to venture a little further out, but we had proceeded but a short distance ere we were stopped by Gen.

Martindale, who was out on the same expedition, with his staff. He informed us that in consequence of a scouting parting being captured the day before, we would have to return. We reluctantly complied, and, after visiting Hall's Hill, Gen. Porter's headquarters, and Minor's Hill, Gen. Morrel's, we returned to camp.

The Camp has been alive with rumors of our being ordered to reinforce Gen. Sherman at Beaufort. There has been a number of division drills lately, with the alleged view of selecting the best drilled Regiments for that purpose. As ours is number one in that line, the men are very jubilant at the prospect of being selected. We have as yet received no positive orders, but are daily expecting them. The paymaster is to be here to-morrow to settle our demands, after which we are ready to start. The men are all very anxious to go.

James Quinn, who announces himself as "The Pennsylvania Artist," has established himself on this side of the Potomac, and occupies a part of the late residence of Commodore Jones, where he is doing a rushing business in the way of ambrotypes, &c. Should the army remain in this region for any length of time, he will reap quite a harvest.

I am happy to say that the health of the Company and Regiment are in the best condition. No cases of small pox have appeared since the death of Boultie. A few cases of fever are the only occupants of the Hospital. Two of my men were among the number, but both are improving finely, and one of them (D. W. Kemble) is almost well. The 7th Maine Regiment in our Brigade, has a sick list of 160, while ours this morning was but 27.

I desire to return my thanks, heartfelt and sincere, to my friends for their hearty and liberal response to my appeal. The blankets, stockings, &c. were received and distributed among the men, although some delay occurred in getting them from Washington. My men were very grateful for them, as they will render them comfortable in a measure. May kind Heaven reward you all.

Hoping my next letter will be dated further south, I remain

Yours, &c.
J. P. S. G.

* * * * *

Camp Griffin, Va.,
November 26, 1861.[27]

DEAR WILVERT:—Last Wednesday was a gala day for the soldiers on this side of the Potomac, it was a grand review, by General McClellan, of all the Volunteer troops encamped on the Virginia side of the river.—Never before, in this country, has there been assembled together such an immense body of armed men, as were reviewed then, on the "sacred soil" of Virginia. The review was held in some large fields between Munson's Hill and Ball's Cross Roads. From Munson's Hill, the view of the large army, passing before the President, Secretaries Cameron and Seward, General McClellan, with the Generals of the different Divisions, was magnificent, and I thought as I saw the seventy-five thousand men before me, men who were willing to die for their loved flag, that if they were at once marched on to Manassas, we should have an easy victory, the peace of our country restored and an end would be put to this unjust, cursed war.

The President, with the Secretaries above mentioned, on horseback, did not reach the ground until after twelve o'clock. They were followed by several regiments of cavalry, together with a mounted brass band. I did not have the pleasure of being close enough to the President to discern his features, which fact took away considerable of the day's pleasure.

I would suppose there was over thirty thousand civilians, looking at the review.—You can imagine, the road I passed over was about six miles, which was completely filled with vehicles of all sorts, from the finest barouche to a common furniture car, full of men, women and children, all trying their best to be on the ground first, so as to have the best position to obtain a sight of the grand affair. There was any number of ladies and gentlemen out on horseback. The ladies were elegantly dressed, some, *a la milataire*, and others in the highest style of fashionable art.

Sergeant Major Hendricks accompanied me, and while we were looking at the "bold soldier boys," a rabbit passed us, when the Major gave chase and soon returned, bringing the long-eared gentleman as prisoner. This capture of "secesh" hastened on the departure for camp.

---

27. *Sunbury American*, December 7, 1861.

On our way back many were the exclamations of the ladies, as they passed us, concerning the rabbit—the Major was asked so many questions, that he got tired answering, so that finally he held the animal up that they could all see it and take that as answer to all questions. Obe boy wanted to trade his horse on the rabbit, but on examination Hendricks concluded that his "*haus*" was more valuable than the old quadruped of the boy. The rabbit was brought to camp and next morning it was nicely served up, by Rigby, the Captain's cook, just in time for the Captain's breakfast, as he returned from picket.

The following are the Divisions and Batteries that were present at the review:

Gen. McCall's division with ten infantry and one cavalry regiment, and two batteries of artillery.

Gen. Heintzelman's division, with seven infantry and one cavalry regiments and two batteries.

Gen. Smith's division, with ten regiments of infantry, one cavalry and two batteries.

Gen. Franklin's division, twelve regiments of infantry, one of cavalry and three batteries.

Gen. Blenker's division, eleven regiments of infantry, one of cavalry and two batteries.

Gen. Porter's division, thirteen regiments of infantry, two cavalry and three batteries.

The boys in our Company are all very well. The health of the regiment is so good that it is observed by all visitors, whether civilians or soldiers. Out of the regiment there is but five in the Hospital, and those are cases that are not dangerous.

Yours fraternally,
H. D. W.

* * * * *

Camp Griffin,
December 9, 1861.[28]

Dear John:—Things move on [illegible phrase] here that there is nothing interesting to write about. We occupy the Camp we selected when we made the last advance. Save an occasional reconnaissance and plenty of picketing, we do nothing but drill and build huts, at both of which arts our Regiment are adepts. When not on other duty, we have a Regimental drill from 9 A. M. to 12 M., and a Brigade drill from 1 to 4 P. M. We get on picket duty an average every six days. On the day of the grand review at Bailey's Cross Roads, one half of our Regiment, including my company, together with parts of the 7th Maine, 33d and 46th New York, were detailed to extend and advance the picket lines of our (Smith's) Division. This prevented us from getting to the review, but we improved the time, and our lines now run about a half mile beyond Lewinsville. The extension brought a considerable amount of forage inside the lines, and the morning after an *observant* officer *might* have discovered the heads of sundry chickens protruding from sundry haversacks. It is needless to say Company C's were *empty.*

As some of your readers may not understand the method of picketing, I will endeavor to give you an idea of it as practiced here. The detail is made the evening before, and twenty-four hours rations for each man cooked. At 3 o'clock next morning, the men are roused up, knapsacks packed with a blanket, haversacks filled, rifles loaded, and you start for the general rendezvous. After the whole force arrives you start for the main reserve where the men are counted off in four equal reliefs, the first of which goes immediately to the outposts, and relieves the men there. The second relief goes to the special reserve half way between the main reserve and outposts, while the third and fourth remain at the main reserve until their turn comes to move. All this must be accomplished before daylight, so that at that hour the Rebels would be most likely to make an attack, fresh men are at every point. The first relief remains at the outposts until 12 M., when they are relieved by No. 2, while No. 3 takes their places at the special reserve, No. 1, returns to the main reserve. At 6 P. M., No. 3 goes

---

28. *Sunbury Gazette*, December 21, 1861.

to the outposts, No. 4 to the special, and No. 2 to the main reserve. The last change is made at 12 M., when No. 4 goes to the outposts and No. 1 to the special reserve. The men are fond of the duty in fine weather, but when it rains, which it does nearly every other day, it is very unpleasant. Fires are now allowed at the reserves, which are—the special, about half a mile, and the main a mile, from the outposts. It requires 850 men every 24 hours to do the picketing for our division. No one but a General or staff officer is allowed to pass the lines or along them, passes not being respected. Signals are used by which we can tell a friend or enemy, as soon as they are in sight. If a friend, they can approach within hailing distance; if enemies, within reach of your rifle. Last Friday a week was the most disagreeable time we have yet experienced. It rained hard all day and night, and was very cold. I had command of the first relief, which went to the special reserve at 12, M. By that time most of us were wet through, so I took possession of a minister's house, nearby, where I quartered my men until morning.

Adventures on the line are numerous, and we not unfrequently meet with open and avowed Secessionists, particularly among the ladies. I took dinner with one the other day, who was exceedingly indignant at the little respect the men had for the fences, declaring she would shoot them if they burned any more rails. As she was young and good looking, (only about eighteen, John) I did my best to pacify her, but I found it an exceedingly difficult job.

On last Friday, a reconnaissance was made by parts of McCall and Smith's divisions, for the double purpose of getting forage, and ascertaining the whereabouts of the Rebels. Our Brigade was marched over near Lewinsville, and held as a reserve. We remained there until the wagons containing forage, returned and announced the success of the expedition, when we returned to camp. They got 102 wagons of corn and 35 of hay and oats, besides penetrating as far as Hunter's Mills, driving in the enemy's pickets, and capturing several prisoners.

We have received no orders to go into winter quarters, but most of the men have built themselves substantial log huts, with "California fire places," which render them quite comfortable. Each man, or mess is their own architect, and the styles are various. To-night the weather is so warm that I am sitting without fire, and my tent open.

The health of my company and the entire regiment is good. I have but two men on the sick list, and they have but colds. Peter Wolf is almost well. The sick list of the regiment is about 40, none of them dangerous. The 7th Maine, in our Brigade, is not so fortunate, as for the last two weeks they averaged a death a day. They are improving, however. The men are very bitter against their Surgeon, and I have heard a number say they blamed him for the great mortality. With kindest regards to all friends, I remain

Yours truly,
J. P. S. G.

* * * * *

The Battle of Dranesville, December 20, 1861. (Credit: Library of Congress)

Camp Griffin, Va.,
December 29, 1861.[29]

Dear John:—I had fully expected to pass this Sabbath evening amid my friends at home, but on applying for a furlough I was very politely informed by Gen. Brannen that "the exigencies of the public service would not permit him to grant it." So Christmas and the holidays

---

29. *Sunbury Gazette*, January 4, 1862.

have been thus far spent in Camp, waiting like Micawber, for "something to turn up."[30]

Christmas was spent in a manner entirely different from that in which most of us were accustomed to spend it. No drilling was done, and the men scattered about as their inclinations led them. Most of us, however, dined on turkeys furnished by the sutler at $1.75 apiece. The day was very pleasant, and in the evening the New York 33d gave a Ball on their parade ground. As I sat in my quarters I could hear the familiar "all hands round" "swing your partners," sung out in a manner that showed they were going in with a will. There were no ladies present, nor was there a bar-room for the young men to frequent, and everything passed off finely. In one division of ten thousand men I did not on that day, see a single person intoxicated.

The particulars of the fight at Drainesville, I suppose, reached you as soon as it did us. The "long roll" sounded in our Camp about 12 M., [illegible phrase] me the first gun opened. [The following sentence is obscured by a water mark]. We double quicked it for six miles to [illegible word] Hill, just above Vienna, [illegible word] there to await for further orders. Drainesville was still four miles off and after a short rest, were very anxious to go on. We remained there until [illegible word] when we returned to Camp. The march was a hard one, but the sound of the cannon and musketry nerved the men to the task. It was a complete victory and is an additional proof of the bravery of Pennsylvanians. I conversed with several prisoners of the 10th Alabama and 1st Kentucky, and they admitted their loss to be very heavy. On Christmas I met a citizen of Drainesville, who informed us that they buried 160 bodies the day after the fight. The Rebels did not return for several days, but now they have about 15,000 men in that vicinity. How long they will remain there is a question that will be decided shortly.

There is a rumor prevalent in Camp that our Brigadier General Brannen is to be ordered elsewhere. He is one of the best officers in the service, and we should very much regret to lose him. Probably he will take us with him. I hope so.

---

30. Another literary reference, this time to the character Wilkins Micawber from Dickens's *David Copperfield*.

Gov. Curtin, Gen. Cameron, Bayard Tayler[31] and other noted Pennsylvanians visited the Reserve Corps to-day. The Governor made a most excellent speech complimentary of the bravery of Gen. Ord's Brigade. According to the late Act of Assembly he had ordered the word "Drainesville" to be inscribed upon the colors of the Regiments. They deserve it, and will yet have more battle fields to place thereon.

A barrel of fine sour krout [sauerkraut], presented, I learn, by your esteemed fellow-citizen, W. I. Greenough, Esq., to my company, arrived safely in Camp last evening. It was most acceptable I assure you, and relished by the men to-day, more highly than anything that could have been furnished them. Many thanks for this solid token of his remembrance.

The men are all in good health. Not a man on the sick list for a week but Peter Wolf, who is almost ready for duty. My Company is the most healthy in the Division, that I could learn of. We owe this in a great measure to the kindness of the friends at home.

Two of my men have been detailed on extra duty: H. D. Wharton, at Brigade Head Quarters, and John D. Colvin, on signal duty at Washington.

The familiar strains of "Old Hundred" as excellently performed by the Band of the 7th Maine, and the taps of the drum remind me that it is tattoo. So with love to all friends, I remain

Yours,
J. P. S. G.

* * * * *

Post Naval Academy,
Annapolis, Md.,
January 24, 1862.[32]

DEAR FRIENDS:—I arrived here yesterday with the regiment, all safe. We are for the present quartered in the building of the Naval Academy. We have excellent quarters, and are well situated. We expect

---

31. Bayard Taylor (1825–1878) was a noted poet, literary critic, and travel author from Chester County, Pennsylvania. In 1862 he was appointed to the Diplomatic Corps as secretary of legation at St. Petersburg.
32. *Sunbury Gazette*, February 1, 1862.

to go on board this afternoon, but I do not think we will leave here before to-morrow some time, probably not before Sunday. I have been in town only a short time, but it presents few objects of interest, being one of the antiquated cities so common in the southern States. Everything bears the impress of other generations.

The 11th Regiment, P. V., is quartered here. They have been here for four months, and have received no pay. [I visited George Kiehl] this morning in the hospital; he is suffering from Neuralgia. He expressed a hearty wish that he was with me. I was walking up the pavement this morning, and noticed a fine looking soldier on guard, parading up and down his beat with a true military tread. Imagine my surprise, when I came opposite, to hear him exclaim, "why, how are you[,] Captain?" I looked up and here was Theodore Robins. He looks well, and makes a fine looking soldier. John Clement also came to see me. He has not been well, but is getting better. Cyrus Swope also visited me.

We have received our new arms. They are the Springfield Rifles, and are a most beautiful arm. The officer at the armory said they were the best in the world. I am much pleased with them as are also the men. My men are all well and in good spirits.

I will write again soon. Direct all letters to Co. C., 47th Regiment, P. V., Key West, Florida. Remember me to all friends.

Yours,
J. P. S. GOBIN.

* * * * *

Steamship *Oriental*,
Chesapeake Bay,
January 27, 1862.[33]

Dear Friends:—As you will see by the heading of this, we are at last afloat, and on our way. We started from Annapolis to-day about 12 o'clock, and as I write we are traveling swiftly down the Bay. The Regiment was gotten on board without an accident of any kind, and

---

33. *Sunbury Gazette*, February 8, 1862.

the men are all well and in excellent spirits. In about 7 or 8 days we expect to land at Key West, nothing unusual happening.

We are all extremely glad to leave Annapolis, as it is one of the most distressed looking towns, as well as one of the dullest I ever saw. Our boat, the *Oriental*, is a new iron ship, splendidly fitted up, and perfectly safe. She is hired by the Government at the rate of one hundred dollars a day. Her captain is a young man strictly pious, and a perfect gentleman. He was married last week, and has his wife on board; she is quite young—does not look to be over 16 years old.

I suppose we will all have a nice attack of sea-sickness before we get through. However, I think I can stand it.

The pilot takes this letter back to Baltimore with him to-night, so I will have to close. The lamps are lit, and it is quite dark out. All of you write soon and often to Key West, until further notice. I will write again shortly, if I can get a chance to send it ashore. If not, I will write as soon as I get on shore. Remember me to all friends, and may God watch over you.

Yours,
SHINDEL.

* * * * *

Letters from the Taggart Guards
Company B, 34th Pennsylvania Volunteer Infantry
(5th Reserves)

Soon after the Bull Run defeat, amid fears of an imminent attack on the capital, the 34th Pennsylvania Volunteers (5th Reserves), including the Taggart Guards, moved from their camp at Piedmont, Virginia, to Washington. First, they returned to Camp Curtin for a short time to recruit and reequip, and then on August 8 the regiment marched south to a camp established for the Pennsylvania Reserves at the Washington suburb of Tennallytown in Maryland. There, the Reserves were organized into brigades, with the 5th Reserves constituting the 1st Brigade along with the 30th Pennsylvania (1st Reserves), 31st Pennsylvania (2nd Reserves), and 37th Pennsylvania

Volunteers (8th Reserves). Brig. Gen. John Fulton Reynolds assumed brigade command. On September 14, the 5th Reserves went to Washington to escort an entourage including Gov. Curtin, President Lincoln, and Gen. McClellan back to camp, where they reviewed the entire Reserve Corps. On October 10, the Pennsylvania Reserves relocated to Camp Pierpont at Langley, Virginia, where they established formal schools of instructions for the commissioned officers. During this time in camp, the 1st Brigade was called out twice for movements toward Dranesville on October 19 and December 20. In the latter advance, they reached the field too late to share in the 3rd Brigade's successful engagement against the Confederates. Otherwise, the Taggart Guards spent this period engaged in routine camp duties, drilling, and the construction of forts to protect the approaches to Washington.[34]

Camp Pierpont,
November 6, 1861.[35]

Dear Old Gazette.—It is a long time since I have taken up my pencil to let you know our whereabouts, but of course you have found out from other sources that the P. R. V. C., are on the sacred soil of Virginia, and on the right of the Grand Army of the Potomac. Our regiment, the 5th, is on the right of the 1st Brigade, so our friends at home and in Point township will see that when the fight does come off we will perform an important part. Our right extends to within half a mile of the river, and we have things just as near right as possible to give the Secesh a warm reception; so let them come when they think fit, for with our gallant old Colonel at our head, the old Keystone will have no cause to find fault with her sons.

In Camp we have nothing of more importance than the regular routine of duty—drilling, guarding, and picketing. The picket duty is not dangerous, as the Secesh are fifteen miles from us at least. They seem to give the Reserves a wide berth. Wherever we go we have tried hard to see some of them, but they are very scarce on our line. Company B has been favored with a sight of but few of them in arms. In our reconnaissance of the 18th of last month we saw some fine

---

34. Bates, *Pennsylvania Volunteers*, 1:665–666.
35. *Sunbury Gazette*, November 16, 1861.

girls at [Dranesville]. They said they were sorry that we had come out to disturb them—that there never would be a Union again—no, never, never. But when we fell back on the village again, and stayed over Sunday, they seemed to have a better opinion of the boys, and not so opposed to the Union.

Coffee and salt were very scarce in and about the village. Coffee could not be got at any price, and salt was worth $9 per sack, so they will have to eat their food without salt. Some of the folks among them treated us well and wished us luck. Our teamsters fed their stock with hay that had been in the hands of the Secesh. We came upon them so suddenly that they had to drop it. We had a right nice march on the way out. Company B being on the left flank of the regiment, was detached as skirmishers, and were forced to make the whole distance through the woods, with knap-sacks on, and forty rounds of cartridges in our boxes, so you may believe it was warm work, and the loads on our backs felt like lumps of lead before we halted.

I see in some of the papers from home of efforts making to send blankets to the soldiers. If they are all as well supplied as the 5th Regiment of Reserve they would not know how to take care of them, for we have more baggage than we ought to have. It takes about forty teams to haul our baggage, and every man has more than he can well carry. So our friends who want to send us blankets had better wait until we go into winter quarters. But socks would come good now, and almost every one of the boys would like a present of that kind from home.

We had our old friend, Major Taggart, to spend the evening with us on the 3d, and he pleased us all with news from home. He visited our Chaplain, and distributed some books among the boys to pass away the time and impart religious knowledge.

The Washington papers have just come. I hear the newsboy singing out—"Charleston taken—five thousand prisoners taken!" Of [course] the Fleet has not yet reached Charleston. Smart boy that, and he sells his papers quick, the boys taking the joke all in fun, telling him to go ahead and do the best he can, as long as he is for the Union.

Mr. Youngman, the soldiers in our company are pleased with the *Gazette* and its course, and hope that you will continue to tell what you think of those who oppose the war and the Administration. The rebel sympathizers have not got the nerve to fight or do anything but growl at the Administration. They are laying up treasures in the minds and hearts of the right feeling citizens which will be handed down from generation to generation. So continue on in your course and the P. R. V. C. will back you to the number of fifteen thousand.

I would like you to let us know through your paper why Northumberland County don't pay anything to the families of the married volunteers? If the reason is that our old county has gone over to the rebels, then I, for one, am content. Tell us what has become of the $1500 that was to be raised by the *patriotic* men of Northumberland County. Let them know that their course is commented upon freely by the men of families here. They should consider that soldiering is not so pleasant a business at this season of the year, lying out in tents, that the married men can be content to have their families suffer, while those at home, surrounded by all the comforts, toast their shins by a good coal fire, and reap the benefits we are fighting for.

We have a fine company of men, willing to do their duty. They will compare favorably with any in the Reserve. The guard house is not necessary for us. We have not had one fight in the company. We live together in perfect harmony, and it would do you good to see them at night circling around a camp fire, and listening to some veteran boatman making his trip to Baltimore in some storm when the waves run as high as flour barrels. I wish some of our friends in Point township could come down and see their boys. They are all well and make the best kind of soldiers.

Good bye, for this time. Send us on the paper whether we write again or not. To all those who have taken the old constitution and the old flag close to their hearts, give a soldier's blessing, and for those who think the constitution is torn, and our flag is no better than any other piece of muslin, pass them by. They may stop your paper, but you will live and thrive when they are forgotten.

Your friend,
OLD SOLDIER.

* * * * *

Camp Pierpont,
December 21, 1861.[36]

Dear Old Gazette:—I take up my pencil to give our friends a little sketch of the maiden fight of the Pennsylvania Reserves on the 19th.

When we came off Brigade Drill the day before, our gallant old Colonel said "I want my command to be ready to march at half past eight to-morrow morning." Of course his command was ready, and marched at the time appointed, at the head of the Brigade, out the Leesburg pike as far as the Difficult Creek. There we filed left and marched about three quarters of a mile, halted[,] and stacked arms. The men, in the meantime, employed and amused themselves in different ways—building fires and making coffee, some throwing the shoulder stone, and other discussing the object of our march. We discovered that we had been marched out there as a reserve to the third Brigade, which had gone out on a foraging expedition towards [Dranesville].

Everything was going on finely; even Company Q were enjoying themselves as well as could be expected in the absence of their Captain; they having a very spirited skirmish with a rabbit, in which there were no lives lost, the rabbit retreating in good order. But soon the boom of a cannon was heard in the distance, when the order was given to fall in and march. It was discovered that our artillery could not cross the creek in the direction we were marching; so the order was given to right about to the pike. About this time a volley of musketry was heard, which made the men very anxious. Accordingly we filed left and made for the creek, not waiting to measure the water. Our Captain went in and his men were not backward in following him, for they were all eager for the fray. After we got on the pike[,] we began to meet the teams with hay, and to receive news of the fight. We then did some tall marching. It was "forward—double quick"—and we needed no further command. The trouble was to keep the boys from getting ahead of their files.

The first thing we met that looked like work was a lad belonging to the Bucktails, with two balls in his leg, supported between two comrades. We asked him how the fight was getting along. He said,

---

36. *Sunbury Gazette*, January 4, 1862.

"fine—we have licked them." He had the balls in his hand, the Doctor having extracted them.

The head of our column then came in contact with three suspicious looking men with muskets, inquiring the way to Centreville. We inquired where they belonged, and upon their replying, "to the 10th Alabama," they were told that we would take care of them. One of them attempted to run, but was knocked down and secured, so it will be some time before they see Alabama again.

It was mortifying to us to be too late for the fight. The Bucktails and their [illegible word] having done the work so well there was nothing for us to do. [An extended illegible phrase follows, obscured by a large water stain.] killed and wounded. The rebels carried off some of their dead, but our boys hurried them up so that they had to drop their wounded and make for tall timber. There were some curious expressions made in regard to the wounded. One of our boys discovered a man who had lost his head by a cannon ball. He said he hunted around for the head, and could not account for its absence, unless its owner had sent it off to get shaved.

Some of our men were excused on the morning of the march; but when they heard the firing, three of them put on their harness and came out to us. The three were Alonzo Copp, Willard Eckert, and James R. Little. Such is the stuff that Company B is made of.

I suppose our General understood his business, but it strikes me that for a reserve we were stationed rather far from where the work was done. Seven miles are rather far to march to get into a fight, but if ever any poor fellows tried hard to be on the spot, the 5th did. It was not our fault, for we made seven miles in one hour and twenty minutes. As we were the reserve in the morning, so we were the reserve on our return to camp, the 5th being the rear-guard, reaching camp at half past 10, P. M., having made a march of twenty-five miles. If we did none of the fighting, we had some of the work to do. The folks at home, and the Secesh, by this will find that the P. R. V. C. don't go out foraging without having some men to load the wagons.

It appears from letters found on the battle ground, that the Secesh were aware of our men coming out foraging, and started from Centreville at two o'clock in the morning, so as to meet them. The

Secesh returned to Centreville, about the same hour in the afternoon, rather the worse for their visit, leaving blankets, overcoats, haversacks, and everything that was loose about them. We left their dead on the battle field and brought our own home.

Charley McGregor tells me the Bucktails will send their dead home to their friends. Col. Kane, of the Bucktails, was wounded three times during the engagement, twice with musket balls, and once from the explosion of a shell, but he fought on through it all. One of the privates went through the whole fight, and walked back to camp, with a musket ball through his cheek. The Bucks had their blood up, and there was no stopping them. They, with the rest of the Pennsylvania troops, are of the right stuff, for troops that can march twenty-five miles, and then fight for two hours and put five thousand rebels to route, are able to do almost anything.

Mr. Editor, I hear rumors from home that some of the folks there are making free with our Captain's name. If they knew what his Company think of him, and how he is regarded by the Regiment, they would hide their heads in shame and confusion. But, poor fellows, we pity them—they have not the heart to fight for their country, but have the spunk to backbite those who have gone to fight the enemy and are not at home to give the lie to their slang. Let them ask men that have been among us what they think of Company B? Ask Philip Gibbons and John Kapp, if there is anything wrong in officers or men. But there is no use for me to say any more on this subject. Our Captain does his duty without fear or favor; but he don't command the army of the Potomac—so they need not expect him to break up the 5th Regiment because he can't have things as he wants them.

There is something wrong with the Express Company. It appears to me that I having read notices in the papers that the express would carry soldiers' packages for half freight. If it is half freight they charge us, God help those that must pay full freight. The box of stockings came safe, and were good ones, like the ladies who sent them. The kindness of the ladies at home sends a gleam of sunshine across our path, and cheers us on in the good work we have in hand. The boys of Company B unite in sending their thanks for this and past favors, and hope they may live to repay in part, if not in full, the kindness of the ladies of Northumberland and vicinity, and to show by their conduct on the battle field that they are in earnest in the matter, and that our country's flag to them is a sacred thing which, in their sight, dares not to be touched by rebel hands.

Yours truly,
OLD SOLDIER.

* * * * *

[The following letter from a Northumberland Volunteer was handed to us for publication.]

Camp Pierpont, Va.,
January 30, 1862.[37]

We still occupy the same camp that we did three months ago; but it has a different appearance now from what it had at that time; for then the fences were all in good condition, and our tents were pitched in the centre of at least fifty acres of good wood land. Our tents have never been moved since, but now there is not a stick of wood within one quarter of a mile distant, only here and there a tree standing among the tents, which would be dangerous to fall in any direction, on account of the injury they might do. As for rails or fences, I don't think there is either of them between the Chain Bridge and our out-post picket line, unless it is a few rails that some of the boys have reserved for bed ticks in preference to the hard ground. *That is, the kind of feathers I sleep on.*

All of company B are in good health now, with the exception of two or three that are on the sick list, having bad colds. There are none in the hospital. I suppose you have heard that John Smith, belonging to the Cameron dragoons, a son of Mr. James Smith, of Point township, was very poorly with the typhoid fever. His brother James D. Smith, and a young man named Louden, were down to see him last week. They also paid us a short visit. They returned home on Monday last. I wish that more of our friends could come down and see how well we enjoy ourselves. We have splendid officers, Taggart, Wells and Slater. Three better men don't inhabit the earth, and there is our

---

37. *Sunbury Gazette*, February 15, 1862.

respected Col. S. G. Simmons, whom all of the boys in the Regiment are proud of.

We all keep close to our tents [in] such weather as this. We have had but one clear day since the thirteenth of the present month, and that was last Sunday. It has been raining more or less all that time, with the exception of one night when it hailed and snowed. Company B was on camp guard that night. It is raining here to-day as usual, and the mud, in and about the camp, ranges from three to six inches deep, and over about the artillery regiment it is much worse. This would be rather an unfavorable time for an onward move. But in case such a thing should be called for, we are ready. I saw in the *Philadelphia Press* of yesterday that the Pennsylvania Reserves were expected to be attacked. It seems strange that we, being on the extreme right and the farthest in advance, never knew anything of it till we saw the account in the papers. But I guess if the rebels come here to raise a *muss*, they will find something pointed at them out here on a hill, that they will have some trouble with.

I suppose you would like to know in what kind of style we live here. I will try to tell you. Early in the winter the most of us built log huts, and roofed them, some with poles, taking earth and throwing it over top; others made a kind of shingles for roofing, and some are built partly with logs, with the tent stretched over the top. A small camp stove inside makes them warm, comfortable, and agreeable. On these stoves we do all our cooking. *It will learn us to keep house in case we should happen to be so unlucky as to be old bachelors!*

Coffee is the principal beverage we use here in camp, and if a soldier has to do without his coffee a day or two he thinks it awful hard living. But that is something that don't happen while we are in camp, unless the wind blows contrary for our stoves, and causes them to smoke, so that we are obliged to throw the fire out of doors in order to hold possession of the tent. But while the wind blows contrary to us, it blows favorable to somebody else, which will only go to illustrate the truth of the old proverb,—"It's an ill wind that blows nobody any good."

I hear the Quarter Master hollowing, "Company B, fall in for your bread!" It appears to me that I love the sound of that man's voice much more when he calls out "bread and beef," than when he sings out "crackers and pork." It's a wonder that they never had any of these cast iron pies to sell in some of the stores around home. There being such a quantity of them used here a person would naturally suppose they should command a good price, the same as sugar and coffee. But, however, they are a very good thing to gnaw at while on a march, or even when a person gets out of employment. We can just take a haversack full of them, and eat a whole day, and not founder ourselves either, for they are considered wholesome food. But we are supplied with fresh bread nearly all the time, and a good part of the time we have beef; so we have no reason to complain.

Captain John Croly, of company Q, started from this place yesterday afternoon on a visit to Northumberland. I suppose he will enjoy himself very well among his old friends of that place. His first Lieutenant will take charge of his company during his absence. Now I will close for this time. Give my kind regards to all my friends. Adieu till you hear again.

From your cousin,
PETER.[38]

* * * * *

Camp Pierpont, Va.,
January 30, 1862.[39]

Friend Youngman:—Having a few leisure hours I will address a few lines to you about the Northumberland boys, for I know you and the friends are always glad to hear from them; but as you have had a description of the camp, and where we are now stationed, that would be nothing new to you. The 5th Regiment P. R. C. still hold the right of the Grand Army of the Potomac, and I think always will. The Boys are all well, excepting a few that have bad colds, which we are all liable to take anywhere; but in every other respect they are well and eager for the fray. We have had a little alteration made in mounting

---

38. The writer is likely 2nd Lt. Peter Vandling, Company B, 5th Pennsylvania Reserves. See Bates, *Pennsylvania Volunteers*, 1:675.
39. *Sunbury Gazette*, February 8, 1862.

guard. Before this last week there were so many detailed out of each company as guard around the camp, but now a company at a time act as Camp Guard, and as last Friday was Company B's turn, they acted as Camp Guard. It was not a very pleasant duty to perform, for it had been raining all day before, and rained all the next day. You may well know that it was not pleasant. The boys, however, did it willingly, and without grumbling; they know that good soldiers won't grumble at anything they are ordered to perform. We cannot expect fine weather all the time, so we must take our chance with the rest. We have had some very unpleasant weather since we have come on the Sacred Soil; in fact, we cannot expect any better this time of the year. We all know that the Colonel will not ask us to do duty when it is not fit, only in cases where strict military discipline requires it, and these are camp and picket guard. Yesterday was the first fine day we have had for some time. The Colonel thought that a little exercise would be good for the men, so he ordered each commanding officer to supply his command with ten rounds of blank cartridges, and go out and practice in firing and drilling. I think the men were none the worse of it.

We have no reason to believe that a fight will come off soon. I was very much amused this morning by the news-boy coming into camp upon an old nag which looked as if the crows would carry her out of camp before he could sell his papers. The boy's mouth was stretched open from ear to ear, hollowing, "the Pennsylvania Reserves to be attacked!" I tell you, he soon sold out his papers; but I see that the rebels have really meditated an attack on Gen. McCall's Division. If they attack the Reserve they will find there will be no more Bull Runs. We have had several visits from our friends from home, and you can well imagine how well we were pleased to receive the friends we have been parted from so long. Nothing pleases us more than to receive a friend. We are all anxious for all our friends who can possibly do so, to pay us visits. It is not only pleasant to receive them, but to receive their kind letters. You ought to see the boys when the Orderly hollows, "fall in Company B for letters!" and the smiling faces and pleasant looks of those who are among the lucky ones.

Our Regiment I think is about one of the most healthy in the Reserve. There are but a few cases of sickness in it, and these are slight ones, principally fever and ague. The 5th is composed of some very good fighting material, and they hold a post of honor which will never be deserted in the thickest of the fight. I think there will soon be a fight, for there will shortly be a grand move of the army of the Potomac, and then the blow will be struck, and followed up till the Stars and Stripes wave over every city, town and village in Rebeldom.

C. W. S.[40]

* * * * *

Letter from Isaiah S. Gossler
Company K, 32nd Pennsylvania Volunteer Infantry
(3rd Reserves)

The general experiences of the 5th Reserves were shared, and briefly recorded, by two other Northumberland County residents who enlisted in different Reserve regiments. The first, Isaiah S. Gossler, a thirty-one-year-old boat builder from Sunbury, joined Company K, 32nd Pennsylvania Volunteers (3rd Reserves) on May 27, 1861, while the unit was assembling in Bucks County. The company initially encamped at Easton, Pennsylvania, until it went to Harrisburg and was officially mustered into serve as the 3rd Reserves on July 27. Then, the regiment proceeded to the Pennsylvania Reserves camp at Tennallytown on August 2, where it was organized along with the 33rd (4th Reserves), 36th (7th Reserves), and 40th Pennsylvania Volunteers (11th Reserves), under the command of Brig. Gen. George G. Meade. On October 9 the regiment relocated to Camp Pierpont near Langley, Virginia, and settled into routine picket duties, fort construction, and occasional skirmishing, while also participating in the several movements against Confederate forces at Dranesville. Gossler's lone missive to the hometown newspapers during this period was sent from Camp Pierpont.[41]

---

40. The author is possibly Pvt. Christian Starrick. He enlisted in Company B, 5th Reserves, on October 9, 1861, and was killed at the Battle of Fredericksburg on December 13, 1862. The only other initials that match is Pvt. Charles W. Scout, but he was discharged from service on a Surgeon's certificate on August 7, 1861. See Bates, *Pennsylvania Volunteers*, 1:676.

41. Bates, *Pennsylvania Volunteers*, 1: 609–610.

Camp Pierpont,
Fairfax Co., Va.,
November 3, 1861.[42]

E. WILVERT, Dear Friend:—At your request, and to fulfil my promise made by me to keep you posted in the movements of our regiment. And as to-day is Sunday, the day of rest to the soldier as well as the civilian, I can think of nothing with which to pass the time more profitably than by describing to a friend some of our regiment's movements. About the longest march we have had was August 6th, we marched as body guard for Gen. McCall on a reconnaissance as far as the Falls, a distance of 12 miles. We arrived back at camp about dark, marching 24 miles on one of the hottest days of the season. Nothing of any consequence occurred until the 23d, when we were ordered out with the other Penn. Reserve Regiments for a grand review by the President and Gen. McClellan. It was a beautiful sight.

The intervening time is taken up by the men performing fatigue duty, cutting down woods, building forts, &c. on the 11th of Sept., the greater portion of the regiment were clearing and cleaning ground so as to extend the limits of our camp. About 4 o'clock on that day, cannonading was heard in the direction of Chain Bridge; we received orders to pack one day's rations and fill our canteens with water and be ready to fall into line at a moment's notice, while doing so, the Adjutant came into camp, his horse in a perfect foam. The orders came and we were fully armed and on the march, as all thought to our first fight, in twelve minutes. Soon afterwards the Artillery passed us and took the lead, when the whole line moved in order towards the Chain Bridge. When the head of line reached there, we were brought to a halt by meeting the Sixth Wisconsin Regiment coming back. We returned and arrived at camp at 9 o'clock, when three cheers were given to Gen. McCall and three to Horatio G. Sickles, our loved Colonel.

October 14th, a sad and fatal accident occurred. A Battery of Artillery was stationed on the hill in front of our lines, and as usual, many were looking on. A young man was lying down, his head resting on his right arm. Orders were given for the first time for "ground

---

42. *Sunbury American*, November 16, 1861.

arms," our muskets were all loaded with ball and three buck-shot. One was accidentally discharged, the ball passing through the young man's arm near the elbow joint, making a compound fracture, passed through the tent and into the heart of an elderly man, who was writing a letter home, he staggered out of the tent and fell dead. The body was sent home the next day, escorted part of the way by two of our companies and band.

About 12 o'clock P. M., on the 18th our cooks were ordered to prepare two day's rations. On the 19th, the whole Division moved out the Leesburg pike and all thought we would soon see a fight. The Kane Rifles[43] (one of the Reserves,) taking the lead and acted as scouts for the Division. After marching about 7 miles, we halted, formed in line of battle, stacked arms and retired to rest and sleep; the ground for a bed and the canopy of Heaven for our covering. The next day was passed in lounging about. Towards evening the Colonel sent to camp for two day's more provision. On the morning of the 21st, our company and Co. E. were ordered on picket duty 3 miles further, where we arrived at daybreak, formed our reliefs, posted the men. After breakfast[,] squads of 2 and 3 started in search of contraband food (at least so we called it). It was not long before potatoes and cabbage arrived. Before the rest returned[,] firing of cannon was distinctly heard.—Fight somewhere, was the cry, and it was not long before Adjutant Johnson came and ordered us to march to the road to join company E., and march to join our regiment. Before we reached the road the provision scouts joined, some with chickens, geese and ducks, and we passed a place where some of the boys had a porker skinned and quartered, which they had to leave. One party came in with a small porker and found us gone, they dropped hog, and started double quick until they caught us, thereby cheating the company out of [a] splendid banquet. We joined our regiment and marched back to camp. Two day's rations were ordered and the men to rest so they would be ready to march at a moment's notice. We received the news

---

43. 13th Pennsylvania Reserves (42nd Pennsylvania Volunteers), also known as the "Bucktails," commanded by Col. Thomas L. Kane.

of Col. Baker's death and the loss [at] Balls Bluff on the 23d.[44] It was a great blow to us, for we afterwards heard that we were within 7 miles of that doomed band of heroes and no show for us to march to their assistance.

At the present writing, it is cold enough to make us feel for overcoats and a little fire.

Respectfully, Your Friend,
I. S. GOSLER.

* * * * *

Letter from William Seiler
Company B, 35th Pennsylvania Volunteer Infantry (6th Reserves)

The second correspondent, William Seiler, was originally from Lower Mahanoy Township but enlisted in Company B, 35th Pennsylvania Volunteers (6th Reserves) from neighboring Snyder County on May 28, 1861. The regiment organized at Camp Curtin on June 22, and then went to Camp Biddle at Greencastle on July 12. The day after the battle at Bull Run, the regiment left for Washington, marching via Harrisburg and Baltimore, and arriving on July 24. They were formally mustered into federal service on July 27 and then moved to the Reserves encampment at Tennallytown. Organized as part of the 3rd Brigade under Col. John S. McCalmont, along with the 38th (9th Reserves), 39th (10th Reserves), and 41st Pennsylvania Volunteers (12th Reserves), the regiment participated in the reconnaissance against Dranesville on October 19 to drive away enemy pickets and procure forage supplies, as well as the advance on December 20, during which the 3rd Brigade formed into line of battle, with the 9th Reserves holding the right flank, the 6th Reserves in the center, and the 42nd Pennsylvania Volunteers (1st Reserves) on the left with the 10th and 12th Reserves in support. Advancing down the Leesburg Pike, the brigade received artillery fire before

---

44. The Battle of Ball's Bluff, on October 21, 1861, resulted in a Union defeat and the death of Col. Edward D. Baker, a former Illinois congressman and then-current U.S. senator from Oregon who was a close personal friend of President Lincoln.

they crossed a field and ascended a sloping hill to confront a force under Brig. Gen. James Ewell Brown (Jeb) Stuart. After exchanging several volleys, the Reserves charged and drove the Confederates from the field. The affair at Dranesville, although minor in size, became the first battlefield victory for the Pennsylvania Reserves.[45]

[The following letter is from one of the Volunteers of Lower Mahanoy township, in this county, serving in the Company of Capt. Roush, of Union county, in the 6th Regiment Pennsylvania Volunteers. Boys who talk and act as the writer does will not fail to make good soldiers:]

Camp Pierpont,
November 6, 1861.[46]

DEAR FATHER:—Having received my pay and having a little leisure time, I write you the following. We are still in Virginia, and expect an advance movement. The weather is rough and cold. Great military operations are going on. Many are drills, and beautiful are the reviews we have down here.

You will find twenty dollars enclosed in this letter which I have not present use for, and as a dutiful son I consider it right to send it to you, which I ask you to take care of for me. If you need it use it yourself. I am well so is John. We are both getting along first rate and like the life we are now leading better than part of our life previous to this.

All the boys that went back are cowards, for they could all have got $13.00 per month and needed not to have worked hard.

No more at present, from your affectionate son.

WILLIAM SEILER.

* * * * *

---

45. Bates, *Pennsylvania Volunteers*, 1: 692–693.
46. *Sunbury American*, November 16, 1861.

Letters from the Augusta Rangers
Company I, 58th Pennsylvania Volunteer Infantry

In November 1861 another local recruiting effort in Sunbury resulted in the formation of a company that styled itself the Augusta Rangers. Led by Capt. John Buyers, a thirty-three-year-old farmer, whom the local press regarded as "an officer in whom every confidence can be placed," the Augusta Rangers would eventually become Company I of the 58th Pennsylvania Volunteers when that unit finally organized at Camp Curtis in Philadelphia on February 13, 1862 (early press reports had speculated that the Rangers would be assigned as Company F of the 38th Pennsylvania, 9th Reserves, but that company ultimately was raised in Meadville, Crawford County). Company I actually reflected a consolidation of recruits from both Northumberland and Luzerne Counties, since neither location had raised a full quota of men.[47] While still stationed in Philadelphia at the end of January 1862, Capt. Buyers had the unfortunate occasion to write home to the parents of company member Henry K. Conrad, who had enlisted on January 23 and then died the very next day in a Harrisburg hospital. That sad duty, however, was tempered somewhat by a message of thanks that Buyers also passed along to the women of Sunbury for their donation of mittens to the company.

Headquarters,
Philadelphia, Pa.,
January 24, 1862.[48]

MR. & MRS. DANIEL CONRAD.—*Dear Friends:*—It was with feelings of deepest grief that we heard of the death of your son Henry K. Allow us to share in your feelings, for rest assure[d] your son was with us as a brother, and we had vainly hoped that we would go hand in hand through this struggle for liberty. But the God of nations chose differently, and in His all wise Providence cut off your son just in the bloom of military glory. He was a brave, reliable youth, an ornament to his company, and beloved by all who knew him. We are

---

47. Bates, *Pennsylvania Volunteers*, 2:285; *Sunbury Gazette*, November 2, 1861.
48. *Sunbury Gazette*, February 1, 1862.

sorry that circumstances were such as to prevent us from following his remains to their resting place. We, the Augusta Rangers, wish to express our deep sense of grief at the loss of our brother soldier, whom we loved and admired, and will ever hold in grateful remembrance, your loss is his company's as well as our loss. But Henry has gone to a better, and brighter home; his virtues have found more congenial companionship among the soldiers of a purer world.

The Augusta Rangers,
per J. BUYERS, Capt. Com.

* * * * *

Headquarters,
Philadelphia, Pa.,
January 24, 1862.[49]

To the Ladies of the Sunbury Knitting and Sewing Society:

Allow me on the part of my company, to tender to you our most grateful thanks for the favor of twenty-three pairs of mittens, which they were pleased to send us by the hands of Miss Maria Fisher. We are much pleased with the gift, but much more by the thought of being remembered by friends at home.

Augusta Rangers,
per J. BUYERS, Capt. Com.

* * * * *

Letters from Chaplain Peter Rizer
79th New York State Militia
(Cameron Highlanders)

After returning from Manassas, the 79th New York Highlanders went back into camp at Kalorama Heights and engaged in digging defensive fortifications while efforts were made to replace the 198 casualties they

---

49. *Sunbury Gazette*, February 1, 1862.

sustained at Bull Run. Most importantly, the War Department appointed Colonel Isaac I. Stevens as regimental commander (he was later promoted to brigadier general on September 28). Surprisingly, the appointment caused a mutiny to erupt within the 79th New York on August 14, as the men felt slighted in not having been granted a say in the replacement of their beloved Colonel Cameron. As well, they resented being forced to remain in the field while most of the three-month New York men were allowed to go home (this despite the fact the 79th had signed three-year enlistments). The grievances were eventually resolved, but it is surprising that Chaplain Rizer made no mention of the incident in his correspondence home.[50]

What Rizer did describe in much detail, however, was the 79th New York's participation in the Port Royal Expedition. After being posted near Lewinsville, Virginia, in September, where they engaged in several successful skirmishes, the regiment was attached on October 21 to the 2nd Brigade (under Stevens) of Brig. Gen. Thomas W. Sherman's Expeditionary Corps, the Army component of a joint land-naval force under both Sherman and Naval Flag Officer Samuel F. Du Pont. The expedition intended to target the South Carolina coast around Port Royal. The regiment proceeded to Annapolis and then to Hampton Roads, Virginia, where they boarded the Army transport Vanderbilt *and embarked for Hilton Head, South Carolina. The expedition was battered by storms, which scattered some of the vessels and caused the loss of the Army's landing boats (effectively eliminating their participation in the planned assault), but on November 3 the fleet reached the entrance to Port Royal Sound. After some preliminary maneuvering, the warships attacked the two forts guarding the entrance to the sound, forcing the Confederates to surrender.*[51]

In Bivouac, near the Chain Bridge,
Fairfax County, Va.,
Headquarters, 79th Reg., N. Y. S. M.
September 7, 1861.[52]

H. B. MASSER, ESQ., *Dear Sir:*—In lack of the usual facilities, my writing must be limited and condensed. Our Regiment, under Col.

---

50. McKnight, *Blue Bonnets O'er the Border*, 30–42.
51. McKnight, *Blue Bonnets O'er the Border*, 47–52.
52. *Sunbury American*, September 14, 1861.

Stevens, though less than 500 effective men, was ordered here on last Tuesday night, from Camp Hope. Intelligence had been received that the enemy was advancing and had shown much impudence. In less than two days an immense Federal force was assembled at this point, ranging about a mile along the banks of the Potomac, and extending about a mile and a half inland. Gen. Smith has command, with his Headquarters on the main road leading to Leesburg. Col. Stevens has command of the left wing, numbering 4,000 or 5,000. By Thursday evening formidable breastworks were thrown up on the highest hill, which is an admirable military selection, and commands a wide range of country. In the Fort, which includes an area of about two acres, and in my judgment, is superior to Fort Corcoran, there are many 32 pounders, and one 68-pounder. Outside there is a trench to be used as a rifle pit. In front there are numerous masked batteries, surrounded by felled timber, which will very materially impede the enemy's progress. The timber has been nearly all felled for some distance in and around the intrenchments.

In our vicinity are other forts, and I understand that all along the line of the Potomac there are ample preparations made to receive the enemy. Here on the left, at an elevation from which you can plainly see the dome of the Capitol, some seven or eight miles distant, we have also breastworks, rifle pits, and many pieces of ordnance. It is highly probable that all these preparations, which have been made in an incredibly short time, operate to hold the enemy in check. Yesterday and the day before, a rebel flag could be seen at a distance of about two miles from our lines, and we were in hourly expectations of an attack. But up to this (Saturday) morning we are in *status quo*. The impression seems to be gaining ground that the Rebels are beginning to see that the call for 400,000 Union troops is a sober reality, and that with them discretion would be the better part of valor.

You may rest assured that our Government is truly in earnest now, and that General McClellan is the man for his work. I can see the most manifest improvement in our military operations. Col. Stevens, as well as Gen. McClellan, is a rigid disciplinarian. He told me the other day, that he was "a perfect Oliver Cromwell on the subject of religion in the army," and that he felt greatly the importance of a chaplain, especially when going into action. "If you cannot pray *with* the Regiment," said he, "I want you to pray in secret, for I have the most implicit confidence in prayer." I have noticed, also, that since the battle of Bull Run, no movements are made on the Sabbath, as had previously been the case.

Yesterday, a Captain of the 5th Wisconsin Regiment, quartered on the same hill with us, went out some two miles scouting on horseback, and happened to fall in with four rebel scouts. He was immediately ordered to surrender. The Captain, putting his hands behind his back, apparently to present his pistols, cocked them, and drawing them round, one in each hand, instantly fired them both, and killed the two mounted scouts. Those on foot then fired at him while he was retreating in full gallop. One shot took effect slightly in his left arm, and the other penetrated both cheeks, without, however, doing the slightest damage to a good set of teeth. The wounded Captain is not much hurt.

I saw two live rebels under arrest day before yesterday at the Headquarters of Gen. Smith. They had an impudent appearance.

God grant that this wicked rebellion may soon be put down.

Yours, Truly,
P. RIZER, Chaplain 79th Reg.

P.S. Capt. H. Ellis has been promoted, and is now Major, vice McClellan, resigned.

* * * * *

Hampton Roads, off Fortress Monroe,
On board the steamship *Vanderbilt*,
October 22, 1861.[53]

To the Editor of the Sunbury Gazette—*Dear Sir:*—On my return to Washington City, last Saturday, I learned that the 79th Regiment, New York Highlanders, had received orders to report themselves at Annapolis, and that they had passed through a few hours previous to my arrival, with as much haste as necessary; I gathered up my baggage

---

53. *Sunbury Gazette*, November 2, 1861.

where I had left it, and started in the 2½ o'clock, p. m. train, of the B. and O. Railroad. The same evening, after an interview with Governor Hicks at the Junction, I found myself at the Annapolis Navy Yard, where I met Gen. Stevens, and sundry other officers, who gave me information in regard to our regiment. The men with very few exceptions, were already embarked, and the vessel lay in the roads, a few miles down the Severn. After a good night's rest, and breakfast next morning at the City Hotel, (Sabbath,) I attended divine service in the Presbyterian Church. Sometime during the night, the steam tug *Fanny* hove in sight, and by day light on [illegible phrase] I found myself in the magnificent ship *Vanderbilt*, plowing the waters of the Chesapeake for this point. Our vessel is said to draw 5000 tons, and cost one million of dollars. She is owned, together with the three others, by Cornelius Vanderbilt, of New York, and is hired to the Government at $2000 a day. Her engines are of huge dimensions, and her steam power is immense. Besides the 79th New York Highlanders [illegible phrase] Michigan Regiment on board, numbering altogether 1500 troops. But what about the Expedition? I will tell you *something* about it, but not everything you would like to know, for we are, as yet, under sealed orders.

Three Brigades left Annapolis, viz: the 1st, under Gen. Wright; the 2d, under Gen. Stevens; and the 3d under Gen. Veile, the whole division numbering about 12,000 men, and commanded by Gen. Sherman. Gen. Stevens' Brigade, with which I am associated, contains the following Regiments, viz: 79th New York, under Lieutenant Col. Nobles, 8th Michigan, under Col. Penton, Round Heads, under Col. Leasure, and 50th Pennsylvania, under Col. Christ. By joining several other divisions at this point from New York and Philadelphia, we are to form an immense fleet, numbering many thousand troops. Among all the guesses about our destination, it seems most probable that the government is about to make a demonstration simultaneously by sea and land, for the purpose of putting down, if possible, the great rebellion, which I regard as the most wicked which history has ever recorded. If our fleet, by the favor of God, who can have no sympathy with treason, should succeed in drawing off a portion of the Gulf States troops from Virginia, Gen. McClellan's [A]rmy of the Potomac might march with less hesitancy towards Manassas or Richmond. But let us wait patiently for results, putting our trust in God, and keeping our powder dry. We must not be so sanguine as to relax any exertions, because "the race is not to the swift, nor the battle to the strong," saith the Scripture. I am satisfied, however, on one point, viz: that nothing but the special interference of Divine Providence to inflict further chastisement upon our wicked nation, will give even temporary success to the Southern Oligarchy. It is well known that Jeff Davis and his clan have declared in their secret councils, that the *people* must be made *subjects* before they can be properly governed. Hence they are willing in their extremity, to accept a *protectorate* from some European monarchy. Are there any sympathizers with the ambitious and aristocratic oligarchy in your region, who, for the sake of immediate peace, would betray the Democratic party into a recognition of the Rebel Anarchy? I cannot call secession a government, for it has neither foundation nor consistency. Then let such sympathizers count the cost of recognition in view of generations yet unborn. God grant that this country may long continue to be the asylum for the oppressed of all nations. And this it will be only so long as "the Star Spangled Banner in triumph shall wave, o'er the land of the free and the home of the brave."

The scenery here is grand and imposing. Both nature and art combine to produce wonder and awe. Fortress Monroe bristles with more than 600 cannon, and looks sufficiently frowning towards the land of secession. Add to this the immense fleet now lying in line, with gigantic paddle wheels ready to make the ocean foam with their stroke, and the distant shores of the rebel land looming dimly on the horizon, and how can you resist the impression of sublimity. We are still awaiting orders to sail, at 2½ o'clock, P. M. I hope this may reach you in time enough for your next issue.

Yours, truly,

P. RIZER,
Chaplain, 79th N. Y. Highlanders.

* * * * *

Headquarters, 79th R. N. Y. Highlanders
On board the steamer *Vanderbilt*, off Fortress Monroe,
October 26, 1861.[54]

To John Youngman, Esq., Editor of the Gazette, *Sunbury, Pa.*—DEAR SIR:—We reached Hampton Roads from Annapolis on Tuesday morning, having lain at anchor for some time during Monday night, on account of unfavorable weather. Since our arrival, we have been coaling, and making sundry other preparations for the expedition. But now I notice the Blue Peter has been hoisted on nearly all the vessels in our Fleet, and this is a sure signal that we will soon sail.

The following vessels are here, and with some others not named, belong to the expedition, viz: *Baltic, Atlantic, Ocean Queen, Coatzacoalcos, Belvidere, Winfield Scott, Ariel, Ben De Ford, Empire City, Illinois, Marion, Ericson, Cahawba, Roanoke, Star of the South, Matanzas, Oriental, Parkersburg, Potomac, Locust Point* and *Vanderbilt.* There are transports, which will be supported by a number of armed war vessels, which I cannot now name. The whole expedition is placed jointly under General Sherman and Commodore Dupont,[55] the former to command the land, and the latter the naval forces. The force will consist of many thousands.

Our Steamship, the *Vanderbilt*, is engaged by the Government, at $2000 per day, and measures from stem to stern 340 feet. She has a 90-inch cylinder, with 12 feet stroke, and is said to draw 5000 tons. Her surf and other boats, which are numerous, measure 25 feet and upwards. Capt. Lefevre is Master. On board we have two Regiments, viz: the 8th Michigan, and 79th N. Y. Highlanders, under Lieut. Col. Nobles, commanding. We are in the 2nd Brigade, under Gen. I. J. Stevens, who is with us. The number of persons on board the *Vanderbilt* may be put down at 2000, which would include all classes and ranks.

This morning I was very unexpectedly gratified to see John H. Rogers, Esq., of the Mechanics' Bank, and two other gentlemen from Baltimore, come on board. They intend to spend several days at Old Point Comfort.

---

54. *Sunbury Gazette*, November 2, 1861.
55. Brig. Gen. Thomas West Sherman (1813–1879) and Flag Officer (Commodore) Samuel Francis Du Pont (1803–1865) jointly commanded the Port Royal Expedition. Du Pont was later promoted to Rear Admiral.

Yesterday I went ashore in company with Rev. Mahon of the 8th Michigan, who had a funeral to attend, and I spent several hours in and around Fortress Monroe, whose 600 guns look so frowningly upon the surrounding waters of the Chesapeake. It covers about 75 or 100 acres of ground, and is surrounded by a thick stone wall, and broad deep ditch, which needs no abattis. There is a hotel, and there are stores, and quite a number of other buildings. I passed through the Fortress from one gate to another, without any interruption from the soldiery, who are stationed everywhere. I suppose my uniform and badges served as a passport. Near the parade ground, and elsewhere, I saw Live Oaks and Catalpas growing. At the post office, I was addressed, unexpectedly, by a familiar voice, and soon recognized Rev. Holman, Chaplain of the 48th Pa. regiment. At his invitation, I accompanied him to their camp 3/4 of a mile distant, and was introduced to Col. Nagle, and several other Pennsylvanians. If I had not been pressed for want of time, I should have visited the desolated village of Hampton in that vicinity, which will long bear the stamp of Vandalism, in remembrance of the Rebel Magruder.[56]

The view from the deck of our vessel is very beautiful and interesting at present, as there are so many ships in the harbor. The water is said to average a depth of 10 or 11 fathoms. In front of the Fortress are the famous "Rip Raps," where once stood Fort Calhoun. In consequence of the gradual and continual sinking of the spot, notwithstanding all the efforts of Government to fill it up, the fort has long since disappeared, and nothing is now to be seen in the distance but heaps of stone, and some few unimportant structures. A little further off may be seen "*Sewell's Point,*" where the rebels have a battery, and a considerable number of troops. The order has not yet been given to weigh anchor, but we are expecting it every moment.

Let us hope that this Naval Expedition may prove successful, and that soon treason and rebellion may be put down forever in our great country.

Truly Yours,
P. RIZER, *Chaplain 79th Reg., N. Y. Highlanders.*

* * * * *

---

56. On August 7, 1861, retreating Confederates under Gen. John B. Magruder deliberately burned Hampton, Virginia, allegedly to prevent Union authorities from using the town to quarter troops or contrabands who were then flocking into nearby Union-held Fortress Monroe for safety.

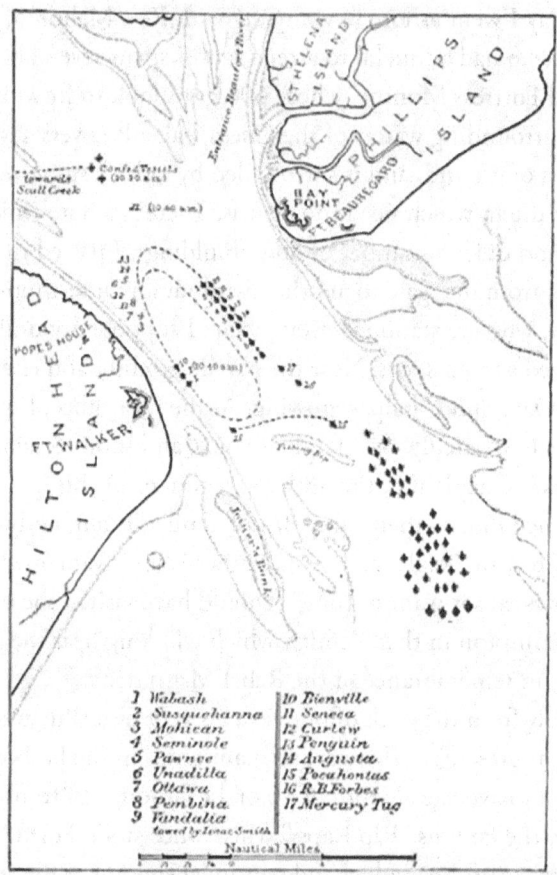

Map of the naval assault at Port Royal on November 7, 1861. (Credit: *Battles and Leaders of the Civil War*)

Headquarters, 79th R., N. Y. Highlanders
Bay Point, St. Philip's Island, S. Car.,
November 12, 1861.[57]

John Youngman, Esq., Editor of the Sunbury Gazette, *Sunbury, Pa.*—DEAR SIR:—On Tuesday morning, the 29th ult., our Fleet weighed anchor and set sail from Hampton roads. I wrote you from that rendezvous, shortly before we sailed, and now I will try to let you hear from me again, as our Regiment is on South Carolina soil.

It may be gratifying to many to receive some information from one of their fellow citizens in regard to the Coast Expedition,

---

57. *Sunbury Gazette*, November 30, 1861.

although, as I suppose, many other correspondents may have anticipated me in some particulars.

In rounding Cape Henry, from whose sandy beach rises a light house, where the Rebels have extinguished the light, we had pleasant weather and a calm sea. Soon the land faded away in the distance, as our noble steamer, the Vanderbilt, plowed the mighty deep with the power of a giant. GENERAL SHERMAN and COMMODORE DUPONT were in combined and equal command. GEN. WRIGHT, GEN. STEVENS, and GEN. VIELE led the three brigades of the whole division, in the order of their respective names here given. The sailing was in the order of a line of march: all the vessels being ranged in three lines, about two miles apart, with the space generally of half a mile or more between each. Our vessel had in tow the sail ship *Great Republic*, which contained 500 horses. The whole fleet was led by that magnificent flag ship, the Wabash, and our steamer being the largest vessel afloat, followed next, in the middle line. The following is a list of the vessels composing the whole fleet, on which you can rely, viz:

War Vessels	Daniel Webster,
Wabash,	Ericson,
Susquehannah,	Ariel,
Mohican,	Empire City,
Seminole,	Illinois,
Pawnee,	Union,
Vandalia,	Winfield Scott,
Unadilla,	Coatzacoalcos,
Ottawa,	Roanoke,
Seneca,	Potomac
Pembina,	Locust Point,
Curlew,	Parkersburg,
Penguin,	Oriental,
R. B. Forbes,	Marion,
Isaac Smith,	Governor,
Pocahontas,	May Flower,
Bienville,	Atlantic,

Augusta,	Baltic,
Sabine,	Ben DeFord,
Vixen,	Star of the South,
Mercury,	Belvidere,
Pettus,	Golden Eagle,
Cahawba,	Ocean Express,
Total, 22	Great Republic,
Transports.	Zenos Coffin,
Vanderbilt (340	Peerless,
Feet long,)	Total, 28.
Ocean Queen,	

Making a total of 50 vessels of both classes.

Now, Sir, you may depend, it was a grand sight, when all these frigates, steamers and transport ships were moving along in regular lines upon the bosom of the ocean. As I looked above and around, with naught but sky and sea to bound my view, I thought

>"My life is one the ocean wave,
> My home is on the deep."

But then I thought of other homes—one on earth and one beyond the deep blue sky. The loved ones of both homes were fresh in my memory. O, tell me not of *home*, when I am far away! Whose eye moistens not? and whose heart throbs not with anxiety at the word? Happy is the man who liveth for a heavenly home.

I was deeply impressed with this truth two or three days after we left Fortress Monroe, for, on Friday, we encountered a severe gale in going around Cape Hatteras, which by evening had increased to a storm. The wind whistled fiercely through our rigging, and the ocean raged and yawned. O, that dark and tempestuous night! It made me consider my principles, and mark well my tendency. I felt that I had embarked in the sacred cause of duty, and that I could trust God for his protection. Then committing myself to his holy keeping, I lay down in my berth, and enjoyed "tired nature's sweet restorer," whilst the heavy timbers of the *Vanderbilt* creaked with the howling storm.

When I arose in the morning, and went to the top of the wheel house, not a vessel of the fleet could be seen, and the *Vanderbilt* was steaming through the waves solitary and alone. Sometime during the night the *Great Republic*, which had been our near companion, was obliged to let go her hawser, and we could not tell what had become of her, or any other ship. What a contrast between the order of our previous sailing in magnificent lines, and the present dispersion! We spent nearly the whole date beating up and down the Gulf Stream, and made but little progress off the Carolina coast. Our object was to get together again if possible, and head for the point of destination. Our noble vessel had weathered the storm without sustaining any injury, but we felt much concern for some of the smaller vessels which had been built for the trade of Long Island Sound, or to be used only as ferry boats, and consequently were unfit for the wide and stormy ocean. By Saturday evening the storm had lulled, and the ocean waves were no longer running mountain high, when some of the fleet again hove in sight.

But what about the *destination* of our Fleet—some 15,000 sailing South. Where are we to land? All the coast in *Secession*, and wherever we may make the attempt, we are sure to meet with armed resistance. Our cause is just. We are going to try to put down treason and rebellion, which is contrary to God's law, and subversive of the best government on earth. Let us then be true to our God, true to our country, and march fearlessly on in the discharge of our duty, land wherever we may.

During the raging of the storm, whilst at dinner, Gen. Stevens announced to us that PORT ROYAL INLET, SOUTH CAROLINA, about fifteen miles about the mouth of the Savannah River, was our destination. And the object of our expedition was to open a convenient and safe harbor for the blockading squadron.

On Sunday we hove in sight of land, and on Monday we had a view of Port Royal Inlet. The transport vessels, which had reached this point with ours, now lay to, awaiting others to come up. From time to time one after another appeared in sight—but not all; for two of the smaller vessels had foundered in the storm, viz, the *Governor* and the *Peerless*. But I understand very few men were lost, as those on board were mostly rescued by the more fortunate vessels. The *Winfield Scott* was obliged to cut away her masts, heave over board nearly all her stores and two guns. Her prow was stoved in. She was saved, however, by the perseverance of Col. Christ's 50th Pennsylvania Regiment, 500 of whom on board, labored incessantly at the pumps. The *Vanderbilt*, with the transports generally, took her position some eight or ten miles distant from shore, and some of the gun boats on Monday evening set out under lead of the *Vixen* to reconnoiter the enemy's batteries and find the channel. One of them received a shot from the Rebel fort on Bay Point, but nevertheless proceeded to place buoys at a number of places. Several shots were exchanged, and three or four rebel steamers showed themselves in the distance. But the cannonading soon ceased and all became quiet again.

Tuesday was profitably occupied by naval reconnaissance's and preparations for the great work to be performed. But as this was not understood by the mass of land troops on board the transports, considerable impatience and anxiety began to be developed. Eye glasses were in constant requisition. Some thought they could see on the two entrenched and fortified points of the Rebel land, evidences of an immense army, which had been collected during our delay in making the attack. Why did not the gun boats pitch right into the Rebel batteries at once, before the enemy had time to rally? This disposition to complain was strengthened on Wednesday, notwithstanding the day proved unfavorable, and the surf ran very high. Commodore Dupont understood his business, however, and waited patiently for the opportune moment. This occurred on Thursday morning at 9½ o'clock. The line of battle was formed in graceful style, by the *Wabash* leading off, and sailing right between the two Rebel batteries, distant from each other about three miles, and separated by Port Royal Inlet at the mouth of Broad River. The battery on Bay Point now opened fire, and the *Wabash* in due time discharged two guns from each of her broadsides, as she sailed along. She was quickly followed by the *Susquehannah*, and other vessels in their turn, until all had joined in the action. Then there was a short suspension, and when the vessels renewed their fire, it was directed mainly towards the battery on Hilton Head Island, which became the scene of intense interest to the thousands of troops congregated on the guards, decks, wheel houses and spars of the numerous transports. For several hours the enemy kept up the firing with great vigor, and some shots were seen to strike our ships, but generally they did not seem to have been well directed; falling either too short or too far beyond the mark. From our side, the deadly missiles were hurled with a perfect storm of fury, and fell like ponderous hail upon the devoted fort. At one time I saw eight shells burst in the air nearly together, immediately over the enemy's head. And this shelling continued incessantly, without the slightest shrinking on the part of our navy, so that it seemed to me impossible for a living rebel to escape with a whole skin, even if he could manage to save his head. When the *Wabash, Susquehannah*, or any of the large gunships opened their broadsides, they appeared like huge monsters whose eyes flashed fire as they disgorged their iron hail with the noise of thunder; and sometimes the dust plowed up by the bursting shells, would rise in the air to meet the curling smoke as it hovered over the battery. During the heat of the engagement, the small gunboat *Mercury* ran boldly right under the enemy's guns, until she was out of their range on the ocean side, and then let fly at the rear end of the battery. Under some circumstances this was a brilliant action.

The battery on Bay Point, called Fort Beauregard, and commanded by Capt. T. Elliott, of the secession army, had been silenced at the first round. An immense rifled cannon is lying near where I am writing, broken asunder, the negroes tell us, by a man of war shot having been sent into the muzzle when loaded and just ready to fire. By the explosion five men were killed, and Captain Elliott was wounded. About 3 o'clock, p. m., Hilton Head battery was effectually silenced, and in a very short time the Union Flag, with Stars and Stripes, was seen flying in triumph upon one of the strong holds of South Carolina. As soon as the announcement was made, our soldiers on ship board waved their caps, and made the welkin ring with loud huzzas. When I saw this exhilarating scene, and hear[d] the Highland band playing "Hail Columbia," I left the top of the wheel house, where I had been for a number of hours, and felt as though I could eat some dinner.

The loss on our side, I am reliably informed, was eight killed and 32 wounded, which is remarkably small, considering that the bombardment lasted 5½ hours. It is impossible at present for us to tell the rebel loss, for they doubtless took many dead and wounded away, when they made their Bull Run flight, which they were enabled to do, by their better knowledge of the surroundings. Had our gun boats been as well acquainted with the channels and outlets, or inlets, as they now are, it is quite probably that the escaping rebels might have been hemmed in. I understand that about 130 dead bodies were found on Hilton Head Island. Here at Bay Point we found one man with the arm shot away, and two more sick. It is said there were about 600 of the enemy stationed on this, and 2000 on the other side. I have taken some pains to be accurate in my statements, but the reports are so contradictory that due allowance must be made for the circumstances.

Our regiment, the 79th New York Highlanders, commanded by Lieut. Col. Nobles, landed on this island the day after the battle, and likewise about 300 marines, under Major Reynolds. The main body of the three Brigades is on Hilton Head Island. We are at the mouth of Broad River, between Charleston and Savannah, about 10 miles south of Beaufort. In addition to opening a suitable and convenient harbor for our blockading squadron, it may be the design to open a cotton port for the benefit of foreign governments, to which a supply of the raw material is becoming a necessity.

Our troops are well, and seem to be highly pleased with their quarters. An immense amount of property was abandoned here by the rebels, so rapid and hasty was their flight. Flour, Bacon, Sweet Potatoes, Rice, Tents, Furniture, Medical Stores, Sugar, &c., have been found in abundance. On this island 23 cannon, some of them of the largest calibre, and on the other, 22 have fallen into our possession, making altogether 45 valuable guns, besides many muskets and rifles.

Capt. Sage, of the Golden Eagle, and Capt. Redell, of the Zenos Coffin, belonging to our fleet, honored us with a visit to-day, and reported that although Beaufort has been abandoned by the white inhabitants, it will not, for the present, be occupied by our troops, because its occupancy would make unnecessary employment for them.

I have been walking up and down the beach, and catching oysters with our men, and find that the southern soldiers must have had fine times. It is a great mistake to suppose they were starving where Yams, Sweet Potatoes, Crabs, Oysters, Clams, Turkeys, Geese, Pork and Venison abound. The climate is delightful. It is so warm that thin clothing is preferable, and many are every day indulging in sea bathing.

About 40 negroes have come in to this fort, and I understand there are hundreds in the vicinity, whom their masters could not persuade to leave the plantations. I could say much more on this subject; but I fear I may tire your readers, Mr. Editor, and therefore must close this epistle. Remember me kindly to all friends.

Respectfully, Yours,
P. RIZER.

* * * * *

Image of the naval bombardment at Port Royal, November 7, 1861. (Credit: Naval History and Heritage Command)

The 79th New York remained in camp near Hilton Head until early 1862, when they returned to the Virginia theater, but by then Chaplain Rizer's service had already ended. Beset by ill health in the southern climate—his condition was sometimes described at the time as the "Hilton Head Fever"—Rizer resigned his chaplaincy on December 9, 1861, and returned to Sunbury to recover. After the war, Rizer continued his ministry at various locations in Maryland, New Jersey, and Oswego, New York. In 1875, Rizer's wife died, rendering a blow from which he never fully recovered. Turning inward, he absorbed his attention with academic pursuits, losing himself in his books and the study of various languages, including Hebrew and German. Peter Rizer's health slowly declined until he finally passed away at the residence of his daughter in Montgomery County, Maryland, on August 25, 1886, at the age of seventy-four.[58]

---

58. Rev. Peter Rizer Biography, Spared & Shared website, https://sparedshared4.wordpress.com/letters/1834-rev-stephen-albion-mealy-to-rev-peter-rizer/ (accessed March 27, 2024).

3

To Key West and the Peninsula, February–July 1862

In the spring of 1862, the Army of the Potomac took the offensive on the Virginia Peninsula, where its ultimate target was Richmond, the Confederate capital. Northern morale remained high, as recent Union successes in the West, including the capture of Forts Henry (February 6) and Donelson (February 11–16) on the Tennessee and Cumberland Rivers, and Union victory at the Battle of Pea Ridge in Arkansas (March 7–8), prompted expectations of a similar outcome in the East that would lead to a swift and successful end to the war. (Bolstering that notion, these early successes were soon followed by a stunning come-from-behind Union victory, led by Brig. Gen. Ulysses S. Grant, at Pittsburg Landing on April 6–7, and the capture of New Orleans, the Confederacy's largest port, on May 1. The Crescent City would stay under federal control for the remainder of the war.)

McClellan landed at Fortress Monroe on March 17, and launched his advance toward Richmond along the York River on April 4. As the Army of the Potomac pushed forward, it was hampered not only by Confederate forces but also inclement weather, inferior roads, geographical surprises not indicated on the army's unsatisfactory maps, and overcautious leadership. Fooled by Maj. Gen. John B. Magruder into thinking Confederate forces were larger than expected, McClellan began a month-long siege of Yorktown rather than risk a direct assault. McClellan's timidity allowed Confederate reinforcements under Gen. Joseph E. Johnston to reach the peninsula. Breaking off the siege after the Rebels abandoned their position on May 4, McClellan fought an inconclusive rearguard action at Williamsburg on May 5 as Johnston continued a retrograde movement toward Richmond. Then followed a series of clashes at Eltham's Landing (May 7), Drewry's Bluff (May 15), Hanover Courthouse (May 27), and Seven Pines (May 31–June 1). After Johnston was severely wounded in the last engagement, the new commander of the Confederate Army of Northern Virginia, Robert E. Lee, revealed his exceptional tactical skills during the Seven Days Battles in late June, a series of almost daily clashes that ultimately stymied McClellan's progress and overall strategy.

Letters from the Sunbury Guards
Company C, 47th Pennsylvania Volunteer Infantry

*B*efore the drama in Virginia unfolded, the War Department began to implement facets of General-in-Chief Winfield Scott's grand strategy to surround and strangle the Confederacy—like a giant Anaconda—by establishing Union forces along the periphery of the South's Atlantic and Gulf coasts. To that end, the 47th Pennsylvania arrived in Key West on February 4, 1862. The regiment settled into Camp Brannan, where it was brigaded

Brigadier General John Milton Brannan, commander of the Department of Key West in early 1862. (Credit: National Portrait Gallery)

with the 7th New Hampshire and the 90th and 91st New York. Most of the time in camp was spent on routine garrison and picket duties as well as daily drilling, including instruction on manning heavy artillery at Fort Taylor. While the camp routines may have become monotonous at times, the regiment still found time for lighter activities with the entire brigade, such as participating in a series of physical contests (foot, sack, and wheelbarrow races as well as a pig chase) in celebration of Washington's birthday on February 22. During this period Capt. Gobin also spent some time on detail, likely due to his legal background, as Deputy Judge Advocate for the Department of Key West. In that position, Gobin supervised all legal (court-martial) proceedings in the department. The 47th remained at Camp Brannan until June 18, when it embarked with the brigade for Hilton Head, South Carolina, arriving on June 22. The regiment went into camp near Fort Walker until July 2, when it was ordered to participate in a movement against Secessionville but did not become engaged. The 47th then shifted base to Beaufort, South Carolina, and was brigaded with the 6th Connecticut, 7th New Hampshire, and 8th Maine. It assumed responsibility for picketing the entire vicinity.[1]

On board SS *Oriental*
Off Great Abaco Island,
February 2, 1862.[2]

DEAR FRIENDS:—Tired of the monotony of a ship life, I will try to pass a few moments in writing to you this morning, and relieve your minds of any anxiety you may have respecting us. We left Annapolis on Monday about noon, and steamed down the Bay, but were compelled to anchor at night on account of the fog. My first night on board the ship passed off pleasantly, and I slept as soundly as though in my log house at Camp Griffen. On Tuesday morning we weighed anchor, and in doing so the chain broke, and the anchor went to the bottom. The wind being dead ahead, we made very slow progress, going by steam alone and only making about eight miles (or knots as sailors call them) an hour. In the afternoon we came in sight of Hampton Roads into which we put to get an anchor of

---

1. Bates, *Pennsylvania Volunteers*, 1:1151; *Sunbury American*, March 15, 1862; *Sunbury Gazette*, March 29, 1862.
2. *Sunbury Gazette*, February 22, 1862.

the Commodore in command of the fleet at Fortress Monroe. We anchored in the midst of the fleet and within a short distance of the Fortress, thus giving us an excellent opportunity to get a sight of that celebrated fortification. It is a magnificent structure, and of the greatest importance to the Government. At least fifty vessels of different kinds were anchored in the Roads. As we came down the Bay in the afternoon[,] we were favored with a visit from the gunboats blockading the Rappahannock. As we moved past the different vessels the sailors would run up the rigging and cheer us with a will, to which our boys, who thronged our decks, would respond heartily.

We remained at Fortress Monroe all Tuesday night, and on Wednesday morning early started again for sea. We passed within a mile of Cape Henry, (now in possession of the rebels,) and were favored with a view of the light ship, wrecked there a few days before we started. She lay upon the beach with her masts all gone but one. At ten o'clock we lost sight of land, and none has gladdened our vision since until this morning, when the Great Abaco, one of the Bahamas, hove in sight, on our weather bow. It presents a bleak and dreary aspect, but we watched it with pleasure.

On Wednesday the sea became very rough, and continued all night and Thursday. About noon on Wednesday the roll of the ship commenced to tell on the men. Nearly every one of them became sea sick. The bulwarks, the deck, and every available spot was filled with them, emptying the contents of their stomachs. At the supper table, I nearly died laughing to see one after another of the officers get up and leave for their rooms. About nine o'clock at night I began to feel rather serious, and as I was resolved that those left should not have a chance to laugh at me, I started for my room. When I got there I found Reese in it, awfully sick and making as much fuss as if he was trying to get his boots up through his stomach. I was laughing at him when all at once it caught me, and oh, Jerusalem, but I was sick. After throwing up all I had in me, and trying hard to hunt something else, I laid down and did not get up until Friday morning. No matter how sick any one became, he got no sympathy. The well ones would laugh at him, knowing there was no danger. On Friday I staggered on deck, and by noon was all right again. The men too commenced coming up, and now all are better than when we started. But of all on board, over 1000, I do not think there were 50 who were not sick.

On Thursday, one of the sailors gave me a piece of sea-weed he picked up. We were then about 150 miles off Savannah, Georgia. You will find it inclosed. Not even a sail was seen on Wednesday, Thursday or Friday, but yesterday one hove in sight, not within hailing distance however. For three days nothing was visible but the sea and the heavens. Occasionally a school of flying fish or porpoises would pass, but nothing more relieved the monotony of the voyage. I fell to reading to pass the time, until yesterday, when I was detailed as officer of the day. This gave me plenty to do, as we are much crowded on board.

This morning we passed the "Hole in the Wall," a natural fissure in the projecting rocks of the Great Abaco. We steamed around it and came on to the Bahama Banks, skirted on the south by the Stirrup Back Islands, or known as such on the charts. In one place, called the Great Harbor, formerly a favorite resort for the Buccaneers that infested these seas, we could see seven vessels at anchor. I was informed they were wreckers, waiting until some vessel foundered, when they make a dart for it. Two vessels under full sail were crossing the Bahama Banks, but as we drew too much water we could not cross, and had to go around them. This morning our Chaplain preached and had quite an audience, but in the midst of his discourse a school of porpoises went by, and this diverted the attention of the boys. The Captain's wife, who with her maid are the only ladies on board, was present. They were only married two days before we started and this is her wedding trip. She is quite young. Does not look to be over 16 years old, and is quite pretty. This evening the light house on the Great Isaacs is visible. We go within about two miles of it.

But it is time to retire. We expect to reach Key West to-morrow night. What is in store for us there, I am unable to say. I hope a descent on New Orleans. I may write more to-morrow, but will put this on board the first passing vessel.

Yours,
SHINDEL.

P.S. The weather is so warm that the men have nearly all thrown off their coats.

* * * * *

Key West, Fla.,
February 6, 1862.[3]

DEAR FRIENDS:—As I could not send off my letter written on board, I enclose this. We arrived here on Tuesday morning and commenced preparations to camp. Our new tents, the Sibley patent, are now all up, and we feel once more at home. We are all surrounded by bushes or scrubby trees, which answer the double purpose of shade and harbors for the mosquitoes. The island of Key West is about 6 miles long, by 1½ wide, and contains 2500 whites and about 1,000 negroes. There are three Regiments here already and some regulars. The 90th and 91st New York, and our own. More are expected, and as soon as they arrive we expect a lively time.

The weather here is exceedingly warm, as much so as it is in July at home. The flowers are in full bloom—oranges, lemons, cocoa nuts and bananas are plenty, and the camp is full of negroes selling them for two cents apiece or three for a picayune, as they style it. The town of Key West is a very pretty one, the houses all being built without chimneys, and many of them without window sash, just shutters, which are closed at night and opened in the day time. Stoves are not used at all in the houses, all cooking being done in an out house.

The box of stockings sent by the Ladies Aid Society, was put on board the ship, and received here in camp last night. Although rather warm here, yet for the sake of preventing sickness we are compelled to wear them. So they come very acceptable, and I am under renewed obligations. The reading matter was particularly acceptable to me.

The mail leaves this afternoon, and I must hasten to close this. I will write again a full account of my impressions here. I have been kept so busy in getting my camp fixed that I have been out but little yet. Last night I attended a Masonic Lodge and made a number of acquaintances.

The men are all in the best of health and spirits. They are busy running around gathering shells, getting oranges, &c. It is hard to keep them at work.

Yours, &c.
SHINDEL.

* * * * *

---

3. *Sunbury Gazette*, February 22, 1862.

Camp Brannan,
Key West, Fla.,
February 16, 1862.[4]

DEAR WILVERT.—With the thermometer at 85° in the shade, it is not a very pleasant undertaking to commence a letter to a friend, but, as I have promised to keep you *posted*, I must do it or *lie* in a position that would not be at all agreeable.

With several members of our company, I attended Episcopal Church last Sabbath—The Church building is a large and beautiful one, and the people deserve great credit for erecting it. The Minister is a strong Union man, and it struck me, on last Sabbath, that he lost no opportunity of displaying his Union sentiments. Some time ago some of the members of this Church were very disloyal, and when the Minister read the prayer "to behold and bless Thy servant, the President of the United States, and all other in authority," they would close the prayer book, and look daggers at him, wondering whom they should hang first—the Minister or *Abe* Lincoln. General Brannen (Captain at the time) hearing of it, put an end to this disrespect, made them take the oath of allegiance, and now they can say "Amen" as loud and as heartily as the best Union men on the island. There is nothing like a little "moral suasion." For the sake of the Church, I am happy to state that only a few of its members were weak enough to show their fondness for Jeff. Davis—the rest of the members were very glad that Gen. Brannen took the matter in hand.

The population of the island is about four thousand, consisting of negroes, Spaniards, and a *few* whites. With the exception of five store keepers, the occupation of its inhabitants is fishing, dealing in fruit and selling hot coffee and cool drinks. There are as many coffee and cool drink saloons here as there are Lager Bier saloons in the Everlasting State of Williamsport, and from that you can readily perceive there is no need of being thirsty. As for intoxicating drinks, they are prohibited—the island being under martial law it is impossible to get even a *smell*, and it is well that it is so, for in this climate there is no telling what amount of sickness its use might produce. The buildings used for stores are very large and airy, but I can assure you that in

---

4. *Sunbury American*, March 15, 1862.

the stores of either Friling & Grant or E. Y. Bright & Son,[5] there are more goods than in all the stores on this island put together. Oranges, coming from Cuba and Nassan islands, are very plenty, and can be bought at three for a sixpence; not such as you folks get at home, but real fresh, juicy fellows that melt in one's mouth equal to the best ice cream made in H. B. Masser's patent ice cream freezers. Fish are very plenty, and can be bought cheap. Thanks to Sergeant Smelser, our company is living high in the fish line. He is company Quarter-Master Sergeant, and on every fish market morning, Peter is at the wharf, and there exchanges our surplus pork and beef for fish; so that the boys have a variety and are content.

Horses and cattle are very small. They come from Cuba. The horses are not near as big as Peter B. Masser's black ponies, and I have seen at home two year old cattle larger than those they use here for beeves.

There *is* an article here, that I believe bothers the whole human race, and that is mosquitoes. Those on this island are not of the common kind, but regular tormenters.—Fix your net[,] work as you may, you will receive their sting before morning. They are great on a serenade too, and if one is impolite enough to go to sleep as they are in the middle of a *glee*, the leader will give you a tickler with his sting that it is impossible to resist; but for my part, I can easily dispense with *that* kind of music, and often wish that they would favor someone else who can appreciate their talents better than I can.

The Fort on this island (Fort Taylor) is a very large one, and is now of the most importance to the government. It is not near finished, but so much so that the rebels dare not venture within the range of its guns.—When finished it will have one hundred and eighty guns, and with those on the embankment on the moat, fronting the town, it will have two hundred and seventy five. Some time since the fort came within an ace of being taken by the rebels, but Capt. Brannen saved it by stratagem. Men were working at the fort, so, to prevent suspicion, the Captain every morning would march a guard from the garrison to the fort, and in that manner before the rebels were aware of it he had full possession of it. Mulraner, formerly

---

5. Friling & Grant and E. Y. Bright & Son were two well-known merchant stores in Sunbury, Pennsylvania.

a Sergeant of the Captain's, who became rich in the rum business, hoisted a *secesh* flag on his hotel, and sent an impudent note to the Captain requesting him to honor the *seven* starts by firing a salute from the fort. Their reply was that if the *rag* was not taken down on the return of the messenger, the Commander would open the guns of the fort on the town, and send Mulraner and his friends to Tortugas to work in the hot sand and giving them time to repent of their folly, preparatory to dangling at the end of a rope. The flag *was* taken down—Mulraner vamoosed the ranch, and is now in command of a company of rebels somewhere near Pensacola. It is tho't that when Gen. Brannan arrives Mulraner's property, which is valuable, will be confiscated.

There are a large number of men-of-war here, and every day more are added to their number. Fifty-seven prisoners were brought in during the last week from Ship Island, besides two prizes, one loaded with turpentine, and the other with arms and machinery that were on the road to New Orleans, for a large steamer that is building there for the use of the rebels.

You need not be surprised to hear of an expedition being sent out from here—everything looks like it—so many vessels in port, more expected and troops arriving every day. There are three regiments here now, the 90th and 91st New York, and our own, besides the Regulars in the fort. If we do go, there will have to be a strong force left behind; for, in my opinion, the most of the Union men here are as treacherous as the men who use the stiletto to stab a friend, at night, from behind.

With the exception of fish and fruit, everything they use comes from the North. They would starve if it were not for the "mud sills," and yet they would try to break up the Government that protects them. Lumber is worth one hundred dollars per thousand feet. Carpenters' wages are three dollars per day but I think they would starve at that, as I see no employment for them. The boys are very well, and are enjoying themselves with the sea bathing. We have received the *American* and *Gazette* three times since our arrival, and they are very welcome visitors, much more so than were the morning papers in Virginia. It is very strange we receive no letters; if the "folks at home" knew how anxious we are to get them they would be a little more punctual.

Yours, Fraternally,
H. D. W.

* * * * *

Camp Brannan,
Key West, Fla.,
February 27, 1862.⁶

DEAR WILVERT:—Gen. Brannan and staff arrived here on Friday last, on the steamer *Philadelphia*. He made his first appearance, to us, on our parade ground, at dress parade, and seemed pleased at the improvement the men had made with their new arms, in the manual. After dress parade he rode [past] the different streets of the regiment, and the enthusiastic cheers given him showed that he was liked, and that the men had perfect confidence in him.

Saturday last, the anniversary of the birth of the "Father of his Country," WASHINGTON, was celebrated in a becoming manner. The whole Brigade was formed in Divisions, which made three sides of a square; the officers in front, while the General and staff were in the centre. A prayer was then offered to the Throne of Grace asking for success to our arms, that this wicked rebellion might be put down, and that we might hereafter celebrate the anniversary of Washington's birth day in peace. The farewell "Address" was then read, after which the Brigade moved in column through the town to Fort Taylor, to be present at the firing of the National Salute of thirty-four guns. Immediately after the salute from the fort, the *Pensacola*, a man-of-war, lying in port, let go all its guns, one after another. The effect was splendid, and the loud barking of its "bull dogs" was dangerous to secesh window glass. The regiments then returned to their different camps, pretty well tired after their march and long exposure to the head of this hot island. After resting, washing and enjoying a *tin* of soup, a holiday was given, and the men were ready to see the fun to be had in the following

---

6. *Sunbury American*, March 15, 1862.

PROGRAMME,

Of the celebration of the 47th Reg. Pa. Vols At Key West, Florida, February 22, 1862.

Music by the Band. Oration by Capt. Gobin.

1st, *Foot Race.*—Two men from each company, to run across the Barrack yard and back. The man making the best time to receive $5, the second best $2.50.

2d, *Wheelbarrow Match.*—Two men from each company to wheel a barrow, blindfolded, fifty yards at a mark or stake. The man coming the nearest the stake to receive $5.00. Second best $2.50.

3d, *Sack Race.*—Two men from each company to run a race of fifty yards in *sacks* up to their necks. The man making the best time to receive $5.00. Second best $2.50.

4th, *Pig Chase.*—Ten men from each company to run after a shaved and greased pig. The men catching and holding it by the *tail* to receive the pig.

Judges were appointed to decide as to the winners of the different feats.

The foot race was very well contested. Jacob H. Keiffer, of our company, came in for the second prize. In a run of four hundred years he would beat all who were in that race. The wheelbarrow match was full of fun, some of the contestants were further off from the stake at the end than when they started. The *big* thing of the day was the sack business. P. M. Randels was in a ring for that—Lanky started well, but when almost to the goal he lost his equilibrium, down he fell; however, a lucky thought struck him, he tried the rolling process, and the consequence was "old Dad" rolled himself into the second prize. The pig race was a failure. There were too many runners for one thing, and another, Mr. Porker being a Secessionist, the sight of so many Union troops rather discomfited him, made him weak in the knees, and consequently he could not run. Everything passed off well. All were pleased, and the ladies, who favored us with their presence, (there was a goodly number of them,) declared they never before enjoyed themselves so much as they did at the celebration of the 47th Penn'a. Vols.

On Monday night, the 24th[,] the Band of our regiment gave a ball for the officers. It was numerously attended by the knights of the spur and tinsel. The ladies were not quite so plenty, however, there was enough to present the form six setts. As for the performance on the "light fantastic toe," I have seen some that was more pleasing to my fancy—it was too much on the "bobbin round" style. The ladies are unacquainted with our northern figures, but to their credit they were willing to learn, and were always ready to fill up a sett so as to keep the ball in motion. I should say all parties enjoyed themselves, for three o'clock of the morning sounded on their ears before any motion was made to move homewards.

On Wednesday night, the 26th, the Band gave a concert. On account of the heavy wind and rain it was not quite so well attended as it might have been. Notwithstanding the storm, the ladies turned out well. Amusements have been very scarce here, and the inhabitants patronize almost anything. Why, some of the boys of our Regiment, got up a negro band of minstrels, and their houses were so crowded that many were refused admittance. The Band cleared over fifty dollars—pretty well for a few hours *blowing*. From the amusements and sea-bathing, you can perceive the Northern "mud-sills" are enjoying themselves, and if they keep it up this island will soon become famous as a watering place—second to neither Cape May or Atlantic City.

The "American" arrives regularly, much more so than letters from home; but five of the latter received since we have been here. The boys were very glad when the paper came, liked Mr. Masser's letter very much, but came to the conclusion that the regiment where the "Augusta Rangers" are, they have a strange hour for beating the *reveille*; the hour specified is the general Army rule for *retreat*.

The boys are very well—they have a strong desire for a little more active service, thinking that when the fighting commences this war will soon be at an end, and they will then have a chance of shaking hands with the good people of Sunbury.

Yours, Fraternally,
H. D. W.

* * * * *

Key West, Fla.,
March 11, 1862.[7]

Dear Friends:—Your letters were received last night and right glad was I to receive them. I have but time to write a few lines, as the mail closes at 6 o'clock tonight, and it is now five. Gen. Brennan has appointed me Deputy Judge Advocate General of the Department of Key West, giving me the Supervision of all law proceedings on the Island. I have Samuel Haupt for my clerk, and it keeps us both busy. I have a splendid office in the barracks—everything nice as can be. It beats the one at home all to pieces.

The weather continues very warm, but I do not mind it any more. The blockading squadron brings in prizes every day, which they catch running the blockade. The other day the *South Carolina* captured a large Steamer, called the *Magnolia*, with $75,000 worth of cotton on board, and on Sunday two schooners loaded with ammunition, soap, thread, needles, &c. The news is glorious. The Mortar Fleet left here last Thursday. By this time they are before New Orleans or Mobile. They are an awful array and are bound to capture anything they attack.

Yours,
J. P. S. G.

* * * * *

Headquarters, Judicial Dept.,
Key West, Fla.,
March 23, 1862.[8]

Dear Friends:—I have just returned from church and although it is bed time, as I have an opportunity to send this North by the prize Steamer *Magnolia* which leaves for New York to-morrow, I will endeavor to ease your minds respecting me.

The weather which all along has been very warm has taken a sudden change, and to-night we are having a regular Norther. To us it

---

7. *Sunbury Gazette*, March 29, 1862.
8. *Sunbury Gazette*, April 5, 1862.

is quite pleasant, but I visited a family in town this evening, and they were all shivering with cold. The ladies sat wrapped up in shawls, and the gentlemen in overcoats. I was considerably amused. They could not believe me in earnest, when I told them it was quite comfortable. I should like to see some of them in the North when we have a foot of snow on the ground and the thermometer ranging accordingly.

The mail arrived yesterday, and by it we received papers up to the 12th inst. The news, with the exception of the exploits of *Merrimac*,[9] continues encouraging. Matters here are coming to a focus. Two batteries of field Artillery have been landed on the Island, and we are drilling our Regiment to the use of them. The men have been supplied with new clothing, brass shoulder scales to protect them from cavalry, and everything betokens a readiness on our part to join in the grand encircling of the monster Rebellion. I recently had the pleasure of examining the Captain and crew of a small schooner that ran the blockade at New Orleans, and escaped to Tampico, from thence here. The Captain was a native of Philadelphia where he had a family residing. His vessel was in the port of New Orleans when Louisiana seceded, she was taken from him, and he had been unable to escape before. He was assisted by a number of influential citizens. He reports the place to be strongly fortified, but represents a strong Union feeling existing. He also stated a number of facts in reference to the battering ram, that were important. Gen. Brannen forwarded the whole party North.

Since the arrival of Gen. Brannen[,] he has been actively engaged in putting this Island in a condition of defense against any foe. The trees are all being cut down, while artillery roads, thirty feet wide, are being run from one part of the Island to another, at different points. Our men have been working hard, but we daily expect 500 contrabands from Port Royal, when we will have easy times. The Island, however, will be rendered impregnable against any assault.

I send you by the *Magnolia* some shells. Last Saturday I took a trip up among the Islands, and the large conch shells in the box I got out of the gulf myself, up at Boko Chique Key. The conches I ate for

---

9. A reference to the CSS *Virginia*, the Confederate ironclad refitted from the Union vessel *Merrimac*, that wreaked havoc at Hampton Roads on March 8, 1862, before dueling the Union ironclad USS *Monitor* to a stalemate the next day.

breakfast last Sunday morning, or rather part of them, as after our pilot had them fixed up, it took some time before I ventured to taste them. They eat first rate, however, nearly as good as oysters.

Yours, &c.
J. P. S. G.

* * * * *

Key West, Fla.,
March 30, 1862.[10]

DEAR WILVERT:—Every Day more or less of the deluded followers of Jefferson Davis appear before the Clerk of the District Court of the United States, at this place, to take the oath of allegiance, and then come to Capt. Lambert, Assistant Adjutant General, to get a pass to leave the island. Their passes are granted when they have the necessary certificates, and, it seems to me, these released traitors grasp their discharges more eagerly than they ever did the ragged currency paid to them by the would-be Southern Confederacy for their *chivalrous* deeds of blood and murder. The oath of allegiance is to the point, but to hit those taking it in the right place, Gen. Brannan has added stronger words, and in conclusion it now reads, "Nor will I give *aid* and *comfort* to the so-called Southern Confederacy."—But what can one expect else of these fellows than breaking the oath. Men who once attempt to break up such a great and pure Government as that of the United States, will not hesitate to do anything, and I expect, before the conclusion of this rebellion, that the most of the rebels who have taken the oath will be under Bragg, or some other *braggadocio* of Davis, Floyd & Co., in arms against us. If they do, my wish is that *they* may be the first to feel the balls of the Springfield rifles belonging to the "mud sills" of the 47th Pennsylvania Volunteers. In releasing these prisoners I think the General in Command is doing what is best, for what is the use of the Government feeding and giving good quarters to a set of rascals, who, at the bidding of their masters, are ready to cut the throats of good Union men, and willing

---

10. *Sunbury American*, April 19, 1862.

to burn and pillage all property belonging to those who differ in opinion with them.

The news from all parts of Florida is very cheering. Pensacola has been evacuated, and now the "Star Spangled Banner" waves over all parts of the city. When the rebels evacuated it they went to the relief of the towns on the coast of Georgia, that they expected would be attacked by one of our many fleets. If they are attacked you may expect to hear of them running, for their new idea of "masterly evacuations" is great with them, and they will be apt to keep it up. At the place they embarked[,] the railroad runs for two or three miles along the water. One of our gunboats, coming up too late to catch, chased them for a while, peppering them as they ran, but *rail* having an advantage over *paddles*, they gave up the chase, not, however, without doing some damage to the engine and train, and making several of the rebels take to the swamps for refuge. The Honorable (?) Mr. Yulee, late United States Senator,[11] was aboard the train.

Commodore Dupont has commenced operations here, and has already planted the Stars and Stripes at Fernandina, St. Mary's, St. Augustine, and other places that I do not remember. The news now here is that the people of the interior are asking protection of Gen. Brannan, and say that Florida was never really out of the Union. They acted the way they have been doing through fear and compulsion. A nice way to get out of the scrape and save their property from confiscation, but it is the old story, and no one but a fool would be gulled by them. To say they were never out of the Union is true, neither were any of the seceded States, for that was never acknowledged at home or abroad. I think General Brannan understands these people perfectly, and the protection he will give them will be a little more powder and ball, unless they humbly beg pardon for the indignities put on him and Lieut. Slemmer, throw down their arms at once, be good and peaceable citizens and come under the authority of the Government as it was before the rebellion broke out. From what I hear this will soon be the case, and then Jeff Davis will have one less *brilliant* in his galaxy of stars.

Our Gunboats are doing good service in the cause; every week they bring into this port three or four prizes. A schooner prize was brought in last Monday, caught on her trip from Havana, or at

---

11. David Levy Yulee (1810–1886), former U.S. senator from Florida.

least on the course from that city, loaded with ammunition. She is a valuable prize. The U. S. Gunboat *Owasco* captured two schooners, off New Orleans, having on board, each, two hundred and fifty bales of cotton; they are lying here now, but will soon be sent North to be disposed of. If our vessels of war are much more successful in capturing prizes we shall soon be able to make up for the loss of the two old hulks that were destroyed by the rebel iron boat *Merrimac*, but all the vessels of the South can never pay for the lives of the poor sailors who were lost in the fight. I have heard sailors here speak of that fight, and they are determined, at the first opportunity, to avenge the death of their comrades with double interest.

The arrival of so many troops on this island has increased the business considerably, particularly that of matrimony. There were two weddings in town this week, and the parties concerned appear to have had a happy time. Their customs are different to those of the North. At home the friends give parties to the happy couple, but here parties are given for three or four nights at the house of the bride. Although the city is under Martial Law, and the Marshal has seized all the liquor, as he supposes, wine and whiskey flowed plentifully, and the effects could easily be seen on both old and young. One old gentleman, as he was trying to keep from the fence, reminded me of the fellow who, on going home at night, having too much on board, was leaning against a large brick building, when a friend called to him, "Tom, do you belong to the Church?" "No, (hic) but I've a leaning that way." So it was with the old gentleman, he didn't belong to the fence, but he had a great *leaning* that way, and it was difficult for him to keep the fence from hitting him.

I suppose the good people of Sunbury will be as glad to hear of the promotion of Sergeant Daniel Oyster to a 2d Lieutenancy, as our boys were last night, when his appointment was announced to them at Dress Parade. After the company marched to their quarters, and were dismissed, three hearty cheers were given that any one might well be proud of, for honest "*Old Mose*." The Lieutenant bears his honors well, but one thing he dislikes, viz: congratulations.

The boys are all very well, and are enjoying themselves at *hard work*, gathering shells, fishing and bathing. There is a rumor that our regiment is going on the main land, if we do it is probably the next time you hear from me it will be from Apalachicola.

Yours, fraternally,
H. D. W.

* * * * *

Camp Brannan,
Key West, Fla.,
April 19, 1862.[12]

DEAR WILVERT:—Having finished a plate of soup, (not a hasty one)[13] enjoyed a piece of ham, cooked in my best style, *fried*[,] and now luxuriating in a pipe of the best *Lynchburg* tobacco, I conclude to indite you a few lines from this most miserable place, Key West.

There are now lying here three very fine vessels captured from Secessia. The cargoes are very valuable, consisting of cotton, coffee, rice, liquor, kerosene and olive oils, leather, and a great many articles of use. I attended the sale of one of the cargoes, and one article I found more numerous than any other—that of hooped skirts. I was curious to know why they had supplied themselves so plentifully with that article, when an old gentleman said that was easily understood, for when the rebels had to run, and in fear of being caught they would make good *hiding* places and then he related a circumstance of a Mexican General who, in running away, found crinoline very convenient as a hiding place, but not secure enough for the Lynx-eyed Americans, as the *brave* gentleman was caught in his wife's trap.

There has been considerable sickness among the troops, but I am happy to state it is abating. Two members of our company, Theodore Kiehl, and H. Wolf, have been in the Hospital, but are now out and almost ready for duty. They take very readily to their rations when they get back to the company, saying the Hospital is a very nice place

---

12. *Sunbury American*, May 3, 1862.
13. This is an obscure but clever reference to a comment made by Winfield Scott during the Mexican War. He wrote to Secretary of War William Marcy, noting that he had received a letter from Marcy just as he sat down to a hasty plate of soup. The Polk administration, hoping to attack Scott's reputation, published the letter, and there followed quite a few political cartoons from the time that featured the hasty plate of soup. For an example, see the Library of Congress website at https://www.loc.gov/pictures/item/2008661471/ (accessed October 6, 2024).

to get well in, but no place for *grub*, as they were as hungry as *wolves* all the time they were in, or rather when they became better. We have lost eight men from our regiment, by death, since we have been on this island. From what I can learn the diseases were mostly contracted in Virginia, but if they have not, it is a wonder that the mortality is not greater among us, owing to the sudden change of climate, the bad water, hot sun and hard work our men are subjected to.

Lieut. Henry Bush, Co. F, in our regiment, died two weeks ago. His company were in the Fort, learning heavy artillery, where he was attacked with typhoid fever—in a few days he was beyond the physician's skill, and now he is sleeping his last sleep in the stranger's cemetery. His funeral was very largely attended by the military and the masonic fraternity, of which he was a member. Lieut. Bush was beloved by his company—they having presented him with a sword a few days before he was taken sick—and in fact was liked by the whole regiment for his kindness and gentlemanly bearing to the men. As soon as the necessary arrangements can be made[,] his body will be sent to Catasauqua, Lehigh County, where his widow and two little children reside.

Since the promotion of Lieut. Oyster, there has been some changes in our company, 2nd Sergeant Beard has been made 1 Sergeant, and Peter Haupt, of Sunbury, taken from the ranks and promoted to 1st Sergeant. Haupt passed an excellent examination, and I am proud, for Sunbury, to say that he is considered one of the A. No. 1's. on drill in our regiment.

With the exceptions of a few slight cases of sickness, the boys are getting along very well and would be perfectly contented if they were at a place where there could be a chance to have a hand in some of the glorious victories which their brothers in arms are engaged in, and away from this detested spot, where there would be something to relieve the eye beside sea-gulls, pelicans and turkey-buzzards. Excuse the shortness of this, hoping ere long to be able to give you an account of a victory in which Co. C, was engaged. Respects to yourself, all in the office and friends generally, I remain

Yours, Fraternally,
H. D. W.

* * * * *

Key West, Fla.,
June 16, 1862.[14]

DEAR WILVERT—

A very sad accident happened here one day last week, which has cast a gloom over the whole regiment. First Sergeant Charles Nolf, Co. I, 47th Regiment Pennsylvania Volunteers, was out on the beach with a few friends of his company gathering shells; in front of them were four of the 90th New York boys with loadened rifles on their shoulders, one of them was carelessly playing with the trigger of his gun, when bang! went off the load, the ball entering the forehead of Nolf, killing him instantly. Great excitement was caused by the accident, and for a time (our boys not knowing the particulars) some of them were determined to avenge their comrade's death, but an investigation pronounced it accidental, when they were satisfied. Nolf was a young man of excellent character, beloved by all who knew him, and it seems hard that he should be hurried into eternity in such a manner, and that too, when the carrying of loadened rifles is strictly prohibited.

There is a family in this city by the name of Fift. One of them, A. Fift, after making a fortune out of his *Uncle Samuel*, (U. S.), thought to make another speck by going to New Orleans to his friend Mr. Mallory[15], one of Jeff Davis' Cabinet (?) in the manufacture of gun boats. Mallory and he went into partnership. After finishing boats, while at Memphis, with a considerable amount of Confederate funds in his pocket, (specie) he gave them the slip. Some of his indignant southern friends followed the double traitor, caught him and immediately hung him, thus saving the United States the trouble of buying an extra rope after this war is over. His brother, who has grown fat off the government, and at the time giving aid to secesh, wishing to visit a cooler atmosphere, and act the part of a nabob in the North, was a few days ago provided with a passage to New York in a Government steamer, while on the same vessel, a soldier, for want of room, could

---

14. *Sunbury American*, July 5, 1862.
15. Stephen R. Mallory (1812–1873), former Democratic senator from Florida and Confederate Secretary of the Navy under Jefferson Davis.

not send a box of sea-shells to gratify the curiosity of his friends at home. You can draw your own inference.

On Saturday, June 4, the troops on the island were reviewed by Gen. Brannan and staff. The *Era*, a paper published by the 90th New York Volunteers, in speaking of our regiment, pays us the following compliment:—

"The 47th Pennsylvania Volunteers, under command of Lieut. Col. Alexander, made a fine appearance. Their marching was perfect and the entire regiment showed the effect of careful drill. A more sturdy, soldierly looking body of men cannot be found, probably, in the service. Col. Good and the officers under his command have succeeded in bringing the Regiment to a state of military discipline creditable alike to them and the State from which they hail. The Regimental band deserves some mention; there are many bands in the service of greater celebrity, whose performances would not bear comparison with that attached to the 47th Regiment."

The paymaster has come at last and paid us off for four months. The sight of money was new to the boys, and most eagerly accepted by them. The Sunbury boys sent most of their pay home to their friends, very glad to do so, showing that, although far away from home, loved ones are not forgotten.

We have received marching (sailing) orders, and before this reaches you, if winds do not play us false, we will be in South Carolina, and probably before Charleston, helping to reduce the place where this foul rebellion first broke out. I will write to you immediately on our arrival, attempting to give you a description of the voyage, and an account of the manner in which Neptune treated the health and *feelings* of the boys. All is hurry and bustle in camp, striking tents, &c., so much so that I can scarcely write. We are all well. None of the Sunbury boys left behind.

With respects to all in the office, and friends generally, I remain,

Yours, fraternally,
H. D. W.

* * * * *

Beaufort, S. Car.,
July 21, 1862.[16]

DEAR WILVERT:—Some evil disposed persons, or those who have no regard for the truth, have written home stories that certain members of our company, myself and Captain Gobin included, had been "engaged in rioting," "disobeyed orders," "killed a citizen," &c., and consequently were to be shot, or other punishment inflicted according to the decision of a court-martial. Such reports are very unpleasant to us, who are far away, offering our lives as a sacrifice for the honor of our insulted flag, and have means to refute the foul reports until *slander* has done its work; while parents and friends are left to an uncertainty, and *sneers* jests of the *sympathizers* are eagerly let loose to hurt the feelings of those who are left unprotected by their sons who are doing *their* part in putting down this rebellion. For the future, it is the wish of our Company, that the friends at home will listen to no more such stories, and believe no reports, unless duly authenticated.

The Sunbury boys of the Band belonging to the 45th Pennsylvania Volunteers, were on a visit to our company last week. Their's were the first familiar faces we had seen since we left Virginia, and I tell you, if the meeting of old acquaintances make the heart throb with you, you can imagine our feelings when we clasped the hands of old friends from home, and particularly the feelings of one who had a brother among the number. They were with us for two days and a night. The experience of Camp-life was exchanged, many a story and joke were given, and from my recollection the small hours of the morning were on us before our eyes were closed in sleep. All things have an end, so with their visit, and if joy was manifested at their arrival, so was an equal amount of grief at their departure. Our fellows promised a return visit, but as our passes were being made out, I received a letter from Lieut. T. D. Grant, leader, dated from the *Arago*, informing me they were on board of that vessel, ready for their departure to Fortress Monroe, so there is "many slip 'twixt the cup and the lip," and while they are off to share in the victory of Richmond, we will bide our time and wait to be in at the subjugation of Charleston.

---

16. *Sunbury American*, August 9, 1862.

That portion of our Regiment to whom was assigned picket duty, on the line nearest the enemy, have returned, being relieved by the 7th New Hampshire Volunteers. Our fellows report the duties pleasant, as it was amusing to see the Georgia sharp-shooters trying to pop the pickets on post, forgetting that our Springfield rifles were of a longer range than theirs, however, they soon discovered it, as could be seen, by the way in which they jumped behind trees whenever our boys returned their fire. Before our party were relieved, two or three companies crossed the river to have some fun, the rebels, not liking the appearance of our bright barrels, skedaddled, leaving our men nothing to do but to burn down the houses they had for protection, and the pay for their trouble amounted to a few red cotton overcoats.

The sight of a lady, since we left Key West[,] is something we had not dreamed of, when last night, four beautiful of the fair, made their appearance, accompanied by some officers, while our regiment was on dress parade. The order for "eyes front" were but half obeyed; and how could it be, when such attractions were on the left. A piece of crinoline is a rarity, and no more wonder, after my experience last night, that the appearance of a lady created such a furor with the miners when the gold was first discovered in California.

Capt. Gobin has commenced his old occupation, that of Judge Advocate. A general Court Martial convened to-day at Beaufort, and from the trial list, I think he will have many weary hours before he is through with his duties.

There is nothing new in the fighting line, however, I hope ere long to give you some of the exploits of the 47th. The boys of our company are all well, this climate seeming to agree with them much better than that of Key West. With respects to all in the office, and friends generally, I remain,

Yours, Fraternally,
H. D. W.

* * * * *

Letters from the Taggart Guards
Company B, 34th Pennsylvania Volunteer Infantry
(5th Reserves)

While the Sunbury Guards settled into occupation duties along the Florida coast, the Taggart Guards prepared for the Union's offensive against Richmond. Initially performing a supporting role with the Pennsylvania Reserves[17] while McClellan moved to the peninsula to begin his drive on Richmond, the 5th Reserves broke camp on March 10, 1862, and moved first to Hunter's Mill, where it bivouacked until March 14, and then to Alexandria. On April 9 the regiment relocated to Manassas, occupying the deserted Confederate positions. While stationed there the 5th was detailed to guard the Orange & Alexandria Railroad from Alexandria to Catlett's Station. On May 7, they were ordered to report to Falmouth, where the regiment encamped until May 25, when the entire 1st Brigade of the Pennsylvania Reserves was directed to cross the Rappahannock River and occupy Fredericksburg. There, the regiment's principal duties included picketing the surrounding countryside and the approaches to the river.[18]

Once he was well into his operations on the Peninsula, McClellan—ever doubtful of his own numerical superiority—called upon the Pennsylvania Reserves to reinforce the Army on June 9. The 5th Reserves moved by transport to White House on the Pamunkey River, then marched along the Richmond & West Point Railroad to Dispatch Station and Mechanicsburg, where they encamped within sight of enemy lines.[19] The day after McClellan initiated the first of the Seven Days' Battles with his attack at Oak Grove on June 25, the 5th was sent across Beaver Dam Creek to picket the line along the left bank of the Chickahominy River. When the enemy advanced in force, however, the regiment was pulled back into line of battle, with the 1st Brigade holding the right flank. The Battle of Mechanicsburg ensued, in which the 5th Reserves lost some fifty casualties. The regiment took part in the battle at Gaines Mill on June 27, when the reserve was forced to go into the fight, and

---

17. At this point, the entire Pennsylvania Reserves comprised the 2nd Division of the Union Army 1st Corps, which was tasked with defending the Potomac River line while the remainder of the Army of the Potomac moved against Richmond.

18. Bates, *Pennsylvania Volunteers*, 1:666.

19. Bates, *Pennsylvania Volunteers*, 1:666. For a thorough account of the Peninsula Campaign to this point, see Stephen W. Sears, *To the Gates of Richmond: The Peninsula Campaign* (New York: Ticknor & Fields, 1992).

then recrossed the Chickahominy on the evening of June 28 and marched via Savage Station and White Oak Swamp to Charles City Cross Roads on June 29. The next day the regiment fought in a severe engagement at Glendale, in which the regiment's commander, Col. Seneca G. Simmons, and the Taggart Guards' leader, Capt. James Taggart, were both killed in action. On July 1, the final clash of the Seven Days took place at Malvern Hill, but the 5th Reserves were not engaged, and then the next day they retired with the Army back to Harrison's Landing and went into camp. McClellan's Peninsula Campaign was over.[20]

Camp Washington,
On board the *Rappahannock*,
May 18, 1862.[21]

Dear Old Gazette:—It is a long time since you and our friends at home have had a word from the Old Soldier. As it is the Sabbath, and a day of rest, I pencil a few lines to let you know that we can hear the whistle of the trains that carry the Secesh to and from their camp in front of us. If we have good luck we will have a chance to try the stuff of the Pennsylvania reserve yet. So far we have been playing the soldier of 1812, doing nothing but eating uncle Sam's grub, and marching from one place to another. It seems to be our luck that when we march[,] the Secesh also move, so that we never meet; but as things look now[,] if they do not "skedaddle," we will have a little brush soon. As I sit writing, the first train from Acquia Creek comes puffing past, and is hailed with a shout from the regiment. The railroad bridge across the Rappahannock will be done soon, and then I suppose the word will be "onward." The Secesh can burn bridges, but there is no other party that can build them as quick as the Union army. Our regiment has done every and anything but fight. We have built forts, dug ditches, built rifle-pits, guarded rail roads, and marched all over the State of Virginia. In our last march from Catlett Station to Falmouth we had a nice time, as the weather was fine and the roads in good marching order, but the most of the way there

---

20. Bates, *Pennsylvania Volunteers*, 1:666–668.
21. *Sunbury Gazette*, May 31, 1862.

was some complaint on account of the shoes. I do not wish harm to anyone, but all the harm I wish the contractors for Government shoes is that they may have to march thirty or forty miles over a rough road, with their own shoes on. We had some talk at Camp Curtin about contractors defrauding the State, but we have taken that all back, and hold up our old pants, blouses, and shoes, which we received from the State of Pennsylvania at Camp Curtin, as patterns of what they should be when we draw them now; and when we draw our rations now we think of the rations we received at Camp Curtin, and think Andy Curtin is a brick, and knows what is good for a soldier.

Our regiment is favored with good health, and the doctor says they are up to their fighting weight, and will give a good account of themselves when they are called. They know how work ought to be done. Company B is in fine trim, and the Captain spares no pains to make them compare favorably with any in the reserve.

I would like to be up in Northumberland County for a few days, and see how the Breckinridgers take Hunter's proclamation, and how they like to drink of the cup they have helped to fill.[22] I think some folks that I might name in the good old town of Northumberland, hereafter when they look back at some of their doings with regard to slavery, such as turning off a preacher because he thinks slavery is a sin, and bringing the Bible to prove that slavery is right, and holding on to it even if the government goes to destruction, will have to repent in sack cloth and ashes, or they, on that great day will be found in the road that leads to h——l, for they could not live in peace in heaven.

But every day brings us news of the old flag, how she mounts over all obstructions, and fort after fort falls, and the American Eagle of to-day is a much prouder bird than it was one year ago. Now she looks from the flag-staff of the *Monitor* and *Nugatuck*. One more victory, and then on to Charleston, and then we will soon hear that the mud-sills of the North have conquered a peace with their *friends* in the South, and that the glorious old Union that has been tried in

---

22. On May 9, 1862, Maj. Gen. David Hunter, Department of the South, issued General Order 11, declaring all slaves in the department (which covered Georgia, Florida, and South Carolina) to be free. On May 19—the day after Old Soldier made his comment to the *Gazette*—Lincoln issued a proclamation revoking Hunter's order. The term "Breckinridgers" referred to local Democrats in Northumberland County with pro-Southern sentiments who voted for John C. Breckinridge in the 1860 presidential election.

the fire and found to be pure gold, will have the respect of the world, and be hailed with joy by the down trodden of all nations.

I can almost see from the *Rappahannock* how some of the men look that would ask us last year this time, "what do you think of your President? He will be a nice man to quell a rebellion. He talks of enforcing the laws. He can talk but he never can do it." Now I suppose they will change their tune, and some of the same men would even take an office under Old Abe. Yes, they may talk of all the good Presidents from the foundation of this government, and Old Abe is ahead of them all. He is the greatest man of this age or any other; so thinks the army, so thinks the navy, and the rest of mankind. Good bye for this time.

Yours, Truly,
OLD SOLDIER.

* * * * *

Camp before Richmond,
June 15, 1862.[23]

Friend John.—When we started for Richmond, we got on board the transports six miles below Fredericksburg. While laying below the landing, waiting for some of the other boats, our band played some national airs, Dixie included, which made the darkies, who had gathered to see us embark, almost wild with delight. They clapped their hands, jumped about, made all kinds of motions, and cut all kinds of capers. All along our route down the river, the negroes seemed to be our only friends. They were gathered at every place where the channel was close to shore, some down on their knees praying for us, and some with their babies in their arms. Old[,] gray[-]headed and all kinds came flocking to the river to see the Union folks. The universal cry was—"God bress the Union folks—I is glad you is come—Is Massa Linkum wid you?"

The only thing on our route that seemed surprising to our company was to find at the White House landing some friends from home in the shape of Susquehannah boatmen—Henry Long, Thomas

---

23. *Sunbury Gazette,* July 12, 1862.

London, and Bobby Fletcher. They all look well and happy, and say they are making money.

JUNE 24th, '62.—*Friend John.*—To write this letter I sit down in the sand, in the middle of a cornfield, about half a mile from Mechanicsville, the extreme right of the Grand Army. We have considerable fun getting under arms and going out to the picket lines to support the pickets. Yesterday there was some firing. We went out but did not get a shot; but it looks like work now, and we may have a fight soon. I hear musketry on the right as I sit penning this. The balloon is up trying to find out what they are at.[24] There is a rumor in camp that the rebels are getting out of Richmond as fast as they can. The news was brought in by contrabands. So says Rumor, but she is an old dame what seems to have lost the confidence of the army.

There goes another volley of musketry. The boys lay still and await orders. Perhaps we will have a fight before night. Last night while the 1st was out on picket, a "bould son of Erin" came to the lines from the rebel side, and when he got among our boys, he said—"Bless God, I am under the stars and stripes once more!" When we were down yesterday, supporting the pickets, our artillery sent about forty shells over the river, which made the Secesh get up and dust themselves, and skedaddle for the timber, without sending us one shell in return. We can hear their drums beating every morning, but we have no drumming on our side of the Chickahominy. Our bands will forget how to play. We occupy the right, the same position we held at Pierpont. This is the hardest place we have inhabited since we have been soldiering. Potatoes, when you can get them, are two dollars per bushel; fresh pork 25 cts. Per lb., and other things in proportion—say, milk, 25 cents a quart.

The white folks have all gone to Richmond, with a few exceptions. There are a few negroes left, and some very poor white folks. The country around here is left desolate. The soil is sandy, and the great river Chickahominy is, where we are, about as large as

---

24. The Peninsula Campaign witnessed the first use of hot-air balloons to conduct aerial reconnaissance for the Army. An observer would ascend about five hundred feet, while the balloon remained tethered to a winch on the ground, and make observations of enemy movements.

Chillisquaque creek—the land on its banks low and swampy. We have found plenty of places to cross when the word is given.

We met our old friend, Lieut. Col. Frick,[25] in our march from Chickahominy station. He looks well and in good spirits, but had not much time, to talk with us. He piloted us out to the picket line, and bid us good-bye, as he had to march with his command to some other point of the line. We have some talk with the secesh pickets occasionally, but should any of our men have Sharp's rifles which they want to try, they let fly, and then the firing goes on. There has not been any one wounded since we have been here.

Verily, much soldiering makes the boys smart, for since we have been here some of them have come in with haversacks full of sweet potatoes. Ask them where they got them, and you cannot find out; but if you go out into the fields you find they have dug up the seed that the secesh planted.

The whole army was rejoiced to see the Reserves join them, and well they might be, for our Regiments look as large as some of the Brigades, and we are all fat and in good fighting trim. We were one day too fast for the rebel cavalry that made the dash on our rear. We had marched up the day before. Had they happened to meet us in their route, they might have gone home with fleas in their ears. As it was, the other Regiments in our Brigade were ordered out, and drove them off, or rather they left when our men came in sight. The whole thing came from our being so kind as to send the rebel Mrs. Lee into the enemy's lines with a flag of truce, and she told them all about our rear, and, rumor says, piloted them in their route.

Bang! There goes a shell within about three hundred yards to our left, so I will close, and my next I hope will be from Richmond.

Yours,
OLD SOLDIER.

* * * * *

---

25. Jacob Gellert Frick (1825–1902), a native of Northumberland County, was lieutenant colonel of the 96th Pennsylvania Volunteers during the Peninsula Campaign. Commissioned colonel of the nine-month regiment 129th Pennsylvania Volunteer Infantry, he earned the Medal of Honor for gallantry at Fredericksburg and Chancellorsville.

To the Citizens of Northumberland having Friends and Relatives in Company B, 5th Reg't. Pa. Reserves.

Camp near City Point Landing,
July 4, 1862.[26]

SIRS:—We have participated in the hard fought battles in front of Richmond, and send you a list of casualties as far as can be ascertained at present. The enemy attacked our brigade (1st, 2nd, 5th, and 8th Reg'ts. P. R. C.) on the afternoon of the 26th of June, and we held them in check until re-inforcements arrived, about 9 o'clock. We slept on the battle field that night, and on the 27th fell back towards the Chickahominy, formed in line, and fought another battle. (I will give a complete list below of our killed, wounded, and missing, with the different dates.) After fighting about three and a half hours, reinforcements came up, and our Division fell back across the Chickahominy at Woodbury Bridge. We encamped near the Chickahominy on the 28th, and on the 29th fell back again covering our wagon trains. On the 30th we formed in line, and fought a battle at White Oak Swamps. On the 1st day of July we fell back near the

Union defenders at Ellison's Mill during the Battle of Mechanicsville on June 26, 1862. (Credit: *Battles and Leaders of the Civil War*)

---

26. *Sunbury Gazette*, July 19, 1862.

James River, under cover of the gun boats. A hard battle took place here, but our Division was not taken in, the men being entirely exhausted. There has been almost continual fighting from the 26th of June till the 3d of July, but our Regiment was only in three battles. They were hard fought though, from the fact that our Regiment musters but 350 men. When we get settled again we will try to send a more correct account. These are as near the facts as we can get at present. Our Colonel was killed on the 30th, in the afternoon, during a charge, and the Captain fell about the same time.

Yours Respectfully,
CHAS. WELLS, 1st Lieut., Co. B.

LIST OF LOSSES IN COMPANY B

On June 26th:—
1. John McNeer, wounded, arm, slight (present)

On June 27th:—
2. James M. Phillips, head, severely (present)
3. James M. Bennet, head (missing)
4. Joshua C. Newberry, neck, slightly (present)
5. James E. Morgin, wrist, slightly (present)
6. James A. Keefer, hand & side, severely (on transport)
7. Frederick Winkleman, knee, slightly (present)
8. Josiah Trumphore, head, severely (present)
9. Amos Garman, arm (present)

On June 30th
10. Capt. J. Taggart, breast & leg, severely (missing)
11. Joseph Hogan, neck, dangerously (missing)
12. David Hawk, finger shot off (on transport)
13. Joseph C. Casson, breast & neck, serious (present)
14. Lafayette Vandling, bowels, supposed mortal (missing)
15. William Black, shoulder (missing)
16. James Throp, head, slightly (present)

MISSING, NOT KNOWN WHETHER KILLED OR WOUNDED.
1. Edwin N. Kline,
2. Joseph Martin,
3. William Eckert,
4. Alonzo Capp,
5. Benjamin Evert,
6. John H. Gibbons,
7. William Jarrett,
8. William Starrick,
9. William Smith.

* * * * *

Letters from the Augusta Rangers
Company I, 58th Pennsylvania Volunteer Infantry

The Augusta Rangers went to the Virginia Peninsula as well but performed a supporting role in the rear. On March 8, the 58th Pennsylvania broke camp in Philadelphia and proceeded, half by water transport and the remainder by rail, to Baltimore and then transport south, to Fortress Monroe. Arriving the next day, the regiment settled into Camp Hamilton. Their arrival coincided with the clash at nearby Hampton Roads between the USS Monitor and CSS Virginia (Merrimac), which caused considerable excitement in camp. On May 10, the 58th participated in an expedition to Norfolk, along with an infantry column that included the 10th, 12th, and 99th New York, 1st Delaware, and 16th Massachusetts, plus an artillery battery and a battalion of mounted rifles, all under the command of Maj. Gen. John E. Wool. Upon arriving the next day, the column discovered the Confederate entrenchments abandoned, so they quickly took possession of the city and the surrounding towns of Portsmouth, Newtown, and Gosport, including the Navy Yard. After performing provost guard duty for several days, the 58th marched to Portsmouth and settled into camp to perform routine picket and guard duty.[27]

27. Bates, *Pennsylvania Volunteers*, 2:265–286.

Major General John Ellis Wool (1784–1869), commander of the Department of Virginia, where the 58th Pennsylvania served in 1862. (Credit: Library of Congress)

Camp Hamilton,
March 19, 1862.[28]

To Miss ------. I hope you will excuse my delay in acknowledging the receipt of eight pairs of stockings, and twenty pairs of mittens, for my Company, from the ladies of Sunbury, through Miss M. A. Fisher. Although nearly one month has elapsed, my men have not forgotten the pleasurable feelings which the reception of this welcome gift awakened, for I assure you such kind remembrances from home are not forgotten. So let me, on the part of my Company, return my warmest thanks to the ladies of Sunbury, for their useful gift; and, also, to you, personally, for your kind wishes for myself and Company—pledging to the fair ones at home, that the *Augusta Rangers* will carry the Stars and Stripes in honor wherever ordered—and if the God of war should

---

28. *Sunbury Gazette*, March 29, 1862.

see fit to return them in safety to their homes, they will have the glorious consolation of having done their duty.
Most Respectfully,

Your Humble Servant,
J. BUYERS.

* * * * *

Camp Hamilton, near Fortress Monroe,
March 31, 1862.[29]

JOHN YOUNGMAN, ESQ.,—Dear Sir:—If I had the leisure time it would afford me much pleasure to tell to my friends at home, through the medium of your paper, the wanderings, and doings, and sight seeing of the Augusta Rangers, but as my time is rather limited they will not be much troubled in this respect; and as we are limited in our correspondence about the army and its movements, your readers will pardon me for not being very communicative on that point. My company has improved very much as soldiers since leaving camp Curtin, and I am pleased to say that every move we have made since, has improved our condition. We are living more pleasantly now than we have lived at any time since we are in the service. Our camp is beautifully located on the bank of Mill Creek, directly opposite to and about half a mile from Fortress Monroe, with a view of the latter place, also of the mouth of Chesapeake Bay, of Hampton Roads, the mouth of James River, the mouth of Elizabeth River, of Sewell's Point, near Hampton creek, and within sight of the ruins of Hampton, with hundreds of sailing vessels and steamers in the distance. Among the latter, the celebrated *Monitor*—alias, the Yankee Cheese Box, alias, the Terror of the Waters, and most certainly the saviour of many lives and much property in this neighborhood. We got here just too late to see the fight between the *Monitor* and the *Merrimac*, and many curses will have to be answered for on that account. Well, it was provoking, for it must have been a beautiful sight. The boys have seen more of military life here than they ever saw before, surrounded as they are by thousands of troops of every arm of the service—from the fifteen inch gun, and the well-handled batteries of Nim and Griffin, down to the

---

29. *Sunbury Gazette*, April 12, 1862.

well-handled Minie, accompanied with all the pomp and show, and paraphernalia of war. They have also seen much destruction.

On Sunday last my company was detailed as part of the grand guard, a part of which I stationed on the out-skirts of Hampton, or rather the ruins of Hampton, under charge of Lieut. Jackson, the remainder under my charge along Hampton creek, with the main post at Hampton bridge, distant from our camp from two to two and a half miles. I have met with much destruction of property, but never any equal to the ruins of Hampton, that once rich and beautiful town so utterly annihilated that not one whole house remains. In looking after my sentinels, it became necessary for me to go through the greater part of the ruins, and while doing so, the many bright hopes and princely fortunes now blasted forever, that once clustered around this beautiful spot, presented themselves so vividly to my mind, that as I sat among these ruins, just as the dawn of day began to show them in all their horror and gloom, in the weakness of my nature I cursed the rebels who caused this destruction. Your readers will remember that Hampton was the principal resort of the first families of Virginia. It was built almost exclusively of brick, while the grounds and walks, and trees and shrubbery were beautifully arranged, situated on Hampton Creek, one further mile from its entrance into Hampton Roads, surrounded by a level and fertile country, and accessible by boats drawing twelve feet water. The only sheltered post to be found here for our guards was in an old wooden building partly torn down, where Gen. ------ and staff, (whose brigade were on their way elsewhere,) were glad to accept of a berth on the floor along with the men. Said General met one of my men next morning carrying a part of his rations (being a piece of dry bread) to an old negro who lived nearby; stopping the guard he asked for the bread for himself which was given him, when he seated himself by a well nearby, and made his breakfast on bread and water. Now, in the name of heaven, what is the use for the tender-fisted gentry of the South to contend with such men? Part of our duty while on guard along Hampton creek was guarding five large buildings filled with contrabands, just opposite Hampton. One of said buildings was the late residence of John Tyler, who I am ashamed to style Ex-President.

I was pleased to hear of the confirmation of Doctor McCoy[30], by the Senate, as a Brigade Surgeon; he has become deservedly popular here. Doctor Fisher left our camp a few days since, with the 57th regiment, and camped with said regiment two miles beyond Hampton. He is in good health, being more fleshy than I have ever seen him.

The Augusta Rangers are well pleased with this place; there is only one reported this morning unfit for duty. We are getting along very well with company drill—so much so that I am becoming proud of their performances. But I am sorry to say that we are not having the Regiment drill we should have, notwithstanding which the boys are anxious to meet the rebels.

It is singular how a soldier's life will alter the dispositions of men: the majority of my men are growing somewhat impatient, and, as the boys say, *spiling for a fight*—yet, while at home, they are quiet and peaceable citizens, and while here are living a more sober and orderly life than some of them were used to at home, but the continual use of arms, and practice of the art of fighting, make them cool, daring, and somewhat reckless.

The general character of the soldier, after he has learned to drop the citizen and become the soldier, is to be admired. Possessed of a new sense of honor, candid and free, cool and daring, they seem to move above the sordid meanness of mankind generally, in an atmosphere peculiarly their own. I am afraid that many will find to their sorrow, should this war continue long, that it will be quite as difficult to drop the soldier and become the citizen as it was to drop the citizen and become the soldier.

I feel like giving you an account of the doings of the army here, but must refrain. A large body of troops passed in review before Gen. Wool the other day, among the rest the Augusta Rangers. When on dress parade of the same day, we received a written compliment from the good old General, for our correct marching and soldierly bearing. The 58th Regiment is very fortunate in having good, comfortable tents—six Sibleys to a company, while the line officers have two marquees to a company.

We have some difficulty in getting wood for cooking purposes, having to bring it from beyond the picket lines, and take it from those

---

30. Dr. Robert B. McCay of Northumberland. See his letter to the *Sunbury American*, July 5, 1862, on page 278.

men only who have not professed allegiances to Uncle Abe's government. Our government don't buy any wood in Dixie. Our rations are good and generally plenty of them, consisting of good bread just one day old, baked at the fort by details from the army, with plenty of beans, rice, potatoes, sugar, coffee, with candles and soap, good water within a few rods, and everything to make us comfortable, except, as I mentioned above, the want of plenty of fuel. I was afraid the want of fire would tell badly upon the health of the men, but I was mistaken, as the company was never more healthy than at present, while the men appear to be improving in health and spirits every day.

I just received a note from one of my sick men at home, in Luzerne county. He was a very good old soldier, and much respected by all the company. He left us at Philadelphia, crying as he left, showing by every move that his heart was with his country. The poor old patriot says in his note: "Dear Captain, please Sir, mark me not a deserter." God bless him. He is one of three of my men who are absent from the regiment. We now number eighty-two enlisted men in camp, but there is over one hundred enlisted men in the regiment from my company. I am unable to tell your readers anything about our future movements, neither when, where, or how we may move, but hope we may ever be able to render a good account of ourselves.

It has become a noticeable fact that the privates of my company are more apt at learning, and have become better booked up on the drill than the majority of other companies in the same length of time. This is to be attributed in part to the fact of our having several good old soldiers in the ranks, and also to having good and efficient Sergeants, while our 1st Lieutenant, A. Jackson, a lawyer by profession, and resident of Wilkesbarre, is one of the most accomplished officers of the regiment, well booked up in military affairs, gentlemanly and kind, and I am pleased to say continues to improve on acquaintance. Our 2d Lieutenant, J. R. Searle, of Luzerne county, has proven himself every inch the gentleman, willing and attentive; so you see that I am ably sustained.

Sending the respects of the Augusta Rangers to all our friends.
I remain Yours Truly,

JOHN BUYERS.

* * * * *

Camp Hamilton,
April 21, 1862.[31]

H. B. MASSER, ESQ.
Dear Sir:—Nothing of particular interest has passed with the "Augusta Rangers" for some days past. And we have still to cronule [sic] "all quiet at Fortress Monroe." Our regiment has been engaged for a few days improving the Camp, and I am pleased to say, that we have now the most beautifully encamped regiment, I ever saw. Our company, in the course of their fixing up, did not forget your humble servant; but of their own free will and a kindness of disposition, which was very pleasing, they sodded the front of both the marquees—laid a brick pavement from the walk to the entrance—planted five beautiful trees in front, and otherwise beautified the whole premises. While it must be born in mind that the greatest part of the above material had to be carried from half to one mile. The men improved their own premises also. And I do assure you it was truly refreshing to all concerned to turn from the continual use of arms and wearying drill, to the gentle and wholesome work of peace such as that named above. Just two days, spent in this way, did the men more good than all the services and moral lectures, that could be talked to them in a month. They go back to their drill, truly rested, with renewed energy and a more cheerful spirit. The health of the Company is good. This is a healthy place. Some years ago it was quite a resort for invalids. Gen. Jackson and John C. Calhoun spent many summers here, while beauty and fashion reigned supreme.

But what a change this rebellion has wrought within one short year. Now, not one family to be found in the neighborhood who is not engaged in the war. Not one farm being cultivated, not a team passing over the road except war teams, in fine nothing meets the view throughout this beautiful country, but war [materiel] and negroes. Going further into the Old Dominion, a farmer may be found here and there, lingering about his premises. A few of them professing true fealty to the Union, but a vast majority holding on to their property with one hand and nursing the rebellion with the other. There is much more ignorance among the white agricultural population here than I had supposed. Among the few that remain[,]

---
31. *Sunbury American*, May 3, 1862.

we have not found any possessed of a fair amount of intelligence. For example, one old gentleman and lady, living on a beautiful farm of four hundred acres, between Hampton and Newport News, and owning much other property and many slaves, we found neither of them able to read writing, while the old lady could not tell her age, because, as she remarked, the leaf of the old Bible, which had it on, was torn out. While being ignorant about outside matters generally, they do not redeem their character in the least by being good farmers, for I have not met with a well worked farm in this part of the country.

If our war friends in the west have as fair a prospect of success before Corinth as our army has before Yorktown and neighborhood, the bulk of the rebellion will soon be crushed out, providing those in the South engaged in warring against our Government do not get too much aid and comfort from their Northern friends. I have reason to know that this kind of feeling, shown so many places in the North, give the rebels great encouragement, and make our work much more difficult.

We have just heard of the taking of New Orleans. I hope it is true. It has created much rejoicing here, while it leaves the war map [to] have the appearance of giving to the men in this peninsula the main balance of the work, and no one has a doubt but what they will do it.

The boys are in good spirits, and thanks to the many letters and papers from home, for assisting to keep them so. They look eagerly for every mail, while every mail brings more or less for them. But I hear some complain. This should not be. I would most respectfully call the attention of their friends to this matter. It is a duty you owe to your sons, your brothers, or your husbands, to talk to them frequently through the mails. It should afford you much pleasure to do so, while you will be doing them much good.

Your readers will pardon me for not giving them any army news. I can only tell them that we are not allowed to write about the army movements.—But, say some people, who have troubled me in this respect, your letters are never opened—you can write what you please. Let me say to all such, that when my honor as an officer becomes so much doubted that my mail matter must be overhauled, I shall resign, which I certainly would not like to do as long as my health permits me to keep my place, which I hope it will do until this grand fight is well finished.

Sending the respects of the Augusta Rangers to all their friends, let me remain,

Yours, respectfully,
J. BUYERS.

* * * * *

H. B. MASSER, ESQ.,[32]

DEAR SIR:—I see a mistake in your paper, which was made in writing you about the Gosport Navy Yard, which I would beg leave to correct. It was the Rebel Government which employed only three hundred and fifty hands in the yard. Our government employed on average about one thousand in it.

I am now stationed with my Company in Portsmouth, and composes part of the Provost Guard of the city. We are quartered along with Company F, in a building formerly used as a depot and warehouse. It is beautifully situated on the bank of the river. And the most aggregable quarters we have had since being in the service. Six companies of our regiment are in Norfolk, and four in this place. We have two stations in this city. Capt. Brown of Company A., commanding one, while I have charge of the other. The boys are very much pleased with the berth, and well they may be, for this is the first house they have had as quarters since the latter part of January. And last night was the first night I have passed inside of a building since the latter part of February.

We came here to relieve the 1st Delaware, the latter regiment having been ordered elsewhere—Just this moment, I received orders to march, the orders of the 1st Delaware are countermanded.—Some strategic movement on hand.

We have become the traveling brigade—having marched in six different directions within a month. The boys think we are being trained for Zeigle's command. (He being called the travelling Major). The Company continue in good health.

---

32. *Sunbury American*, June 14, 1862. The letter itself was undated.

Letters for my company will still be addressed to Portsmouth, and they will follow the Regiment.

Yours, &c.,
JOHN BUYERS

* * * * *

Portsmouth, Va.,
July 6, 1862.[33]

Friend John.—As many false stories have been circulated at Sunbury concerning this company, I would state to you that we are getting along very well—a few more than usual complaining of being unwell, but only one sick enough to stay in the hospital. The boys are in good spirits, and not at all disheartened by the late fight of McClellan's. Our army at Richmond was roughly handled—had seven days' hard fighting against great odds. They are now resting under the protection of the gun boats, just below Fort Darling, and may require reinforcements before moving. We have every confidence in McClellan, but his command is too weak. Our men did everything that men could do, but they had to contend against a superior number of men, three-fourths of whom were maddened with powdered whiskey, while the officers were desperate.

We have marching orders, and are only waiting for green troops to relieve us. I feel anxious to get nearer Richmond, and expect to engage in the fight. If the Rebels make another stand at Richmond, we will have in that neighborhood the greatest battle on record. The Union sentiment in Eastern Virginia does not appear to brighten much, while the rebel army is becoming desperate, but I believe our government is just as safe now as ever. The Union cause *must triumph*. The darkest hour is just before day-light, and that day-light, followed by the sun-rise of peace, is not far distant.

Yours,
J—.[34]

* * * * *

---

33. *Sunbury Gazette*, July 19, 1862.
34. The letter is from Capt. John Buyers.

Camp near Portsmouth, Va.,
July 31, 1862.[35]

Friend John.—I intended writing you in time for this week's paper, but could not get it down. I have nothing particular to tell, yet I know that those about Sunbury who have friends with the Augusta Rangers would like to hear from them as often as practicable.

It is useless for me to try to give you any general war news. I will only report progress for our own company and Regiment. It is now full ten o'clock on Thursday night—raining and very dark—not a light to be seen except a few in the officers' quarters—the men wrapped in peaceful slumbers—and not a sound to be heard except the steady tread of the faithful sentinel, whose quiet gun reports all right.

Imagine your old playmate sitting in his Marquee at this time, with his thoughts for his only company, and those thoughts wandering off towards home, and settling down upon the good old times when we went journeying together, and enjoyed the beauties of nature.

These is no scenery around here to compare with that about Sunbury, while the cultivation of the land here is miserable—nothing to compare with that about Sunbury, except in flowers and strawberries. The flowers here are beautiful, and the strawberries were most excellent. But the more important articles, as grain, grass, potatoes, &c., are indifferent. The only kinds of garden truck that equals ours are tomatoes and onions.

My company has had a good chance to test the qualities of all kinds of vegetables around here, and, like wise men, they have improved it. They do much grand guard duty, (or picket, it is called,) and while doing so they present their compliments to many rebel farmers, whose property they are guarding, and generally take part of their pay out in garden truck, chickens, &c.

Our Regiment is doing all the guard duty that is being done between the Elizabeth and Sangamond rivers, taking care of rebel property, seeing that the mails are being regularly carried between Norfolk and Richmond, and that all common carriers are not disturbed in their peaceful avocations, from Norfolk westward—and doing all other things that good and faithful servants of the Richmond

---

35. *Sunbury Gazette*, August 16, 1862.

government should do. Now if the same course is being pursued by the Union army generally, we may expect our reward, and that reward will be a long and bloody war, wound up with a successful rebellion.

But I am pleased to see a different state of things inaugurated by Gen. Pope[36], and endorsed by our good old President. God grant that Pope's style may come in vogue down this way soon. Slight glimmerings of it have already appeared, and have been hailed by all the military with rapturous applause. We hail it as the harbinger of a short war and a quick return to our peaceful homes. The kid glove business is about played out, and we expect soon to be invited to wade in, the whole union army will do it with a hearty good will, and make the benighted traitors board them while doing the work. It may be hard work to beat repentance into their darkened souls, but it must be done.

The general health of our company is good, not one in the hospital. We are still encamped in a grove, near Portsmouth. Since I wrote to you, we have had a short raid, up the country. On Tuesday last some of the patrol reported the rebels advancing in force over the Sangamond River. The long roll beat at quarter past one o'clock P. M., and at half-past one o'clock the regiment was on its way toward the Sangamond, with one days['] rations provided. Your humble servant was honored with the command of two companies consolidated for the time, forming the color company. Our boys were the first in line, God bless them.

Finding the report false, or the rebels having retreated, we returned to camp reaching here a little after daylight, on Wednesday, somewhat tired, but right side up with care.

It is getting late, and I must close. Those wishing to write to the company will still address to camp near Portsmouth, Va.

Yours, Respectfully,
J. B.

* * * * *

---

36. Maj. Gen. John Pope (1822–1890). He earned successes in the Western Theatre early on in the war leading the Army of the Mississippi, and pursued a harsher policy towards Confederate civilians, but met ignominious defeat during the Second Bull Run Campaign after being brought east to command the Army of Virginia.

Letter from Thomas D. Grant
Regimental Band, 45th Pennsylvania Volunteer Infantry

During the spring campaigns of 1862 a trio of Northumberland County soldiers checked in with the Sunbury newspapers for the first time, updating their hometown on their activities and wellbeing. The first to write was Thomas D. Grant, a twenty-seven-year-old store clerk who had been the leader of Grant's Cornet Band, a popular instrumental group in Sunbury before the war.[37] On September 15, 1861, the band enlisted as an ensemble and was designated as the regimental band for the 45th Pennsylvania Volunteers, which organized at Camp Curtin on October 21. Two days later the regiment traveled by rail to Washington and went into camp along the Bladensburg Road. On November 3 the regiment was ordered to Prince Frederick, Maryland, to oversee peaceful elections in that district. After returning to camp, the 45th departed again on November 19 aboard the steamer Pocahontas *for Fortress Monroe. It remained in camp until December 6, then embarked for Port Royal, South Carolina. There, the regiment participated in the occupation of the Sea Islands. Grant's letter from March 15 described the unit's activities up to that point. The band was collectively discharged from service by general order on September 27, 1862.[38]*

Fort Drayton,
Otter Island, S. Car.,
March 15, 1862.[39]

DEAR JOHN:—Having a leisure hour this afternoon, I will endeavor to drop you a few lines, in fulfillment of my promise to let you know how we are getting along "down in Dixie." Since leaving Harrisburg, our career has indeed been a shifting one, and I will give you a brief history of it.

---

37. Grant and his band were briefly referenced in Wharton's letter of July 21, 1862, on page 240.
38. Bates, *Pennsylvania Volunteers*, 1:1057–1058, 1072–1073.
39. *Sunbury Gazette*, March 29, 1862.

On the 21st of October last, our Regiment, the 45th Pennsylvania, left Harrisburg, bound for Washington, D. C., where we arrived on the 22nd, about 4 o'clock, P. M., and were quartered last night in the "Soldier's Retreat." Next day we marched out of the city and encamped about a mile and a half from it on the Bladensburg Road. We remained here but three or four days and marched to Camp Hale, near Bladensburg. While at this Camp, we were placed in the Brigade of Gen. O. O. Howard.

As regards Washington, I have scarcely anything to say, we not being permitted to enter the city, and my only view of it being from the dome of the Capitol, which through the kindness of Col. Welsh, I was permitted to visit in company with several of the Sunbury boys. While at Camp Hale, we participated in a grand review, which took place on the parade ground near the city, on the 28th of October, I believe. It was the most splendid sight I ever beheld. In passing in review, I had a fair view of Gen. McClellan and Staff. The General and his entire Staff were in full uniform and mounted on splendid horses. On the 5th of November our Brigade, composed of the 45th Pennsylvania, 4th Michigan, 2nd New Hampshire and 5th Rhode Island regiments, was ordered into Maryland to protect the Union men in the holding of their election. Our regiment marched to Prince Frederick, the county seat of Calvert County, a distance of sixty miles from Bladensburg. We made the march in three days. On the 2d day we marched 27 miles; every man carrying his arms, a heavy knapsack and two days provisions in his knapsack. This you must admit was pretty good work for raw troops. We remained a day at Prince Frederick, and on the 7th started on [illegible phrase] where we arrived on the 9th, pretty well "used up" as soldiers say. Camp Hale being very unhealthy, we moved, on the 18th, to within about a mile of Washington, on the farm of J. C. Rives, Esq. Our stay here was very short, as on the 19th we received orders to proceed to Fortress Monroe, via Baltimore. We left for Baltimore about midnight, arriving there about 11 o'clock, A. M., on the 20th, and embarked on board the Steamer *Pocahontas* (since wrecked off Cape Hatteras in Gen. Burnside's Expedition.) We arrived at the Fortress next day about 3 o'clock, P. M., landed and marched out to "Camp

Hamilton," and encamped. In marching out to Camp, we were reviewed by Maj. Gen. Wool and Staff.

To the kindness of Dr. McCoy, now medical Purveyor of that post, I am indebted for an interior view of the Fortress, and a very interesting description of it. From the Fortress we could see the batteries at Newport News, Sewell's Point and Craney Island. Through a glass I distinctly saw floating over the latter, the accursed ensign of treason.

We remained at Camp Hamilton until the 6th of December, when we embarked on board the Transport Steamer *Cosmopolitan*, bound for Port Royal, where we arrived on the 9th, after a delightful passage. The weather was so pleasant that there was but very little sea-sickness among the men; but for myself, I felt seriously inclined to "cast up accounts," and pay tribute to old father Neptune; but I presume, the old gentleman, knowing that I would again pass over a portion of his dominions, postponed the settlement. I supposed I will catch it next time. Before landing at Port Royal, we received orders to proceed with five companies of our regiment to this point, where we arrived on the 11th, bringing with us five large guns for the fort.

This point was occupied by rebel troops, previous to the capture of Port Royal, and quite a large fort (earth works) constructed; but after the taking of Port Royal they abandoned it after bursting their guns and setting fire to the wood-work of the fort. Little damage was done by the fire, and in a short time we had our guns mounted and things put in order. The works are considered quite strong, and are enclosed by a ditch twenty feet wide in which piles, eight feet high, are driven.

There are quite a number of "contrabands" on this island and others arriving almost daily. I witnessed a scene a few days ago that for brutality exceeded any thing I ever beheld. I was called from my tent to see a log of negroes that had just arrived. Among the number was a woman with a little child—around the neck of the woman was an iron yoke, a heavy chain connecting it with an iron band around her ankle. She had attempted to escape and was thus hobbled to prevent her running, as it would instantly throw her down upon her attempting it. She, however, managed to get to our Camp, where she was soon released from her bonds; but not until nearly every man in the regiment had seen her and vented curses on the wretches who do or permit such cruel acts. The woman says she has had these chains on her three months.

On Wednesday last, part of our regiment was sent out on a scouting and foraging expedition, and on Thursday morning very early they divided into two parts, intending to make a simultaneous attack upon a house in which it was said a rebel picket was stationed. Owing to a dense fog and the negro guide taking one party the wrong road, they unfortunately came together, and before they could recognize each other, fired upon each other, the result of which was sad indeed. Capt. Rambo, of Company K, and Corporal Reichert, of the same Company, were instantly killed, and one Corporal and six privates of that Company, wounded, one of whom died last night; one of Company G and one of Company H were slightly wounded. Captain Rambo was from Columbia, Pa.—an excellent officer and highly esteemed by his Company and Regiment. The bodies of the Captain and Corporal Reichert were sent home in charge of Lieut. Fassler. This sad disaster cast a gloom over our Camp, and it will be long before it is forgotten. It was indeed a sad sight when the killed and wounded were borne from the boats, and one which I trust it may be long ere I again behold.

On Thursday, very heavy firing was heard in the direction of Savannah, and I have since heard that three of the rebel gun-boats were captured by our fleet near Fort Jackson. We are in daily expectation of hearing of the capture of Fort Pulaski and Savannah.

The success our army has met with in different places, leads us to hope for a speedy termination of this war. God grant that it may be so, and that we may again return to our happy homes. How long we will remain at this post I cannot of course tell, but from present appearances it will not be long.

With every mail comes that truly welcome visitant, the *Gazette*. Please accept my sincere thanks for your kind remembrance of the absent. Should you have any difficulty in finding substitutes for the two subscribers who have lately stopped your paper, let me say to you that they will be forthcoming as soon as we are once more in old Sunbury, as the *Gazette* and the *American* are the kind of papers that those who are now in the service of their country prefer having. All the Sunbury boys in our Regiment are in good health, and desire to be kindly remembered.

Very truly,
G.

* * * * *

Letter from George W. Kiehl
Company D, 11th Pennsylvania Volunteer Infantry
(Three Years)

The second author, George W. Kiehl, had enlisted in Company D of the reorganized 11th Pennsylvania Regiment when that unit assembled in early August 1861. Even though the company was mainly recruited from Jersey Shore, Lycoming County, it contained several Sunbury men. Now serving for three years, the 11th Pennsylvania remained in Camp Curtin, Harrisburg, until November 27, when it moved to Baltimore and then to Annapolis, where it was attached to the forces of the Middle Department under Maj. Gen. John A. Dix until April 1862. While at Annapolis the 11th engaged in guard duty along the railroad lines, served as provost guard for the city and Naval Academy, and provided large details for fatigue duty. On April 9 the regiment was ordered to Washington, D.C., where it arrived the next day and was quartered at Soldier's Rest. The regiment then went to Manassas Junction on April 17 to guard the Manassas Gap Railroad until May 12. In early June the 11th participated in an expedition to Front Royal.[40] Kiehl's lone missive to the Sunbury Gazette *was sent in late March 1862 while the regiment was stationed at the Annapolis suburb of Crownsville.*

Crownsville, Anne Arundel Co., Md.,
March 26, 1862.[41]

Dear Editor:—It is a pleasure to me to enclose a few lines to you, informing you that I have received the two last issues of your paper.

---

40. Frederick H. Dyer, *A Compendium of the War of the Rebellion* (Des Moines, Iowa: The Dyer Publishing Company, 1908), 1581–1582.
41. *Sunbury Gazette*, April 5, 1862.

I thank you for your kindness, and I hope that myself and the boys from Sunbury will not be forgotten in future, as the *Gazette* is always a welcome visitor among us, as from it we get the news from home.

Since the death of our gallant captain, J. H. Knox, we have had a captain appointed by the Governor to take charge of our company, whose name is Wm. E. Sees, of Harrisburg. He is an able and kind commander. As I have been acquainted with him in the three month's service, (also in the same regiment with myself) I can recommend him as a good man. He is one of our small P. V. Yankee braves—his height is six feet four inches, and built in proportion, and as fine and brave a looking officer as ever drew a sword; if there are any patriotic boys in Sunbury, or thereabout that feel like serving their country, I recommend them to enlist in Co. D, 11th Regiment, commanded by Captain Wm. E. Sees.

We have been ordered on the railroad from Annapolis, and we are stationed between the junction and the former place, situated in a fine pine grove of trees, and have comfortable quarters for the summer. The boys are enjoying themselves by fishing and shooting ducks; they have also plenty of oysters. But we would prefer going further down in Dixie, for the boys think they have been in bondage long enough, and feel anxious to have a brush with Jeff's boys.

This is a very healthy place, and the boys are all well, being able to eat all the rations furnished them, since they are here, and the duty is light. There are four men detailed every morning for twenty-four hours, and each man has but once through the day to walk one mile, and at night two are on at a time, from six to twelve o'clock, and then relieved by the other two men who walk till six in the morning.

The surrounding country is full of secesh to the backbone. I am not an abolitionist myself, but I have seen enough of the institution of slavery since I am here, and learned enough from information of the inhabitants, to know that it is a curse to them instead of a blessing. I hope that the colored race throughout the world, may speedily see the day of freedom, and I believe that God, who ruleth over all nations, designs the present as the time of their deliverance.

As for the boys who came with me from Sunbury and the country, Serg. I. S., Taylor, Corp. R. B. Taylor, [Theodore] Robins,

Jno. P. Clemens, C. S. Chamberlin, Hiram Manier and Jacob Poff, they are all well, and enjoy themselves happily here.[42]
I remain yours, &c.,

GEO. W. KIEHL, O. S.

* * * * *

Letter from William A. Fetter
Company D, 7th Pennsylvania Cavalry
(80th Volunteers)

The third correspondent, William A. Fetter, of Company D, 7th Pennsylvania Cavalry (80th Pennsylvania Volunteers), reported from Camp Morehead near Columbia, Tennessee, in May 1862. The 7th Pennsylvania Cavalry had initially been authorized by Governor Curtin on August 27, 1861, and recruited throughout the fall, with the soldiers assembling at Camp Cameron in Harrisburg. On December 19 the regiment departed for Louisville, Kentucky, reporting to Maj. Gen. Don Carlos Buell, then in command of the Department of the Cumberland. The regiment was placed in a camp of instruction at Jeffersonville, Indiana, remaining there until the end of January 1862. Then, the 7th moved south to Nashville, Tennessee, to assist in the occupation of the state by Union forces. The three battalions of the regiment were then assigned different duty stations, the first battalion going to Columbia, the second remaining in Nashville for garrison duty, and the third battalion stationed at Murfreesboro and Lebanon. The 1st Battalion, with Company D in tow, moved with a Union column to Chattanooga in June, where they encountered the enemy at Sweden's Cove. On July 1, as the operations in the east were winding down on the peninsula, the 1st Battalion occupied Manchester, Tennessee.[43]

---

42. Of the Sunbury men mentioned in the final paragraph, Sgt. Isaac S. Taylor and Cpl. Robert B. Taylor were both killed at Antietam; John P. Clemens was killed at Fredericksburg; C. S. Chamberlain was wounded at Second Bull Run; Jacob H. Poff was wounded at Antietam, then taken prisoner at the Wilderness on May 6, 1864; and Theodore Robins was wounded at Fredericksburg and later discharged on a surgeon's certificate on June 14, 1863. Only Cpl. Hiram Manier survived the war unscathed and was discharged on June 9, 1865. As for George W. Kiehl, he deserted on September 14, 1862. See Bates, *Pennsylvania Volunteers*, 1:280–282.

43. Bates, *Pennsylvania Volunteers*, 2:1114–1115; Bell, *History of Northumberland County*, 422.

[The following Soldier's Letter was handed to us for publication.]

Camp Morehead,
Near Columbia, Tenn.,
May 11, 1862.[44]

Dear Sir:—I will endeavor to give you some of our doings down in Dixie. We are encamped on the borders of Columbia, a town situated on the banks of Duck river, and a smart place; population about 5000. There are some Union men in the place, and also some of the Devils—a great many of the latter. The ladies of the place (Union) presented General Negley with a splendid flag, which he had hoisted on the court house. Negley's whole brigade (the 7th) participated in the ceremony. It was a splendid sight. After the flag was floating in the breeze, Negley told the people what would be the consequence if it would be taken down. The town would be laid in ashes. He made a splendid speech on the progress of the Union Army, and all passed off very quietly. We are bothered a great deal by the rebels. We are on the go day and night, hardly getting time to sleep. Some time ago we had a trip down to Pulaski, about 35 miles South of this place. On the way down we were attacked by Morgan's devils. They captured some of our infantry, but after making them take the confederate oath they let them go again; but by the time we (the cavalry) got up, they had all left for a place called Lebanon; but there they got hell; (excuse me.) Our regiment, and some of the Kentucky boys, were together. There was quite a smart brush. Morgan and Scott had about 800 men while we had only 500. We took 175 prisoners, and spotted three men, while only two of our men were slightly wounded. The whole brigade went down to Pulaski yesterday expecting to meet Price[45] with 10 or 15,000 men. The rumor is that he crossed the river, and was coming up this way. Well, he will have a good time of it. General Mitchel[46] in his rear and Negley in front, I don't think he will fare as well as he expects. It is the general opinion that the war will end in guerilla warfare.

---

44. *Sunbury Gazette*, May 31, 1862.
45. Confederate Maj. Gen. Sterling Price (1809–1867).
46. Maj. Gen. Ormsby McKnight Mitchel (1810–1862). He later assumed command of the Department of the South at Hilton Head, South Carolina, and direct operations involving the Sunbury Guards (Company C, 47th Pennsylvania). He succumbed to yellow fever at Hilton Head on October 31, 1862.

The first battalion of the 7th Pennsylvania Cavalry is laying here, the balance is laying back at Nashville. I think that we are the only part of the regiment that is attached to Negley's brigade. We are employed scouting and taking spies. The other day we were sent out to Gen. Pillow's place, (by the way I will tell you that he has one of the finest places in this part of [the] country) to take a spy. After we got in sight of the house, we surrounded the woods, and when he came out and mounted his horse, we closed on him in double quick time. We escorted him to headquarters, and after having a hearing before Negley, he was handed over to the Provost Guard; I think he is in irons now. His plea was that Pillow sent him up to see how much his (Pillow's) property was damaged. He said he had passed through all our pickets from the Mississippi up, and at last he was bagged.

This is one of the best countries that we have passed through since we left old Pennsylvania. There is some of the best land I ever saw. But what a lot of *Nigs* is here; they all work out—women as well as men take the plow. It is getting warm here; the sweat is rolling down while I write. The fruit is growing rapidly. Peaches and all kinds of fruit are plenty. The grain looks well, and out in head, and the harvest is coming on fast.

I enjoy myself first rate. I am not sorry that I went into the service. I have seen more since I have been in the service than I would otherwise have seen in a whole lifetime. We have plenty to eat and drink, and plenty of clothing to wear. My health has been very good ever since I left home, although it was said that I was sick, and never would get well again. My wife wrote to the Captain about it; it was all a sham. The health of the company is good now, though we have had some losses in our company; we have lost Capt. Bryson, 1st Lieut. Castell, 1st Sergeant Trombower, and three privates, out of our company, more than any other company lost. I must close my letter. Hoping you are well, I am

Yours, &c.,
WM. A. FETTER.

* * * * *

Letters from Sergeant A. J. Stroh, 9th Iowa Cavalry

Several letters, finally, arrived again from former residents of the county—or, in one case, from the comrade of a former Sunburian who was writing to report on the latter's death. A pair of letters from Sergeant A. J. Stroh, who was then serving in the 9th Iowa Infantry, recounted his military exploits in Arkansas, including a description of the Battle of Pea Ridge. On May 4, 1862, Pvt. Joseph M. Dotson of Company K, 2nd Iowa Cavalry, penned a letter from Corinth, Mississippi, to Sunbury resident George Weiser, informing the elder Weiser of the disappearance and possible death of his son, Peter, during a routine patrol. And lastly, in late June 1862, the Sunbury American *published one communication by former Northumberland physician Dr. Robert B. McCay, who was then serving as a brigade surgeon at Fortress Monroe. Noting McCay's appointment to the Medical Department as "a most excellent one," the* Sunbury American *praised his "abilities and acquirements, which are of a high order, [and] are only second to his modest worth and unobtrusive manners."[47] As the chief administrator for medical supplies at Fortress Monroe, McCay authored a letter of thanks for goods and pleasantries furnished for patient care by the women of Northumberland County.*

Battlefield,
Near Sugar Creek, Ark.,
March 12, 1862.[48]

Dear Nephew:—Yours of February 10th has been received. You have heard, I suppose, ere this, that I had been at home in Iowa, on a visit to my family, to see them perhaps for the last time. On my return to the army I arrived in camp at Cross Hollows, Arkansas, on the 4th of March, and on the night of the 5th we were ordered to retreat, or fall back, as the enemy was upon us. We took up our line of march and fell back to Sugar Creek, and there made a stand, but it was only a

---

47. *Sunbury American*, June 8, 1862.
48. *Sunbury Gazette*, April 5, 1862.

few hours before the enemy attacked Sigel's[49] division, at Bentonville, and drove him in to the main body. That night Price cut us off, and the next day, the 7th, he opened fire on us about 8 o'clock in the morning. The attacking force of the enemy numbered about 30,000, but three regiments of us held him in check on that day, whilst Sigel drove the right of Price's division in our front. Night closed the contest for that day, and we lay on our arms all night at less than half a mile from the enemy, who, it is said, expected to make a mere breakfast spell of our camp in the morning. About daylight the next morning, our batteries opened a destructive fire on them, and at 10 o'clock they began to give way. Our infantry then opened a heavy fire on them, and in less than half an hour the enemy was in full retreat. Then went up cheer after cheer for the Old Flag. In the distance we could see them scaling the heights, and running for life.

The day after the battle was a day of sorrow. Our divisions moved forward, encamped on the battle ground, and commenced burying our dead. The sight was extremely sickening., I saw, lying upon the field, dead men with bodies dreadfully mangled; arms, heads and legs blown off. It was a sight that I never wish to see again, although I expect I shall if I live to participate in another fight. Our loss was large, but the loss of the enemy must be very great. We had 45 killed in our regiment, or about 230 killed and wounded. I thought I had an idea of a battle, but I find I had none.

Well, I will tell you a little about myself in connection with the fight. I was in three destructive files and charges, and did not get a scratch, while four or five fell dead at my side. At one time, while skirmishing down a hill, I was almost cut off before I knew it. In this peril I thought I had only once to die, but that I would try my luck in running; out of five of us two got wounded, one killed, and myself and another got off without a scratch, although the balls came after us like hail, but through the mercy of God I was spared for that time. I had made up my mind, on going into the fight, to resign myself to His will, and do the best I could to keep from being taken a prisoner.

As I said before, there were only three regiments, I believe there was part of four, only about 1600, to five times their odds, but we

---

49. Maj. Gen. Franz Sigel (1824–1902). A German national who participated in the Revolutions of 1848, Sigel delivered his best battlefield performance at the Battle of Pea Ridge (March 8–9, 1862), personally directing the artillery fire that finally routed the Confederate forces.

held them in check all day, until they got reinforcements, when we had to fall back to keep them from outflanking us, but only to give them a fresh turn on the following day, which we did with such triumph as has not been seen in the West before. I think it was a Bull-Run No. 2, on their side, for they went as fast as legs could carry them, and have not showed themselves since. The prisoners we have taken, acknowledge themselves badly whipped.

On the second day of the fight we were held in reserve, but we had done all we could do the first day. In conclusion, all I have to say is that we have whipped them, and that we are willing to try them at any time again, if they try to cut off our retreat. But I don't think he will try that again, or at least he need not do that to make us fight. Inclosed you will find two buttons which I cut from the uniform of a dead secesh.

Your Uncle,
J. STROH.

* * * * *

[The following letter from our late townsman, Sergeant A. J. Stroh, of the Iowa 9th, give a most graphic description of the battle of Pea Ridge, Arkansas.—Ed. Gaz.]

Camp Cross-Timbers,
March 30, 1862.[50]

Dear Sir:—It is with pleasure I address you this Sunday morning, hoping that you are well. I have been sick for some time, almost ever since I arrived in camp from home, with the diarrhea, but I am well now again. I am, however, very thin in flesh, but feel quite well at present.

I have been in one hard-fought battle, where bullets flew as thick as hail, and my comrades fell fast and thick around me; one fell at the first fire right at my side, and the corporal's gun, who stood next to me, was hit while we were lying down waiting for the enemy's approach. We soon put them to flight, our company sustaining a loss, at

---

50. *Sunbury Gazette*, May 3, 1862.

the first fire, of four killed and three or four wounded. We gave them a volley in return which told on their ranks, and then chased them over the hill till we almost came in range of their battery, which threw grape and canister at us. We then retreated, and took a new position on the left of the road, the enemy on one side of a deep ravine and our brigade on the other. We then advanced down the hill under a most deadly fire, the enemy falling back into a small ravine which served as a barricade to them, giving them a great advantage over us; we continued to advance, however, not knowing that we were fighting great odds till we were about being surrounded—they had us nearly outflanked. Our company was on the right as we were faced to the rear, and we fought them by the rear rank twice. At this juncture[,] Six of our company ran out to the right to get a good chance to take aim at them, and I was one of them. I shot a few times, taking deliberate aim as they would raise out of the ravine to shoot; but we had not long to stay, for the first thing we knew we found ourselves out-flanked, and bullets coming in on our right. There were only six of us at this particular place on the extreme right of company and regiment, as it was faced to the rear, and when the regiment fell back we did not see the movement, and were left behind; but upon discovering our position, we soon made tracks up the hill through a perfect hail of bullets. I ran into a small ravine that ran up and down with the ridge down which we advanced. Two of us got off without a scratch, one was killed, two wounded, and I think one taken prisoner, as I did not see him after that. He sent in a letter since stating that he was a prisoner—at least I think the writer of the letter is the same man. I made up my mind to die, for as I raised the top of the hill the balls came like hail from the opposite side, cutting the branches close around my head, and striking the ground all around me, making the dirt fly at my feet.

We took another position still farther west, under or at the point of a round ridge. We had held our ground up to this time, about 4 o'clock in the afternoon, with about 1600 men against 15,000, when they were reinforced by about as many more, who were driven in our front by Sigel. They brought all their forces together at this point, and we were obliged to retreat to an open field. We were not reinforced at any time during the day, and fought them three times, holding them at bay till 4 o'clock, when we fell back about half a mile, and the enemy occupied our position. Both armies lay about three-fourths of a mile apart (just across a field)[,] the pickets coming in sight of each other several times during the night. The next morning was to tell the tale. Price told his men that they had us just where he wanted us, and that we would surrender in less than two hours, but to their great surprise about sunrise, on the eighth, (next day) our batteries opened on them, and before 10 o'clock we had them in full retreat for Springfield, and I did not know but that we would have to drive Price back to Springfield again.

Both armies lay in the shape of a rainbow, at least they moved in that way. When our army got out into the open fields, we could see them crossing the hill to the left of the road in perfect swarms, not stopping to fire a gun on our left, but our right wing was most furiously assailed. The roll of small arms, and the booming of cannon on all sides, for miles along the right, was most terrific. A shout went up for the victory—the Stars and Stripes—cheer after cheer, till it sent terror to the hearts of the poor, God-forsaken wretches. I find great ignorance among the most of them, and on speaking with them they said if they knew we were only fighting to sustain the laws, they would not have taken up arms against the government. Many of them are pressed into the service, those who had been were all marked with a band around the arm to distinguish them from those who entered the service voluntarily.

On the second day of the fight we were held in reserve, and I had a better chance to see and hear what was going on than I had the first day, as one participating in an engagement can see or hear nothing except what is going on in his immediate presence. We had 45 killed in our regiment, and 240 killed and wounded. Many of the wounded have died since the battle. In our company 7 were killed and 13 wounded, 3 of whom have since died.

After the flight of the enemy I passed over the field, and had an opportunity of witnessing all the horrible consequences of war. Here lay my lifeless of comrades with mangled bodies and disfigured faces—faces shot to pieces. Poor fellows who had been merry only the day before lay there in their gore, hardly to be recognized by those who knew them well. During the struggle the day previous, one of our company passed me, and as he ran across the road he gave me one glance—a ghastly look. I saw him so[me] more that day, but upon searching for him next day I found him dead near the place. I think the poor fellow was struck when we met in the road, and he barely got out my sight before he fell dead. I shall never forget that dreadful look he gave me as long as I live; there was something so horrible about it. The Secesh had robbed him of his money, shoes, stockings and cap; this is a game played on both sides.

In conclusion I will tell you something about the wounded. O, Lord, save me from witnessing another battle-field if it can be helped; but this is what we can expect. The horrors of the hospital on the field are indescribable: here lays a man with his leg shot off, there another with his brains protruding and is still alive, there is another with his eyes blown out, another with his [illegible phrase], another with a ball hole through his body, or perhaps three or four of them, and is still sensible, another with both legs shot off, he lives for several days, another shot in the head, the ball just passing under the skin—a slight wound; some with noses shot off, others shot in the mouth. These distressing scenes I have witnessed, but hope I may never see any more like them.

We were told yesterday to hold ourselves in readiness for another brush with the enemy, but how it will turn out I don't know; I believe it to be a hoax.

Yours,
A. J. STROH.

* * * * *

Letter from Joseph M. Dotson
Company K, 2nd Iowa Cavalry

[The following letter was received by Geo. Weiser, Esq., of Sunbury, and handed to us for publication.—ED. GAZ:]

Camp at Corinth, Miss.,
May 4, 1862.[51]

Mr. Geo. Weiser—Respected Sir.—It is with feelings of sadness, mixed with pleasure, that I address you this morning. Your son Peter is no longer with us, although I have strong hopes that he is a prisoner; but at the same time have some fears that the result is different. I will give you the particulars as near as I can: On the 28th of last month, our Regiment, in connection with the 2nd Michigan Cavalry, was ordered out to Boonville, Alabama, to tear up and destroy the railroad at that place. We took a number of prisoners, and Peter and four others were left to guard them. But a number of rebel Cavalry came on them. Three of the men saw them coming, in time to retreat, but for some cause Peter did not get away. I do hope that he is a prisoner, but my reasons for fearing worse is, that the enemy came on a squad of 5 of Company G's men, and killed every one of them. They did not appear to want prisoners.[52]

Peter and I have been associates ever since he came to Iowa. We enlisted at the same time, and I miss his company very much. He requested me that if he should fall in battle, or be taken prisoner, I should inform you of the fact. If I can obtain any information concerning his fate I will inform you.

Yours, with Respect,
JOSEPH M. DOTSON.

* * * * *

---

51. *Sunbury Gazette*, July 12, 1862.
52. Weiser was indeed taken prisoner at Booneville and held until paroled at Aiken's Landing, Virginia, on October 17, 1862. He was then sent to Camp Parole, Maryland, to await a formal exchange, which occurred on January 10, 1863. Weiser served out the rest of his enlistment and was discharged on October 3, 1864.

Letter from Dr. Robert B. McCay, Brigade Surgeon Chesapeake General Hospital, Fortress Monroe

[The following letter from Dr. R. B. McCay of Northumberland, Brigade Surgeon, stationed at Fortress Monroe, acknowledges the receipt of several boxes of delicacies, as well as books, linen bandages, and other matters calculated to add to the comfort and entertainment of our sick and wounded soldiers, forwarded by the ladies of Sunbury, who, from the start, have evinced a degree of patriotic devotion without regard to party, sect or religion, so characteristic of our noble country women:][53]

Chesapeake General Hospital,
June 21, 1862.

MY DEAR MADAM:—

I had the pleasure of opening a box, sent by you, a few days ago, containing a large number of magazines and light works, for the amusement and instruction of our sick and wounded, and several cans of preserves. At the same time come two large boxes filled with linen, bandages, butter, preserves, dried fruit, &c., &c., for the physical comfort of our patients.

Please accept my hearty thanks for this evidence of your sympathy. Over fifteen hundred patients have been treated, in this establishment, during the last three months, many of whom were from Pennsylvania. Some from our own county; several from your town. Yet, amid the multitude of contributions pouring in upon us from all parts of New York, New Jersey, and other States, with bounteous supplies from dear old Philadelphia, her Ladies' Aid Societies and Sunday Schools, from Lancaster, free handed Pittsburg, and our good neighbors of Danville—the *first* evidence of pity for our suffering sick and wounded, the first sign of help from *my* county came with the boxes from Sunbury.

---

53. *Sunbury American*, July 5, 1862.

Everything arrived safely except the butter. The stone jar was broken, and its delicious contents mixed with dried huckleberries! Still, none of it was lost.

It was not a little amusing to watch the wonder-beaming countenances of our wounded Secession prisoners, who stood by to see the boxes opened—They had never seen, or even *heard* of *Apple Butter!* and could not contrive what it was good for. Their tongues soon convinced them, however, that all the good things of this world do not grow in Cottondom.

Allow me again to thank you, and through you the ladies of Sunbury and its vicinity, who have so liberally remembered the poor soldiers.

I am, very truly, your friend,

R. B. McCAY,
Brigade Surgeon in Charge.

BIBLIOGRAPHY

Primary Sources

Newspapers
Cincinnati Gazette (Cincinnati, Ohio)
Columbia Democrat & Bloomsburg General Advertiser (Bloomsburg, Pennsylvania)
New York Times (New York, New York)
Northumberland County Democrat (Sunbury, Pennsylvania)
Star of the North (Bloomsburg, Pennsylvania)
Sunbury American (Sunbury, Pennsylvania)
Sunbury Gazette (Sunbury, Pennsylvania)

Government Publications
Heitman, Francis B. *Historical Register and Dictionary of the U.S. Army*. Washington, DC: Government Printing Office, 1903.
Kennedy, Joseph C. G. *Agriculture of the United States in 1860*. Washington, DC: Government Printing Office, 1864.
———. *Manufacturers of the United States in 1860*. Washington, DC: Government Printing Office, 1864.
———. *Population of the United States in 1860*. Washington, DC: Government Printing Office, 1864.
The War of the Rebellion: Official Records of the Union and Confederate Armies. Washington, DC: Government Printing Office, 1880–1901.

Secondary Works

Articles and Monographs
Andrews, J. Cutler. *The North Reports the Civil War*. Pittsburgh: University of Pittsburg Press, 1955, 1983.
Bates, Samuel P. *History of the Pennsylvania Volunteers, 1861–1865*. Harrisburg, PA: B. Singerly, State Printer, 1870.
Beers, J. H. *Biographical Annals of Lebanon County, Pennsylvania*. Chicago: J. H. Beers & Co., 1904.
Bell, Herbert C. *History of Northumberland County, Pennsylvania*. Chicago: Brown, Runk & Co., 1891.

Blanchard, Charles. *The Progressive Men of the Commonwealth of Pennsylvania*. Volume 2. Logansport, IN: A. W. Bowen & Co., 1900.

Carmichael, Peter S. *The War for the Common Soldier: How Men Thought, Fought, and Survived in Civil War Armies*. Chapel Hill: University of North Carolina Press, 2018.

Clark-Pujara, Christy and Anna-Lisa Cox. "How the Myth of a Liberal North Erases a Long History of White Violence." *Smithsonian Magazine* (August 27, 2020).

Dyer, Frederick H. *A Compendium of the War of the Rebellion*. Des Moines, IA: The Dyer Publishing Co., 1908.

Endres, Frederic F. "Review of *A Radical View: The "Agate" Dispatches of Whitelaw Reid, 1861–1865*." *Civil War History* 22:4 (1976).

Ent, Uzal W. *The Pennsylvania Reserves in the Civil War: A Comprehensive History*. Jefferson, NC: McFarland & Co., 2014.

Floyd, J. L. *Genealogical and Biographical Annals of Northumberland County, Pennsylvania*. Chicago: J. L. Floyd & Co., 1911.

Fry, Zachary A. *A Republic in the Ranks: Loyalty and Dissent in the Army of the Republic*. Chapel Hill: University of North Carolina Press, 2020.

Hesseltine, William B. "The Pryor-Potter Duel." *The Wisconsin Magazine of History* 27:4 (June 1944).

Howe, Daniel Walker. *What Hath God Wrought: The Transformation of America, 1815–1848*. New York: Oxford University Press, 2007.

Jordan, Brian Matthew. *A Thousand May Fall: Life, Death, and Survival in the Union Army*. New York: Liveright Publishing Corp., 2021.4

Jordan, John W. *Encyclopedia of Pennsylvania Biography*. Volume 1. New York: Lewis Historical Publishing Co., 1914.

McKnight, William Mark. *Blue Bonnets O'er the Border: The 79th New York Cameron Highlanders*. Shippensburg, PA: White Mane Books, 1998.

McPherson, James M. *Battle Cry of Freedom: The Civil War Era*. New York: Oxford University Press, 1988.

Nein, Jaqueline B. *Dunkelbergers in America, 1728–1997: The Dunkelberger Genealogy*. Reading, PA: Dunkelbergers in America Association, 1997.

Nicolay, John G. and John Hay. *Abraham Lincoln: A History*. New York: The Century Co., 1890.

Perry, James M. *A Bohemian Brigade: The Civil War Correspondents—Mostly Rough, Sometimes Ready*. New York: John Wiley & Sons, Inc., 2000.

Peters, Thelma. "The Loyalist Migration from East Florida to the Bahama Islands." *The Florida Historical Society Quarterly* 40:2 (October 1961).

Quint, Ryan T. *Dranesville: A Northern Virginia Town in the Crossfire of a Forgotten Battle, December 20, 1861*. El Dorado Hills, CA: Savas Beatie, 2024.

Reardon, Carol. *Pickett's Charge in History and Memory*. Chapel Hill: University of North Carolina Press, 1997.

Sears, Stephen W. *To the Gates of Richmond: The Peninsular Campaign.* New York: Ticknor & Fields, 1992.

Websites and Online Sources

47th Pennsylvania Volunteers: One Civil War Regiment's Story, www.47thpennsylvaniavolunteers.com

"Civil War Reporting and Reporters." American Antiquarian Society, https://collections.americanantiquarian.org/earlyamericannewsmedia/exhibits/show/news-and-the-civil-war/civil-war-reporting-and-report

"Drawing the War, Part 1: Alfred Waud." Emerging Civil War, https://emergingcivilwar.com/2012/03/12/drawing-the-war-part-1-alfred-waud/

FamilySearch, www.familysearch.org

Fold3, www.fold3.com

"Invading Virginia's 'Sacred Soil." Blue Gray Review, https://www.bluegrayreview.com/2011/05/25/invading-virginias-sacred-soil/

"John Merryman Biography." Archives of Maryland (Biographical Series), https://msa.maryland.gov/megafile/msa/speccol/sc3500/sc3520/001500/001543/html/1543bio.html

Political Cartoons featuring Hasty Soup. Library of Congress, www.loc.gov/pictures/item/2008661471/

"The Reported War: Printed Media and the American Civil War." Oregon State University Libraries, https://scarc.library.oregonstate.edu/omeka/exhibits/show/mcdonald/civil-war/war/

"Rev. Peter Rizer Biography. Spared & Shared, https://sparedshared4.wordpress.com/letters/1834-rev-stephen-albion-mealy-to-rev-peter-rizer/

"U.S. Census Bureau QuickFacts: Northumberland County, Pennsylvania." U.S. Census Bureau, https://www.census.gov/quickfacts/fact/table/northumberlandcountypennsylvania/PST045221

"United States Census, 1860," FamilySearch, https://www.familysearch.org/ark:/61903/1:1:MX5J-29Z: Sat Mar 09 13:55:42 UTC 2024

"United States Mexican War Index and Service Records, 1846–1848." FamilySearch, www.familysearch.org/ark:/61903/1:1:QLXQ-R414:Fri Mar 08 23:47:15 UTC 2024

ABOUT THE AUTHOR

John P. Deeben is a historian, government archivist, and genealogist with a passion for Civil War history.

He currently serves as a reference archivist and Subject Matter Expert (SME) for Early American Military Records at the National Archives and Records Administration in Washington, D.C., where he provides research assistance for military records from the Revolutionary War to the early twentieth century. He also frequently lectures and writes about federal records of genealogical interest. His numerous articles have appeared in such national publications as *American Ancestors*, *National Genealogical Society Journal*, *NGS Magazine*, and *Civil War Times*. He has spoken at various national conferences including the Federation of Genealogical Societies (FGS), the National Genealogical Society (NGS), and the Genealogical Institute on Federal Records (Gen-Fed). In 2012 he published *Genealogy Tool Kit: Getting Started on Your Family History at the National Archives* (National Archives Foundation).

A native of Sunbury in Northumberland County, Pennsylvania, John has held a lifelong interest in local history. He has compiled five self-published books about various lines of his family roots within Northumberland County, and researched the histories of several local Lutheran churches. John holds degrees in American History from Gettysburg College and The Pennsylvania State University. He currently resides with his family in North Beach, Maryland.